HOW TO READ A FINANCIAL REPORT WORKBOOK

T0286134

HOW TO READ A FINANCIAL

WRINGING VITAL SIGNS OUT OF

WILEY

REPORT WORKBOOK

THE NUMBERS

TAGE C. TRACY

Copyright © 2025 by Tage C. Tracy. All rights reserved.

Published by John Wiley & Sons, Inc., Hoboken, New Jersey.
Published simultaneously in Canada.

No part of this publication may be reproduced, stored in a retrieval system, or transmitted in any form or by any means, electronic, mechanical, photocopying, recording, scanning, or otherwise, except as permitted under Section 107 or 108 of the 1976 United States Copyright Act, without either the prior written permission of the Publisher, or authorization through payment of the appropriate per-copy fee to the Copyright Clearance Center, Inc., 222 Rosewood Drive, Danvers, MA 01923, (978) 750-8400, fax (978) 750-4470, or on the web at www.copyright.com. Requests to the Publisher for permission should be addressed to the Permissions Department, John Wiley & Sons, Inc., 111 River Street, Hoboken, NJ 07030, (201) 748-6011,fax (201) 748-6008, or online at http://www.wiley.com/go/permission.

Trademarks: Wiley and the Wiley logo are trademarks or registered trademarks of John Wiley & Sons, Inc. and/or its affiliates in the United States and other countries and may not be used without written permission. All other trademarks are the property of their respective owners. John Wiley & Sons, Inc. is not associated with any product or vendor mentioned in this book.

Limit of Liability/Disclaimer of Warranty: While the publisher and author have used their best efforts in preparing this book, they make no representations or warranties with respect to the accuracy or completeness of the contents of this book and specifically disclaim any implied warranties of merchantability or fitness for a particular purpose. No warranty may be created or extended by sales representatives or written sales materials. The advice and strategies contained herein may not be suitable for your situation. You should consult with a professional where appropriate. Further, readers should be aware that websites listed in this work may have changed or disappeared between when this work was written and when it is read. Neither the publisher nor authors shall be liable for any loss of profit or any other commercial damages, including but not limited to special, incidental, consequential, or other damages.

For general information on our other products and services or for technical support, please contact our Customer Care Department within the United States at (800) 762-2974, outside the United States at (317) 572-3993 or fax (317) 572-4002.

Wiley also publishes its books in a variety of electronic formats. Some content that appears in print may not be available in electronic formats. For more information about Wiley products, visit our web site at www.wiley.com.

Library of Congress Cataloging-in-Publication Data is Available:

ISBN 9781394263271 (Paperback)
ISBN 9781394263288 (ePDF)
ISBN 9781394263325 (ePUB)

Cover Design: Wiley
Cover Image: © John Wiley & Sons, Inc.

SKY10082728_082724

CONTENTS

LIST OF EXHIBITS

PREFACE

The first question to ask is why write this book now or maybe more appropriately, what took so long?. To be quite honest, this book had been staring us in the face for years. It lies in the simple concept of setting our keyboards aside, taking a step back, and listening more attentively to what additional accounting and financial concepts our customers would like to understand. The purpose of this book is to extend and expand your knowledge of accounting and financial concepts, topics, and subject matter, keeping within our primary mission of helping you, the reader, digest relatively complex financial content by presenting it in easy-to-absorb, bite-sized pieces.

Since 1980, when *How to Read a Financial Report* (now in its 10th edition) was first released, the book's content and concepts have been well received by the business community and our readers alike, which span the far reaches of the globe. The feedback we've received has been extremely rewarding and enlightening. We appreciate the thousands of compliments received over the past 40 years and have enjoyed learning what topics readers consider to be most valuable. Through all this, one constant has always been present as we continue to see a robust demand for the Excel workbook file, which includes all the financial exhibits presented in the book.

Sometimes it takes a while for an accounting concept or opportunity to sink in, and this book was no different. After having further discussions with my publisher and various third parties, it dawned on me that I must provide more context, insight, and actual examples of financial exhibits to help our readers digest and understand the concepts presented in *How to Read a Financial Report*. Providing the Excel workbook files will offer the in-depth information readers want to gain confidence. As such, the first edition of *How to Read a Financial Report Workbook* has been produced with the following key objectives being kept in mind:

- ✓ First, the content offered in this book is designed to complement *How to Read a Financial Report*, 10th Edition, by presenting different perspectives on core concepts (to improve your knowledge of the content). For example, financial statement connections are covered in both books, but in the workbook, the financial statement connections are evaluated from the perspective of understanding critical business operating cycles (e.g., the sales or purchasing cycle).
- ✓ Second, this book offers a much more thorough business financial case study comparing our example company operating under three different business management scenarios or styles, including a base case, a simple case, and an aggressive case. We have provided additional exhibits, calculations, and number crunching, which offer invaluable insights into how the same example business can generate such widely varying financial statements and operating results.
- ✓ Third, a deeper dive aims to help readers understand trending accounting topics related to recognizing sales and the impact on accounts receivables and deferred revenue, managing inventory levels and establishing values, properly accounting for long-term capital assets, the importance of intangible assets, and insight into just how often accounting estimates are utilized when preparing financial statements and reports.
- ✓ Fourth, bonus material covers extremely important financial and accounting topics related to how a company raises and manages equity. Critical topics involving the cap table (i.e., the ownership summary of the business) and the cap stack (i.e., ownership rights to the assets of a business) are introduced with real-world financial exhibits provided.
- ✓ Fifth and finally, the cash flow cycle is completed with expanded material, tips, tidbits, advice, and insight provided as to how companies utilize different strategies to manufacture cash from the balance sheet along with providing a clearer picture to help you determine if net profits are actually real or imaginary.

This book has been structured to enhance and expand your knowledge of financial reports and financial statements as presented in *How to Read a Financial Report*. It provides additional financial exhibits, case studies, and financial what-ifs and it presents key concepts in bullet-point formats. I explain important concepts by providing important written overviews, but the general idea is to allow you, as a reader, to dig into the numbers in more depth to see a complete link between financial numbers and concepts.

The first part of this book (Chapters 1 through 4) will act as a refresher course with key financial and accounting concepts, including understanding the critical importance of cash flow (Chapters 1 and 3), revisiting the big three financial statements (Chapter 2), providing a summary of financial statement connections in Chapter 4 (but from the perspective of understanding business cycles).

Part Two starts by laying the foundation for our case study of our fictitious business example, but under three different management styles (or strategies). It then proceeds by taking a deep dive into our three management styles for our fictitious business example case study by focusing on four significant balance sheet accounts and how, within our three management styles, the same business can produce such different results. The four significant balance sheet accounts include trade accounts receivables, inventory, long-term assets, and other current liabilities (including accrued liabilities and deferred revenue, a hot topic). I take a balance sheet approach to these concepts and topics to explain the reference I make in previous books as to why the balance sheet is where losses go to hide, cash goes to die, and the BS goes to lie. Part two closes by providing a comprehensive financial analysis for our fictitious business example case study companies.

Finally, I close out the book in Part Three by incorporating bonus material related to understanding such critical concepts as using ratio analysis to evaluate the financial performance of our case study companies, how to manufacture cash from the balance sheet, gaining further knowledge on whether net profits are real or imaginary, and then providing more insight as to ownership structures of businesses and the all-important cap stack.

I present countless financial statements and related financial exhibits in this book as Excel spreadsheets. If you would like a copy of the Excel workbook of the exhibits, please contact me at my email address: tagetracy@cox.net.

I cannot thank my late father and John Wiley & Sons enough for providing me the opportunity to author this book that takes *How to Read a Financial Report* to the next level. Like all the books I've written, this workbook emphasizes that accounting is just as much an art form as it is a science. The funny thing about accounting is that it is really centered on simple algebra logic and equations (e.g., A – B = C, sales revenue minus costs of sales revenue equals gross profit). So, while the math is relatively simple, clearly defining what comprises A (i.e., sales revenue) and B (costs of sales revenue) to produce C (gross profit) takes on a life of its own. To repeat one of the oldest jokes in the accounting profession, when you ask an accountant what 2+2 equals, the proper response is: *What do you need it to be?*

I sincerely hope you enjoy this book and expand your knowledge of the profession, art, and technical aspects of accounting, and reading, writing, and understanding financial reports and statements.

TAGE C. TRACY

Anthem, Arizona
June 2024

Part One

A REFRESHER COURSE IN THE BASICS

1

STARTING WITH THE LANGUAGE OF FINANCE AND CASH FLOWS

Chapter 1 dives headfirst into two critical topics that will be on full display throughout this book. First, I provide a crash course on the language of accounting and finance. Simply put, in order to master reading (covered in my book *How to Read a Financial Report*), writing (covered in my book *How to Write a Financial Report*), and understanding financial statements and reports, it is essential that you learn the basic jargon.

Second, understanding how businesses generate and consume cash is a topic that is of critical importance and always on full display. As such, the second half of Chapter 1 dives right into the importance of cash flow, which is expanded upon further in Chapter 3, with even more insight provided in Chapters 12 and 15. True to our primary mission of translating complex accounting and financial concepts into simple and easy-to-understand tools and ideas, cash flows, the lifeblood of every business, is positioned with added reverence throughout this book to ensure that you remember the golden rule of operating a business: Never, ever run out of cash!

A Crash Course in the Language of Accounting and Finance

If you're heading to France or Italy, it goes without saying that you should brush up on the basics of French or Italian because being able to communicate in the local dialect can improve your travel experience. The same goes for accounting and finance. If you can at least master some basic terminology, it will be less of a struggle to understand financial statements. This section of the chapter covers two buckets of terminology, basic and advanced.

Basic Terminology

Basic terminology is primarily associated with communicating the results of financial statements (from an accounting perspective), with a heavy weighting toward the income statement. Below, I've provided a sampling of the most commonly used basic accounting and financial terminology:

- Top line: A company's net sales revenue generated over a period of time (e.g., for a 12-month period).
- COGS or COS: Pronounced like it is spelled; stands for costs of goods sold (for a service-based business or company that sells both products and services) and costs of sales (for a service-based business). COGS or COS tend to vary directly (or in a linear fashion) with the top-line sales revenue.
- Gross profit and margin: Sometimes used interchangeably, gross profit equals your top line less your COGS or COS. The gross margin (a percentage calculation) is determined by dividing your gross profit by the top line.
- Op Ex: A broad term that is short for operating expenses, which may include selling, general, administrative, corporate overhead, and other related expenses. Unlike COGS or COS, Op Ex tends to be fixed in nature and will not vary directly with the top-line sales revenue.
- SG&A: Selling, general, and administrative expenses. Companies may distinguish between Op Ex and SG&A to assist parties with understanding the expense structure of its operations in more detail.
- Bottom line: A company's net profit or loss after all expenses have been deducted from net sales revenue. Being *in the black* indicates that a net profit is present and being *in the red* indicates that a net loss was generated.
- Breakeven: The operating level where a company generates zero in profit or loss. It can also be used to identify the amount of sales revenue that needs to be generated to cover all COGS/COS and Op Ex.

- Contribution margin: You may hear companies reference the term *contribution margin*. What this generally refers to is the profit generated by a specific operating unit or division of a company (but not for the company as a whole). Most larger companies have multiple operating units or divisions, so the profit (or loss) of each operating unit or division is calculated to determine how much that specific unit or division contributed to the overall performance of the entire company.
- Cap Ex: Cap Ex stands for capital expenditures and is a calculation of how much a company invested in tangible or intangible assets during a given period (e.g., for equipment, machinery, new buildings, investments in intangible assets, etc.).
- YTD, QTD, MTD: These are simple and stand for *year to date*, *quarter to date*, or *month to date*. For example, a flash report may present QTD sales for the period of 10/1/24 through 11/15/24 (so management can evaluate sales levels through the middle of a quarter).
- FYE and QE: These two items stand for fiscal year-end and quarter-end. Most companies utilize a fiscal year-end that is consistent with a calendar year-end of 12/31/xx (which would make their quarter-ends 3/31/xx, 6/30/xx, 9/30/xx, and 12/31/xx). Please note that several companies utilize FYEs that do not follow a calendar year-end to match their business cycle with that of a specific industry. For example, companies that cater to the education industry may use a FYE of 6/30/xx to coincide with the typical operating year for schools or colleges (which tend to run from 7/1/xx through 6/30/xx).

Advanced Terminology

Advanced terminology tends to be centered in references to financial concepts that are focused on cash flows, forecasts, projections, and financing topics (i.e., raising capital such as securing loans or selling equity in a company). With that said, here's a summary listing of advanced terminology to reference.

- EBITDA: This is one of the most used (and abused) terms in finance today and stands for *earnings before interest, taxes, depreciation, and amortization*. A shorter version that is also used frequently is EBIT or *earnings before interest and taxes*. The reason for EBITDA's popularity is that capital sources want to clearly understand just how much earning a company can generate in the form of operating cash on a periodic basis. EBITDA strips out interest, taxes, and depreciation and amortization expense (both noncash expenses) to calculate what is perceived to be a company's ability to generate internal positive cash flow (which is widely used when evaluating the value of a company and its ability to service debt).
- Free cash flow: FCF is closely related to EBITDA but takes into consideration numerous other factors or adjustments such as the need for a company to invest in equipment or intangible assets on a periodic basis (to remain competitive), the required or set debt service the company is obligated to pay each year (for interest and principal payments), any guaranteed returns on preferred equity, and other similar adjustments. FCF can be a highly subjective calculation based on the estimates and definitions used by different parties.

- YOY: YOY stands for a year-over-year change in financial performance (e.g., sales change for the current 12-month period compared to the prior 12-month period).
- CAGR: This stands for compounded annual growth rate and represents a financial calculation that evaluates a financial performance over a number of periods (e.g., sales increased at a CAGR of 15.5 percent for the five-year period of 2019 through 2024).
- Sustainable growth rate: This calculation estimates a company's maximum achievable growth rate by using internal operating capital (i.e., positive cash flow) only. When a company exceeds its sustainable growth rate, external capital such as loans or equity from new investors may need to be secured to support ongoing operations.
- Debt service: Total debt service includes both required loan interest and principal payments due over a period of time.
- B2B and B2C: A company that sells primarily to other businesses is B2B (business to business), whereas a company that sells primarily to consumers is B2C (business to consumer).
- Burn rate: A burn rate is generally used for newer businesses or start-ups that have not achieved profitability and are "burning" a large amount of cash. The burn rate calculates the amount of cash burn a company is incurring over a specific period, such as a month or a quarter. If a company has a burn rate of $250,000 a month (before generating any sales), then an investor could quickly calculate that this company would need $3 million of capital to support it for one year.
- Runway: The runway calculates how much time a company has before it runs out of cash. In our example, if the company has $1 million of cash left and is burning $250,000 per month, it has a remaining runway of four months.
- TTM and FTM: TTM stands for *trailing twelve months* and FTM stands for *forward twelve months*. These figures are often used by parties to help understand a company's annual operating results that are not in sync with its FYE (e.g., how much sales revenue was generated for the period of the QE 9/30/19 through the QE 6/30/20, 12 months of operating history). TTM and FTM can be especially useful when evaluating companies that are growing rapidly or have experienced a recent significant change in business.
- C-suite: The C-suite represents the group of company executive management team members whose titles include the word *chief*. This would include the chief executive officer (CEO), chief operating officer (COO), chief financial officer (CFO), chief technology officer (CTO), chief marketing officer (CMO), chief investment officer (CIO), and other designated chief executive management positions as determined by a company.

Throughout the remainder of this book, I will reference these concepts frequently, so you may want to bookmark this section to help refresh your memory as needed. There's no harm in returning to these lists when you're swimming with the financial sharks out in the open water. There's nothing worse than looking overmatched because you can't even understand basic accounting and financial terminology.

Starting with Cash Flows

Every book that I've written, either by myself or with my dad, has emphasized the importance of three critical concepts that are absolutely essential to understanding financial reports and financial statements. These are

1. Cash flows
2. The big three financial statements
3. How financial statements are interconnected. To avoid disappointing you, I start by emphasizing the importance of cash flow, a concept well worth repeating again and again.

Savvy business managers, lenders, and investors pay close attention to the cash flows generated by a business. ***Simply put, cash inflows and outflows represent the heartbeat and pulse of every business. Without a steady heartbeat and healthy pulse of positive cash flows, a business would soon have to go on life support—or alternatively, die.***

Given the importance of generating cash flows, we cover this topic out of the gate before we jump into discussing the income statement, the balance sheet, and the statement of cash flows (the big three financial statements, covered in chapter 2). However, we would also like to remind you of this simple logic when understanding the big three financial statements. That is and if you remember one important concept for each financial statement, it should be these:

1. *Understand* the income statement,
2. *Trust* the balance sheet,
3. Most importantly, *rely* on the statement of cash flows.

As you work through this book, it will become readily apparent as to why it is essential to not only understand a company's cash inflows and outflows, but also understand how to use this information to better ascertain the financial performance and reliability of a company's overall financial performance.

Summary of Cash Flows for a Business

A business's cash inflows and outflows appear and are reported in a summary of cash flows, most often referred to as the statement of cash flows (one of the big three financial statements covered in Chapters 2 and 3). For our example company introduced in Exhibit 1.1, we use a technology business (a fictitious business I've named QW Example Tech, Inc.) that has been operating for many years. This established business has historically generated a profit on an annual basis but, more recently, hit a bit of a bump in the road as the company pivoted its business interests toward selling more software products and fewer hardware products. Equally important, the company maintains a solid financial condition to ensure the business has ample liquidity and cash to support ongoing operations. The company has a good credit history, and financial lending groups extend loans to it on competitive terms. Its present stockholders would be willing to invest additional capital in the business, if needed.

None of this comes easily, as most business owners will attest. It takes a strong management team and sound business model to generate consistent profits, manage and secure capital (both debt and equity), and for lack of a better term, stay out of financial hot water. Many businesses fail these imperatives, especially when the going gets tough, whether it be from difficult macroeconomic conditions, increased competition, or rapidly changing customer demands.

For the remainder of this book, I will use our fictitious example company, QW Example Tech, Inc., as the basis for presenting, reading, and analyzing financial information, statements, and reports. Multiple years of financial information will also be presented to assist with providing more insight into how to better understand and read financial statements. To add some intrigue and twists to this book, our fictitious example company will be presented in three separate case studies (summarized in depth in Chapter 5), including a base case, a simple case, and an aggressive case. The cases depict the same company and the same financial transactional activity for the year, but under different management at the C-suite level and at the level of the management team responsible for the accounting and financial function.

If you would like to leap ahead and dig into our fictitious example company and gain a complete understanding of each case study, then please jump to Chapter 5. If you would prefer a quick refresher course on the importance of cash flows, the big three financial statements, and financial statement connections, then Chapters 1 through 4 have been designed especially for you.

Before I provide a more detailed explanation of the cash inflows and outflows summarized in Exhibit 1.1, please keep these three points in mind:

- First, the format presented in Exhibit 1.1 is not within the guidelines dictated by GAAP (i.e., Generally Accepted Accounting Principles) but rather has been simplified for ease of review

EXHIBIT 1.1—UNAUDITED SUMMARY OF CASH FLOWS—SIMPLE FORMAT, BASE CASE (SEB)

Dollar Amounts in Thousands

Summary of Cash Flows For the Fiscal Year Ending	12/31/2023
Cash Flows from Profit-Making Activities	
From sales of products & services to customers, which includes some sales made last year	$ 58,261
For acquiring products & services that were sold, or are still being held for future sale	$(19,650)
For operating & other expenses, some of which were incurred last year	$(33,888)
For interest on short-term and long-term debt, some of which applies to different years	$ (407)
For income tax, some of which was paid on last year's taxable income	$ (438)
Net cash flow from profit-making activities during year	$ 3,879
Cash Flows from Other Sources and Uses	
From increasing amount borrowed on interest-bearing notes payable, net of repayments	$ 3,000
From repayments of loans and other amounts borrowed during the year	$ (2,240)
From issuing additional capital stock (ownership shares) in the business	$ 2,500
For building improvements, new machines, new equipment, and intangible assets	$ (5,500)
For distributions or dividends to stockholders from profit	$ (250)
Net cash decrease from other sources and uses	$ (2,490)
Net Cash Increase (Decrease) during Year	$ 1,389

and understanding. This is why the header to Exhibit 1.1 references financial information and not a financial statement. In Chapter 2, we present a formal statement of cash flows in Exhibit 2.3 that is within the guidelines established by GAAP. Of course, one consistency between the exhibits will be that the change in cash between the two years will be exactly the same (which should be expected).

- Second, note that the caption describes this as *unaudited*. This reference is always extremely important to keep in mind because, when a qualified third party (e.g., a CPA firm) is retained to audit financial information, the report issued will clearly state that the financial information has been audited. If no mention is made to the financial information being audited or it clearly states that the financial information is unaudited, this usually indicates the financial information has been prepared internally by the company. This is not to say the financial information is incorrect and/or inaccurate but rather indicates that it has not been examined, evaluated, or audited by an independent third party, so the risk of errors or omissions may be increased.

- Third, in Exhibit 1.1 we reference profit in lieu of income for ease of presentation and understanding. It is important to keep in mind that for most businesses, profit or net profit is synonymous with the term income or net income, which I use interchangeably throughout the book.

Exhibit 1.1 summarizes the company's cash inflows and outflows for the year just ended 12/31/23 and shows two separate groups of cash flows.

Presented first are the cash flows of its profit-making activities—cash inflows from sales and cash outflows for expenses. Second up, we present the other cash inflows and outflows of the business—raising capital from loans or the sale of stock, repaying borrowings, investing capital in assets, and distributing some of its profit to shareowners.

We assume you're fairly familiar with the cash inflows and outflows listed in Exhibit 1.1. Therefore, we are brief in describing the cash flows at this early point in the book:

- The business received $58,261,000 during the year from selling products and services to its customers. It should be no surprise that this is its largest source of cash inflow. Cash inflow from sales revenue is needed for paying expenses. During the year, the company paid $19,650,000 for the products and services it sells to customers while incurring sizable cash outflows for operating expenses ($33,888,000), interest on its debt (borrowed money of $407,000), and income taxes ($438,000). The net result of its cash flows of profit-making activities is a $3,879,000 cash increase for the year—an extremely important number that managers, lenders, and investors watch closely.
- Moving on to the second group of cash flows during the year, the business increased the amount borrowed on notes payable by $3,000,000, repaid $2,240,000 of borrowings during the year, and its stockholders invested an additional $2,500,000 in the business. Together these three external sources of capital provided a net of $3,260,000, which is in addition to the internal $3,879,000 cash from its profit-making activities during the year. On the other side of the ledger, the business spent $5,500,000 for building improvements, new machines and equipment, and intangible assets. Finally, the business distributed $250,000 in the form of a dividend to its stockholders.
- The net result of all cash inflows and outflows is a $1,389,000 cash *increase* during the year. It should be noted that when you see an increase in cash, you shouldn't jump to any conclusions. In and of itself, a net increase in cash is neither good nor bad. You need more information than appears in the summary of cash flows to come to any conclusions about the financial performance and situation of the business.

What Does Cash Flows Summary *Not* Tell You?

In Exhibit 1.1 we see that cash, the all-important lubricant of business activity, increased $1,389,000 during the period (in this case, a year). In other words, the total cash inflows exceeded the total of cash outflows by this amount for the period. The cash increase and the reasons for it are vital information. The summary of cash flows tells us part of the story, but cash flows alone do not tell the whole story. A business's managers, investors, lenders, and other stakeholders need to know two additional pieces of information that are *not* reported in an organization's summary of cash flows. They are:

1. The profit earned (or loss suffered) by the business for the period, which is reported in the income statement.
2. The financial condition of the business at the end of the period, which is reported in the balance sheet.

Now, hold on. Exhibit 1.1 just informed us that the net cash increase from sales revenue less expenses was $3,879,000 for the year. This may lead you to ask, "Doesn't this cash increase equal the amount of profit earned for the year?" No, it doesn't. The net cash flow from profit-making operations during the period does not equal the amount of profit earned for the period. In fact, it's not unusual for these two numbers to be very different.

Profit is an *accounting-determined* number that requires much more than simply keeping track of cash flows. The differences between using a checkbook to measure profit and using accounting methods to measure profit are important to understand. Cash flows during a period are ***hardly ever*** the correct amounts for measuring a company's sales revenue and expenses for that period. To summarize: Profit cannot be determined from cash flows.

Furthermore, a summary of cash flows reveals virtually nothing about the *financial condition* of the business. Financial condition refers to the assets of the business matched against its liabilities at the end of the period. For example: How much cash does the company have in its checking account(s) at the end of the year? From the summary of cash flows (Exhibit 1.1) we can see that the business increased its cash balance by $1,389,000 during the year, but we cannot determine the company's ending cash balance. More importantly, the cash flows summary does not report the amounts of assets and liabilities of the business at the end of the period.

Profit Is Not Measured by Cash Flows

The company in this example sells both products and services on credit. The business offers its customers a short time period (e.g., 30 days) to pay for their purchases. Most of the company's sales are to other businesses, which demand credit. (In contrast, most retailers selling to individuals accept credit cards, debit cards, and other forms of immediate electronic payments instead of extending credit to their customers.) In this example, the company collected $58,261,000 from its customers during the year. However, some of this cash inflow was for sales made in the *previous* year. And some sales made on credit in the year just ended had not been collected by the end of the year.

At year-end, the company had *receivables* from sales made to its customers during the latter part of the year. These receivables should be collected early next year (hopefully). To clarify, some cash was collected from last year's sales but some cash was not yet collected before the year ended, so the total amount of cash collected during the year differs from the amount of *sales revenue* for the year.

Cash disbursements during the year are *not* the correct amounts for measuring expenses. The company paid $19,650,000 for products and services that could be sold to customers. At year-end, however, many products were still being held in *inventory*. These products had not yet been sold by year-end. Only the cost of products sold and delivered to customers during the year should be deducted as an expense from sales revenue to measure profit. Don't you agree?

Furthermore, some of the company's product costs had not yet been paid by the end of the year. The company buys on credit and takes several weeks to pay its bills. The company has *liabilities* at the year-end for recent product purchases and operating costs. Further complicating the situation, the company makes cash payments during the year for operating expenses and interest and income tax expenses, but these are not the correct amounts for measuring profit for the year. At the end of the year, the company has liabilities for *unpaid expenses*. The cash outflow amounts shown in Exhibit 1.1 do not include the unpaid expenses at the end of the year.

In short, cash flows from sales revenue and for expenses are not necessarily the correct amounts for measuring profit for a period of time. Many types of cash flows take place too late or too early so they cannot be used to correctly measure profit for a period. Correct timing is needed to record sales revenue and expenses in the right period. The amounts of cash flows caused by sales and expenses could turn out to be fairly close to the correct accounting amounts—or they could be vastly different. Even slight differences between the cash flow amounts and the correct accounting amounts can cause problems.

Cash Flows Do Not Reveal Financial Condition

The cash flows summary for the year does not reveal the financial condition of the company. Managers certainly need to know which assets the business owns and the amounts of each asset, which can include cash, receivables, and inventory, among others. Also, they need to know which liabilities the company owes and the amounts of each.

Business managers are responsible for keeping the company in a position to pay its liabilities when they come due. In other words, managers have to keep the business *solvent* (able to pay its liabilities on time) and *liquid* (having enough available cash to meet its needs). Furthermore, managers have to know whether assets are too large (or too small) relative to the sales volume of the business. A company's lenders and investors want to know the same things.

In brief, both the managers inside the business and the lenders and investors outside the business need a summary of a company's financial condition (its assets and liabilities). They also need a profit performance report, which summarizes the company's sales revenue, expenses, and profit for the year.

In this chapter, we have explained that a cash flows summary has its limits—in particular, it does not report profit and does not present the financial condition of a business. Nevertheless, a cash flows summary is useful. A different version of Exhibit 1.1 is one of the three primary financial statements reported by every business, which is the statement of cash flows (further discussed in Chapter 2). But in no sense does a cash flows summary take the place of the profit performance report (i.e., the income statement) or the financial condition report (i.e., the balance sheet). The next chapter introduces these two financial statements as well as a more formal statement of cash flows (compared to what has been presented and discussed in this chapter).

A Few Additional Thoughts to Keep in Mind

Over the past century (and longer) the *accounting profession* has developed. One of its main functions is to prepare and report business financial statements. A primary goal of the accounting profession has been to develop and enforce accounting and financial reporting standards that apply to all businesses. In other words, there is an authoritative rule book that businesses should obey in accounting for and reporting profit, financial condition, and cash flows. The established rules and standards are collectively referred to as *generally accepted accounting principles* (GAAP). Businesses are not free to make up their own individual accounting methods and financial reporting practices and should strive to develop and maintain GAAP-based accounting and financial information and reporting systems (applied on a consistent basis). However, two key points need further clarification as it relates to preparing GAAP-based financial statements:

- First, pay close attention to the word *should*. That is, companies should make every effort to develop and maintain accounting systems that are in compliance with GAAP. Here's the *but*: You would be amazed at how many businesses (especially smaller and medium-sized private businesses that are not as sophisticated) will make an attempt to develop and maintain a GAAP-based accounting system and do a fairly good job, but often are not 100% in technical compliance with GAAP (for any number of reasons).
- Second, companies are provided leeway to interpret and apply different accounting methods and guidelines that have been established by authoritative bodies. For example, different GAAP accounting methods have been established to value inventory, including LIFO, FIFO, average cost, and standard cost. I won't bore you with the details explaining the difference between these inventory valuation methods, as the key concept to remember is that similar companies operating in the same industry may in fact use different accounting methods to value basically the same asset (i.e., inventory).

If explaining the basic concept of GAAP previously isn't confusing enough, here's some additional nuggets to chew on as it relates to things getting more complicated these days.

Presently, in the United States, there are continuing developments to adopt separate rules for private companies versus public companies and for small companies versus larger companies. As both an author of numerous accounting and financial books and as a full-time consulting fractional CFO, I can say that I wholeheartedly agree with these efforts as requiring certain smaller and private companies to apply highly technical accounting concepts that do not have a material impact on a business is a step in the right direction. A primary goal of accounting should be to calculate and present the fair economic performance of a company over a period of time (or at a period end). Burying certain businesses in accounting concepts, rules, and guidelines that are overly complex or technical is, without question, counterproductive.

Furthermore, efforts to harmonize American accounting and financial reporting standards with those of other countries keep slogging along. There has been a lot of standardization. Yet, there are several areas of accounting and financial reporting in which there are differences between countries. From time to time throughout this book, I provide more insight into the changing landscape of accounting and financial reporting standards and how it may impact different businesses.

2

A REFRESHER ON THE BIG THREE FINANCIAL STATEMENTS

As noted in the Preface, the primary purpose of Part One of this book is to provide a refresher course on critical concepts covered in *How to Read a Financial Report*, 10th Edition. In the spirit of this objective, Chapter 2 of this book has been dedicated to summarizing the big three financial statements again, including the income statement, the balance sheet, and the statement of cash flows. But a word of caution is best delivered at this point, as one of the key objectives of producing a field guide for *How to Read a Financial Report*, 10th Edition, is to expand, develop, and advance your knowledge of financial reports, financial statements, and accounting. These skills underpin financial information, reports, and statements. Here, you may stop and ask yourself, "What in the world is this guy talking about?" You may believe, and rightfully so, that accounting and finance comprise a relatively boring business function that should be relatively predictable and consistently applied. Well, I hate to burst your bubble, but starting in Chapter 5, I'm going to introduce you to the wonderful world of accounting (or maybe the more appropriate term is "creative accounting") and finance from the perspective of different business operating environments and management teams.

Before we reach Chapter 5, where the real fun begins, I'm going to take this opportunity to revisit the big three financial statements, which will include supporting exhibits for the base case of our fictitious example business. I would also like to note that as you move through this book, it is important to remember that *How to Read a Financial Report*, 10th Edition, takes more of a technical/accounting perspective or approach. In other words, it is a bit more black and white because it provides an understanding of accounting and financial concepts and how the big three financial statements are interconnected. This book is based on more of a real-world business approach that, while it adheres to general or standard accounting rules and guidelines, its primary purpose is to assist with socializing accounting concepts, business operating environments, the production of financial statements, financial analyses and reporting strategies, and business planning from an internal operating or strategic perspective. As I used to tell my dad (who was professor emeritus at the University of Colorado), "That is how you teach it in the classroom, but this is how it is done on the street."

Let's launch into our first topic on the big three financial statements, making sure you have a clear understanding of the role and importance of the balance sheet, income statement (aka profit-and-loss, or P&L), and statement of cash flows. Large or small, for-profit or non-profit, corporations, LLCs, partnerships or sole proprietorships, governments or private businesses, legal or illegal, it doesn't really matter, as this basic concept is always present. That is, all operating entities need to produce complete, accurate, reliable, and timely financial statements on which to base sound business decision-making.

The Financial Reporting Bedrock

It should go without saying that business managers, company lenders and investors, regulatory agencies, and countless other parties need to clearly and concisely understand an organization's financial performance and results in a timely manner. This is common sense, no doubt, but you would be absolutely amazed at how often this basic concept is overlooked or, for lack of a better term, neglected by even the senior-most executive management teams. Maybe it is a result of ignorance, not having enough time, or just being lazy, but as we start our discussion on the big three financial statements, it should become abundantly clear just how important all three primary financial statements are and the key role each one plays.

Before I dive into a more detailed analysis of each of the big three financial statements, a quick overview of each financial statement and the related purpose is warranted:

- ***The balance sheet:*** The financial condition of a business is communicated in an accounting report called the *balance sheet*. In its simplest form, the balance sheet reports the assets a business owns, the liabilities it owes (to third parties), and the net ownership equity (assets minus liabilities), all at a point in time.
- ***The income statement (or P&L):*** The financial performance of a business that reports and measures its profit- or loss-making activities is presented in an accounting report called the *income statement*. In its simplest form, the income statement reports sales, costs of goods sold, operating expenses, other expenses or income, and finally, whether a net profit or loss was generated over a specific period of time (e.g., 12-month period of 1/1/23 through 12/31/23).
- ***The statement of cash flows:*** Finally, the last of the big three financial statements, and often the most important (but least understood), is the *statement of cash flows*. In its simplest form, this financial statement reports a business's sources (i.e., how a business generates cash), uses (i.e., how a company consumes cash), and net change in cash. Similar to the income statement, the statement of cash flows covers a time period that is almost always consistent with the one reported in the income statement.

It should be noted that alternative titles for these financial statements are common. For the balance sheet, alternatives include "statement of financial condition" or "statement of financial position." An income statement may be titled "statement of operations" or "earnings statement" as well as the profit and loss or, more simply, the P&L. For ease of presentation, I stick with the names *balance sheet* and *income statement* to be consistent throughout the book. The statement of cash flows is almost always called just that (but sometimes referred to as just a cash flow statement).

Finally, as you work your way through the book, please remember these definitions for frequently used terms and concepts:

- ***Financial information:*** The term *financial information* is used throughout the entire book and, in its broadest sense, includes all types of financial reports, financial statements, data, analyses, evaluations, assessments, and so on. Generally speaking, I will use consistent terminology throughout this book with a primary focus on producing financial reports and financial statements.
- ***Businesses:*** As previously noted, all types of businesses, organizations, not-for-profits, government entities, and so on should produce financial statements on a periodic basis. Again, for ease of reference and consistency, when I refer to a *business* throughout the book, it is assumed to include any one of the entities identified.
- ***Financial statements:*** The term *financial statements*, in the plural, generally refers to a complete set that includes a balance sheet, an income statement, and a statement of cash flows, and it often infers that multiple years of financial statements will be presented. Informally, financial statements are called just *financials*. In almost all cases, the financial statements need to be supplemented with additional information, which is presented in *footnotes* and *supporting schedules*. One supporting schedule is very common—the *statement of changes in stockholders' (owners') equity*.

The Income Statement (aka Profit-and-Loss or P&L)

First up, I will begin with the income statement, as, for most parties, this is the financial statement that is not only looked to first to quickly assess total sales generated (which is a common measurement of the "size" of a business) and whether a business made any money (i.e., a profit), but, maybe more importantly, is the financial statement that tends to be the most easily understood. Exhibit 2.1 provides an example of a standard externally presented income statement.

The income statement is read in a step-down manner. At the top of the income statement, sales revenue is reported first. Then, as you proceed down each step, a deduction of one or more expenses is reported. The first step deducts the cost of goods (products) sold from the sales revenue of goods sold, which gives *gross profit* (also called *gross margin*—one of the few places you see the term *profit* in income statements). This measure of profit is called *gross* because many other expenses are not yet deducted.

Next, a broad category of general business expenses, often referred to as *operating expenses* or *selling, general, and administrative expenses* (SG&A) are reported in the P&L. In our income statement example (Exhibit 2.1), you see three different operating expenses presented, including SG&A, followed by research and development, and, finally, depreciation and amortization expense. When preparing external income statements, there is no set rule as to how many expenses must be presented. Still, generally speaking, you will find that most external income statements attempt to avoid providing too much detail and limit the list to eight or fewer (unless the business had a very unusual year and elects to provide additional disclosures).

In our business example, the reason I have chosen to disclose three specific expense "buckets" separately is for their importance.

- First, in today's hyper-technology–driven economy, investors are keenly focused on how much a business spends on research and development (an extremely important function). Since our example company is a technology-based business, this expense bucket makes sense to report separately.
- Second, SG&A expense is highlighted to reflect the importance of just how much a business must spend to secure or capture customers and, ultimately, drive sales revenue and to include the costs associated with managing and operating the business. In some cases, businesses will separate total SG&A expenses between direct selling, marketing, and promotional costs versus corporate operating expenses, but in our fictitious example company, I've elected to consolidate these expenses for ease of reporting.
- Third, you will notice that in our income statement example, I have elected to report depreciation and amortization expense (unique noncash expenses) as a separate line item. This is because as I move through the book and highlight

EXHIBIT 2.1—AUDITED FINANCIAL STATEMENTS—INCOME STATEMENT, BASE CASE (SEB)

Dollar Amounts in Thousands

Income Statement For the Fiscal Years Ending	12/31/2022	12/31/2023
Sales Revenue, Net	$ 54,210	$ 59,494
Costs of Sales Revenue, Service	$(12,882)	$ (14,374)
Costs of Sales Revenue, Products	$(11,040)	$ (7,392)
Gross Profit (aka Gross Margin)	$ 30,288	$ 37,728
Operating Expenses:		
Selling, General, & Administrative	$ 22,567	$ 25,289
Research & Development	$ 5,692	$ 7,139
Depreciation & Amortization	$ 1,571	$ 1,643
Total Operating Expenses	$ 29,831	$ 34,071
Operating Income (Loss)	$ 457	$ 3,658
Other Expenses (Income):		
Other Expenses (Income)	$ 0	$ 2,000
Interest Expense	$ 339	$ 407
Total Other Expenses (Income)	$ 339	$ 2,407
Net Income (Loss) before Income Taxes	$ 118	$ 1,251
Income Tax Expense (Benefit)	$ 41	$ 438
Net Income (Loss) after Income Taxes	$ 77	$ 813

See Notes to Financial Statements

Sales revenue (aka the "top line") is always reported first with costs of goods sold then reported to calculate gross profit.

Operating expenses are reported after gross profits and capture general company business expenses.

Finally, after all expenses are reported the company reports its net profit (or loss), often referred to as the "bottom line."

the importance of understanding the statement of cash flows, it is very convenient to segregate noncash expenses such as depreciation and amortization expense as a separate line item in the income statement. It should be noted that businesses may or may not report depreciation or amortization expense on a separate line in their income statements based on the concept of materiality. I have elected to report depreciation and amortization as a unique expense to better help readers understand its impact on earnings, cash flow, and the balance sheet.

The level of detail for expenses in income statements is flexible and highly dependent on the desires of the company's management team to report what they believe is the right balance of providing too much detail versus not enough. From a financial reporting standards perspective, the guidelines are somewhat loose on this point and left open for different levels of opinions.

Finally, I reach the bottom portion of the income statement, where other expenses and income are reported. Interest expense on debt is deducted as well as other non-recurring-type expenses (e.g., in this case, a large loss was incurred to account for obsolete inventory), which generates earnings before income tax. The last step is to deduct income tax expense, which gives net income, the bottom line in the income statement. Undoubtedly, you have heard the term *bottom line* (but this slang is not used in financial statements), as well as *top line*, which refers to total sales revenue. Other terminology you should be aware of include being in the black (generating a profit) or the red (incurring a loss).

Note: Publicly owned businesses are required to report earnings per share (EPS), which basically is annual net income divided by the number of capital stock shares or similar investment units. Privately owned businesses don't have to report EPS, but this figure may be useful to their stockholders.

To conclude our introduction with the income statement, three items should be kept in mind.

- First, the income statement presented in Exhibit 2.1 has been structured for external presentation (as opposed to internal business analysis). I dive into the key differences and importance of income statements prepared for external versus internal parties later in this book.
- Second, it is important to note that of the big three financial statements, the income statement tends to be the most often manipulated or subject to misstatement. The reason for this is that many parties tend to focus on this financial statement to the exclusion of the others, making it the main attraction. These same parties are often not nearly as well versed in understanding the balance sheet and statement of cash flows.
- Third, you will see multiple references to this all-important advice, which simply states: ***Understand the income statement, trust the balance sheet, but most importantly, rely on the statement of cash flows.*** As you work through the financial statements and this book, the importance of the state of cash flows will become increasingly apparent.

The Balance Sheet

The financial statement that is second in line is the balance sheet, which in its simplest form presents the *financial condition* of a business at a point in time (e.g., as of the FYE 12/31/23). Unlike the income statement, which presents a business's financial performance over a period of time, the balance sheet reports and summarizes a business's assets and liabilities, as well as the ownership interests in the residual of assets in excess of liabilities (referred to as owners' equity) at a specific point in time.

The balance sheet shown in Exhibit 2.2 follows the standardized format regarding the classification and ordering of assets, liabilities, and ownership interests in the business. It should be noted that financial institutions, public utilities, railroads, and other specialized businesses use somewhat different balance sheet layouts, but, for the purpose of this book, I will use the standard format presented in Exhibit 2.2 for our overview. This format is generally used by technology companies, manufacturers, distributors, professional service companies, retailers, and the large majority of other business types.

The assets, liabilities, and owners' equity reported in the balance sheet follow generally accepted conventions, which I briefly summarize here. According to long-standing rules, balance sheet accounts are subdivided into the following classes, or basic groups, in the following order of presentation:

Left Side (or Top Section)	***Right Side (or Bottom Section)***
Current assets	Current liabilities
Long-term operating assets	Long-term liabilities
Other assets	Owners' equity

Balance sheets are often presented in a horizontal format, with ***assets*** presented or listed on the left side, ***liabilities*** on the upper half of the right side, and ***net owners' equity*** on the lower half of the right side below the liabilities to emphasize that the owners or equity holders in a business (the stockholders of a business corporation) have a secondary and lower-order claim on the assets—after its liabilities are satisfied. Balance sheets can also be presented in a vertical format with assets listed at the top or first, liabilities listed in the middle or second, and net owners' equity presented at the bottom or third. For ease of presentation, I used the vertical format in Exhibit 2.2.

Roughly speaking, a balance sheet lists assets in their order of "nearness to cash." Cash is listed first at the top of the assets stack. Next, receivables that will be collected in the short run are listed, and so on down the line. In later chapters, I say much more about the cash characteristics of different assets. In like manner,

EXHIBIT 2.2—AUDITED FINANCIAL STATEMENTS—BALANCE SHEET, BASE CASE (SEB)

Dollar Amounts in Thousands

Balance Sheet as of the Fiscal Year Ending	12/31/2022	12/31/2023
Assets		
Current Assets:		
Cash & Equivalents	$ 775	$ 2,164
Accounts Receivable	$ 6,776	$ 8,009
Inventory	$ 3,822	$ 1,706
Prepaid Expenses	$ 600	$ 625
Total Current Assets	$ 11,973	$12,504
Long-Term Operating & Other Assets:		
Property, Machinery, & Equipment	$ 4,000	$ 4,500
Less: Accumulated Depreciation	$ (1,571)	$ (2,214)
Net Property, Machinery, & Equipment	$ 2,429	$ 2,286
Other Assets:		
Intangible Assets, Net	$ 2,000	$ 6,000
Other Assets	$ 100	$ 100
Total Long-Term Operating & Other Assets	$ 4,529	$ 8,386
Total Assets	$ 16,502	$20,889
Liabilities		
Current Liabilities:		
Accounts Payable	$ 1,405	$ 1,459
Accrued Liabilities Payable	$ 1,084	$ 1,258
Short-Term Loans Payable	$ 3,390	$ 2,400
Other Current Liabilities & Deferred Revenue	$ 1,011	$ 1,348
Total Current Liabilities	$ 6,890	$ 6,465
Long-Term Liabilities:		
Loans Payable & Other Long-Term Debt, Less ST Loans	$ 750	$ 2,500
Total Liabilities	$ 7,640	$ 8,965
Stockholders' Equity		
Capital Stock-Common	$ 7,500	$10,000
Retained Earnings	$ 1,362	$ 1,924
Total Stockholders' Equity	$ 8,862	$11,924
Total Liabilities & Stockholders' Equity	$ 16,502	$20,889

See Notes to Financial Statements

Cash & equivalents listed first followed by accounts receivables (highly liquid). Notice the decrease in inventory from the prior year. I'll get to this later.

Tangible capital assets are presented, which include equipment, machinery, furniture, computers, etc.

Finally, other assets are presented. Large increase in intangible assets relates to intangible assets, patents & software acquired.

Trade payables & accrued liabilities listed first followed by current portion of debt.

Long-term liabilities presented next. Notice increase from prior year.

Finally, capital stock is listed next followed by retained earnings. This company raised $2.5 million of capital with stock sales in 2023.

liabilities are presented in the sequence of their "nearness to payment." I discuss this point as we move along in later chapters.

Each separate asset, liability, and stockholders' equity reported in a balance sheet is called an *account*. Every account has a name (title) and a dollar amount, which is called its *balance*. For instance, from Exhibit 2.2, at the end of the most recent FYE ending December 31, 2023, the inventory account had a balance of $1,706,000. It should be noted that the inventory account is most likely made up of multiple sub-accounts, including raw material, work-in-process, finished goods, and other inventory accounts, which, for external reporting purposes, are consolidated to reflect just one value in inventory. This generally holds for most other balances (presented in the balance sheet) as in almost all cases, the dollar figure represents a summation of multiple individual accounts (that are summed together given their similarities in purpose).

A balance sheet is prepared at the close of business on the last day of the income statement period. For example, if the income statement is for the year ending December 31, 2023, the balance sheet is prepared at midnight on December 31, 2023. The amounts reported in the balance sheet are the balances of the accounts at that precise moment in time. The financial condition of the business is frozen for one split second. A business should be careful to make a precise and accurate cutoff to separate transactions between the period just ended and the next period.

A balance sheet does not report the flows of activities in the company's assets, liabilities, and shareowners' equity accounts during the period. Only the ending balances at the moment the balance sheet is prepared are reported for the accounts. For example, the company reports an ending cash balance of $2,164,000 at the end of its most recent FYE (see again Exhibit 2.2). Can you tell the total cash inflows and outflows for the year? No, not from the balance sheet. You can't even get a clue from the balance sheet alone because the flow of cash over a period of time represents the purpose of the statement of cash flows.

Some part of the total assets of a business comes not from liabilities but from its owners investing capital in the business and from retaining some or all of the profit the business earns that is not distributed to its owners. In this example the business is organized legally as a corporation. Its *stockholders' equity* accounts in the balance sheet reveal the sources of the company's total assets in excess of its total liabilities. Notice in Exhibit 2.2 the two stockholders' (owners') equity sources, which are referred to as *capital stock—common* and *retained earnings*. For a number of businesses, it is not uncommon to have different types of capital stock often referred to as common and preferred. The reason companies separate disclosing common and preferred stock is extremely important to understand and will be covered in more depth in Chapter 15 in our discussion on the cap table and cap stack.

When owners (stockholders of a business corporation) invest capital in the business, the capital stock account is increased. Net income earned by a business less the amount distributed to owners increases the retained earnings account. The nature of retained earnings can be confusing; therefore, I explain this account in depth at the appropriate places in the book. Just a quick word of advice here: Retained earnings is *not*—I repeat, is *not*—an asset. Get such a notion out of your head.

A final word or two with the balance sheet. First, when reviewing the balance sheet, keep these thoughts in your head: Are your assets lying to you? and Are your liabilities telling you the truth? For example, in our balance sheet presented in Exhibit 2.2, the value in inventory as of the FYE 12/31/22 is stated at $3,822,000, yet this decreases to $1,706,000 as of the FYE 12/31/23 (a substantial drop). The value of inventory was written down in 2023 (as you will discover later in this book), but it begs the question, did management "massage" the inventory value to be a bit higher as of the FYE 12/31/22 to protect net income?

Second, it is recommended that you become familiar with the term *balance sheet dressing*. No, this is not some special type of side dish served with your seasonal Thanksgiving Day turkey but rather represents the efforts by company executives to manage certain transactions as of the end of a period to present the performance of a business in the best light possible. When I dive into various company performance ratios and analyses covered in Chapters 11 and 12, this will become more apparent.

The Statement of Cash Flows

Finally, we reach the third and final financial statement of the big three, which I like to think of in terms of the Disney movie *Cinderella*. If you recall, the two attention-starved stepsisters (i.e., the balance sheet and income statement) demand all the attention and relegate Cinderella to performing demeaning tasks. However, as the story moves forward, Cinderella blossoms into the most beautiful sister of all as her true, deep, and rich character comes to light. You might think of the statement of cash flows in this same light as, once you truly understand its importance and meaning, you will find that it shines an amazing light on the operating performance of a business.

It might be an overreach, but this analogy drives home a critical concept associated with the big three financial statements. That is, the income statement and, to a lesser extent, the balance sheet, tend to get most of the attention from financial experts. As in today's "time is of the essence" business mindset, the questions that generally first come to mind are: (a) What are top-line sales (and how much did they grow)?, (b) What's the company's bottom-line profit?, and (c) How financially strong is the company? All good questions, but none of these addresses the most important question of all—can the business generate enough cash to support ongoing operations? This, in a nutshell, represents the essence of the statement of cash flows.

Earlier in this chapter you were introduced to the two hardcore financial statements that are included in the financial report of a business, Exhibit 2.1 (income statement) and Exhibit 2.2 (balance sheet). These two provide a comprehensive summary of the financial performance and financial condition of the business. This is not the end of the story, however. Financial reporting standards require that a *statement of cash flows* also be presented for the same time period as the income statement.

This third financial statement, as its title implies, focuses on the cash flows of the period. The cash flow statement is not "better" than the income statement or balance sheet. Rather, it discloses additional critical information that supplements the income statement and balance sheet.

Exhibit 2.3 presents the statement of cash flows for our business example. Similar to the income statement, the statement of cash flows reads from the top down, and has three primary parts, or layers: cash flows from *operating* activities, cash flows from *investing* activities, and cash flows from *financing* activities.

Cash flows from *operating* activities refers to revenue and expenses (as well as gains and losses) during the period that culminates in the bottom-line net income or loss for the period. In short, "operating" refers to the profit- (or loss) making activities of the business and, as you can see, represents the first amount reported in the statement of cash flows (at the top of the statement). After this, companies generally report noncash expenses, such as depreciation and amortization expense, along with reporting changes in the company's current assets and current liabilities realized during

EXHIBIT 2.3—AUDITED FINANCIAL STATEMENTS—STATEMENT OF CASH FLOWS, BASE CASE (SEB)

Dollar Amounts in Thousands

Statement of Cash Flows **For the Fiscal Years Ending**	**12/31/2022**	**12/31/2023**
Net Income (Loss) after Income Taxes	$ 77	$ 813
Operating Activities, Cash provided (used):		
Depreciation & Amortization	$ 1,571	$ 1,643
Decrease (increase) in Accounts Receivables	$(1,122)	$(1,233)
Decrease (increase) in Inventory	$ (333)	$ 2,116
Decrease (increase) in Other Current Assets	$ (50)	$ (25)
Increase (decrease) in Accounts Payables	$ 155	$ 54
Increase (decrease) in Accrued Liabilities	$ 118	$ 42
Increase (decrease) in Other Liabilities	$ 217	$ 469
Net Cash Flow from Operating Activities	$ 634	$ 3,879
Investing Activities, Cash Provided (Used):		
Capital Expenditures	$ (250)	$ (500)
Investments in Intangible & Other Assets	$ 0	$(5,000)
Net Cash Flow from Investing Activities	$ (250)	$(5,500)
Financing Activities, Cash Provided (Used):		
Dividends or Distributions Paid	$ 0	$ (250)
Sale (Repurchase) of Equity	$ 0	$ 2,500
Proceeds from Issuance of Loans (i.e., Debt)	$ 0	$ 3,000
Repayments of Long-Term Loans	$ (750)	$(1,250)
Net Borrowings (Repayments) of Short-Term Loans	$ 560	$ (990)
Other Financing Activities	$ 0	$ 0
Net Cash Flow from Financing Activities	$ (190)	$ 3,010
Other Cash Flow Adjustments - Asset Impairment	$ 0	$ 0
Net Increase (Decrease) in Cash & Equivalents	$ 194	$ 1,389
Beginning Cash & Equivalents Balance	$ 581	$ 775
Ending Cash & Equivalents Balance	$ 775	$ 2,164

See Notes to Financial Statements

Statement of cash flows begins with information from the income statement including net profit or loss & depr./amort expense.

Net cash flow from operating activities presents a company's ability to generate or consume cash from internal operations.

Net cash flow from investing activities is presented next. Note the significant investment made in other assets (acquisition of intangible assets).

Net cash flow from financing activities is presented last. The company raised money from both debt and equity sources.

Ending cash balance agrees to the balance sheet (a proper check and balance).

the reporting period. Once all this activity is reported, net cash flow from operating activities is reported, which in our example amounts to a positive $3,879,000 for the FYE 12/31/23.

This next statement may sound counterintuitive, but it is especially important to understand: When a company's asset value increases over a period of time, this represents a use of cash (i.e., cash is consumed and decreases during the period). Likewise, when a company's asset value decreases over a period of time, this represents a source of cash (e.g., inventory is sold, the value is reduced, and it is turned into cash when the customer pays). On the liability side of life, a liability increasing in value over a period of time represents a source of cash (the opposite of the asset relationship), and a liability decreasing in value over a period of time represents a use of cash (e.g., vendor obligations due are paid, consuming cash).

As you work through the book, these concepts will become clearer and emphasize a critical concept in business financial management. That is, in order to improve liquidity and cash flows, businesses need to make sure they don't overinvest in assets (that consume excess cash), and that they also utilize appropriate credit sources from vendors, third parties, future customers (e.g., receiving deposits), and so on to leverage their liabilities to improve cash flows. What this means is that smart business operators know exactly how far they can push vendors, suppliers, lenders, and so on to provide extra or extended terms to retain added cash inside a company to support ongoing operations.

Next up in the statement of cash flows is the section referred to as cash provided or (used) in *investing* activities. This section generally reports how a company spends or invests large amounts of cash/capital in long-term investments such as equipment or machinery additions, investments in intangible assets such as software development, and so forth (i.e., what long-term investments are being made by the company). In our example company, one item that should clearly catch your eye is the $5,000,000 investment made in intangible assets during the FYE 12/31/23. As we will discover later in the book, this investment was part of a large acquisition of intangible assets the company made from another business to drive future growth.

The final section in the statement of cash flows presents cash provided or used in the *financing* activities of the business. This section is designed to clearly disclose how a company finances its business operations from sources of cash other than operating cash flows (previously discussed). The information reported in this section relates to both how a company secures cash/capital (debt or equity) from external parties and how cash/capital is deployed as a return to the external parties. For example, in our example company, you will notice that $3,000,000 of new debt was secured during the FYE 12/31/23, while at the same time, $1,250,000 of old debt was repaid during the same period. You may ask what these transactions relate to, so I'll go ahead and give you a hint. The company raised new debt of $3,000,000 (along with selling equity, raising another $2,500,000) to fund a large intangible asset acquisition of $5,000,000. As part of its new debt facility, the company was required to pay off an existing loan (thus the repayment or use of $1,250,000 for debt).

At the very end of the statement of cash flows, a simple summary calculates the net increase or decrease in cash and adds this to the beginning cash balance, which then presents the final ending cash balance.

As we close our summary-level discussion on the statement of cash flows, it's worth visiting (and remembering) two critical concepts:

- First, you will notice that in our example company, a net profit of $813,000 was generated, compared to a net increase in cash of $1,389,000 being realized during the FYE 12/31/23.

If you've ever asked how the net increase in cash during a given period can be greater than the profit generated, the answer lies in the statement of cash flows. Rarely will you find a situation where the net profit generated equates with the exact same amount of net cash increase during the same period, as cash inflows from sales revenue are almost always higher or lower than the actual sales revenue recorded during the period, and actual cash outflows for expenses are typically higher or lower than the amounts of expenses recorded for the period.

- Second, I would direct you toward our previous thoughts on understanding the income statement, trusting the balance sheet, and, most importantly, relying on the statement of cash flows. In effect, the statement of cash flows acts as the glue that ties or connects all the financial statements together. It starts by reporting net profit or loss and depreciation and amortization expense (both from the income statement). Then, it captures all the changes in a company's assets and liabilities to produce a net increase or decrease in cash, which, when added to the beginning cash balance, results in an ending cash balance (which ties to or should agree with the cash balance reported on the balance sheet). In effect, the statement of cash flows acts in the capacity of a self-regulating series of checks and balances to help parties better understand a company's economic model and ability to generate reliable positive cash flows (the ultimate purpose of a business).
- If you are still somewhat confused or hazy with the statement of cash flows, fear not. I've dedicated an entire chapter to this financial statement in Chapter 3, as it is always helpful to dive deeper into a business's financial transactions that provide sources of cash, as well as those financial transactions that consume or use cash.

3

TAKING A DEEPER DIVE INTO THE STATEMENT OF CASH FLOWS

Cash Flows: Why Three Different Numbers?

As with all books I've authored, you will notice one constant message or topic that is always, and I mean always, emphasized. And that is the importance of understanding how businesses generate and consume cash during an operating period such as over one month, one quarter, or one year. This book is no different, as in order to understand the concepts and decipher the exhibits presented, you must develop a reasonable level of understanding and confidence in how companies manage cash resources and what constitutes the primary sources of cash (i.e., where cash comes from) and uses of cash (i.e., where cash goes) during a period of time. This, my friends, is the primary reporting purpose of the final big three financial statement, the statement of cash flows, and why, yet again, an entire chapter (as eluded to at the end of Chapter 2) is dedicated to this subject matter to help you master your knowledge of how businesses generate and consume cash.

To start, it would be helpful to revisit a critical concept in understanding the statement of cash flows to provide a clear picture as to why a company's net bottom-line profit does not equate to its increase or decrease in cash during the year. Yes, this is a valid question, so, to assist you with understanding this concept better, I'm going to build you a bridge (to get from one point to the next) by directing you to three key data points related to our example company's cash flows and break down each one in more depth:

- Recall from Exhibit 2.1 that our example company generated net income after income taxes of $813,000 during the FYE 12/31/23. Simple enough. Total sales revenue less all direct costs of sales revenue, operating expenses, and other expenses equals net bottom-line profit. Does this represent a source of cash for our example company? Absolutely, but does it represent the only source? Absolutely not, as will become evident through the remainder of this chapter.
- Please turn your attention to the middle of Exhibit 2.3 presented in Chapter 2 and notice that per the statement of cash flows, our example company generated net cash flow from operating activities of $3,879,000 during the FYE 12/31/23. So how did our example company generate only $813,000 of net bottom-line profit yet produce $3,879,000 of cash from operating activities? The answer lies in the second section of this chapter titled "Changes in Assets and Liabilities That Impact Cash Flows from Operating Activities."
- If you review Exhibit 2.3, you can see that our example company's net cash balance increased during the FYE 12/31/23 by $1,389,000, which compares to net bottom-line profit of $813,000 (higher) and cash flow generated from operating activities (much lower). Here, the answer lies in the third section of this chapter titled "Completing the Statement of Cash Flows with Investing and Financing Activities."

Before you dive into the remainder of this chapter, please take a moment to read the statement of cash flows presented in

Exhibit 2.3 (in Chapter 2) from top to bottom. I'll make you a wager here. I bet you understand the second and third sections of the statement (*investing* activities and *financing* activities) better than the first section (*operating* activities). Indeed, your reaction to the first section might be that it's all Greek to you, which by the way, is nothing to be embarrassed about as the first section is often the most difficult to understand.

Also, as you work your way through the balance of this chapter, it is essential to remember that business managers have a double duty. First, they must earn a profit, and second, they must convert the profit into cash as soon as possible. Waiting too long to turn profit into cash not only potentially reduces the company's value because of the time value of money, but more importantly, if a company runs out of cash and becomes illiquid—let's just say this is not a place you want to end up. As such, business managers should be clear on the difference between net profit reported in the income statement and the amount of cash flow generated from profit during the year. Creditors and investors should also keep a close eye on cash flow from profit (operating activities) and management's ability to control this important number.

Changes in Assets and Liabilities That Impact Cash Flow from Operating Activities

The main question on everyone's mind seems to be: Why doesn't net profit simply equal cash flow? In our example, the company earned $813,000 net income over the year just ended. Why didn't earning this amount of net profit generate the same amount of cash flow? The first section in the statement of cash flows provides the answer to this question. It shows us that the company generated $3,879,000 cash flow from operating activities compared with its $813,000 net income for the year. Cash flow from operating activities is quite a bit higher than net income for the period.

To help understand what is causing this difference and to reconcile the two amounts, I direct you to Exhibit 3.1, which lists the balance sheet accounts of our example company to close out the prior FYE 12/31/22 and at the end of the current FYE 12/31/23; it includes a column for changes between the two years. (You might compare the informal balance sheet here with the formal layout of the balance sheet introduced in Exhibit 2.2.) This section of the chapter focuses on the first section of the cash flow statement, which explains the determinants of the company's cash flow from operating activities (i.e., its profit-making or profit-seeking activities) during the year. Cash flow from operating activities is driven by changes during the period in the assets and liabilities affected by the revenue and expenses.

To get from net income to the resultant cash flow, I have to make *adjustments* to net income. The adjustments are triggered by changes during the year in the company's operating assets and liabilities (i.e., the assets and liabilities directly involved in recording sales revenue and expenses). Such adjustments are listed in the statement of cash flows, just after the net income. I look at these adjustments in the order shown in the company's statement of cash flows.

Changes in operating assets and liabilities affecting operating cash flow

1. ***Accounts receivable:*** At year-end the company had $8,009,000 uncollected sales revenue, which is the ending balance of its accounts receivable. The $8,009,000 is included in sales revenue for determining profit, but the company did not receive this amount of cash from customers. The $8,009,000 is still in accounts receivable instead of cash at year-end. However, the company collected its $6,776,000 beginning balance of accounts receivable. The $6,776,000 collected minus $8,009,000 not collected results in a $1,233,000 negative impact on cash flow. See the third adjustment in the cash flow statement (Exhibit 3.1). In short, an increase in accounts receivable hurts cash flow from profit.

EXHIBIT 3.1—CASH FLOW FROM OPERATING (PROFIT-MAKING) ACTIVITIES, BASE CASE (SEB)

Dollar Amounts in Thousands

BALANCE SHEET	12/31/2022	12/31/2023	Change
Assets			
Cash & Equivalents	$ 775	$ 2,164	$ 1,389
Accounts Receivable	$ 6,776	$ 8,009	$ 1,233
Inventory	$ 3,822	$ 1,706	$(2,116)
Prepaid Expenses	$ 600	$ 625	$ 25
Property, Machinery, & Equipment	$ 4,000	$ 4,500	$ 500
Less: Accumulated Depreciation	$ (1,571)	$ (2,214)	$ (643)
Intangible Assets, Net	$ 2,000	$ 6,000	$ 4,000
Other Assets	$ 100	$ 100	$ 0
Total Assets	$16,502	$20,889	
Liabilities			
Accounts Payable	$ 1,405	$ 1,459	$ 54
Accrued Liabilities Payable	$ 1,084	$ 1,258	$ 174
Other Current Liabilities & Deferred Revenue	$ 1,011	$ 1,348	$ 337
Short-Term Loans Payable	$ 3,390	$ 2,400	$ (990)
Loans Payable & Other Long-Term Debt, Less ST Loans	$ 750	$ 2,500	$ 1,750
Total Liabilities	$ 7,640	$ 8,965	
Stockholders' Equity			
Capital Stock	$ 7,500	$10,000	$ 2,500
Retained Earnings	$ 1,362	$ 1,924	$ 563
Total Liabilities & Stockholders' Equity	$16,502	$20,889	

STATEMENT OF CASH FLOWS FOR YEAR	12/31/2023	Adj. #	
Net Income (Loss) after Income Taxes (Exhibit 2.1)	$ 813		
Operating Activities, Cash Provided (Used):			
Depreciation & Amortization			
for Depreciation Expense	$ 643	(1)	
for Amortization Expense	$ 1,000	(2)	
Decrease (increase) in Accounts Receivables	$(1,233)	(3)	
Decrease (increase) in Inventory	$ 2,116	(4)	
Decrease (increase) in Other Current Assets	$ (25)	(5)	
Increase (decrease) in Accounts Payables	$ 54	(6)	
Increase (decrease) in Accrued Liabilities	$ 174	(7)	
Increase (decrease) in Other Liabilities	$ 337	(8)	
Net Cash Flow from Operating Activities			$ 3,879
Investing Activities, Cash Provided (Used):			
Capital Expenditures	$ (500)		
Investments in Intangible & Other Assets	$(5,000)		
Net Cash Flow from Investing Activities			$(5,500)
Financing Activities, Cash Provided (Used):			
Dividends or Distributions Paid	$ (250)		
Sale (Repurchase) of Equity	$ 2,500		
Proceeds from Issuance of Loans (i.e., debt)	$ 3,000		
Repayments of Long-Term Loans	$(1,250)		
Net Borrowings (Repayments) of Short-Term Loans	$ (990)		
Net Cash Flow from Financing Activities			$ 3,010
Net Increase (Decrease) in Cash During the Year			$ 1,389

2. ***Inventory:*** Notice the rather large decrease in the company's inventory during the year. This may or may not have been a smart business decision. Perhaps the business needed a smaller inventory to adjust to changing market conditions, where customers are more interested in purchasing the company's services and software than its products. In any case, the $2,116,000 inventory decrease positively impacts cash flow. The quickest way to explain this is that inventory is an investment in both products that are in the process of being manufactured and those that are finished and being held for sale. Increasing an investment means putting more money into the investment. Decreasing an investment means reducing the amount of money allocated to that investment. See the fourth adjustment in the cash flow statement. In short, a decrease in inventory helps cash flow from operating activities.

3. ***Prepaid expenses:*** During the year, the company paid $625,000 for certain operating costs that will benefit next year and, therefore, were not charged to expenses during the year. See the ending balance in the company's prepaid expenses account. The company paid $625,000 on top of its operating expenses for the year. However, the company had $600,000 of prepaid expenses at the start of the year. Those costs were paid last year and then charged to operating expenses in the year just ended. Considering the beginning and ending balances in prepaid expenses, the company experiences a $25,000 drain on cash during the year. The $600,000 not paid minus $625,000 paid has a $25,000 negative impact on cash flow. See the fifth adjustment in the cash flow statement (Exhibit 3.1).

4. ***Depreciation and amortization:*** During the year, the company recorded $643,000 of depreciation expense, not by writing a check for this amount but by writing down the cost of its property, machinery, and equipment. This write-down is recorded as an increase in the accumulated depreciation account, which is the contra or offset account deducted from the property, machinery, and equipment asset account. These long-term operating assets are partially written down each year to record their wear and tear during every year of use. The company paid cash for the assets when it bought these long-term resources. The company does not have to pay for them a second time when it uses them. In short, depreciation expense is not a cash outlay in the year recorded and, therefore, is a positive adjustment, or so-called add-back for determining cash flow from profit. See the first adjustment in the cash flow statement. Similarly, the company recorded $1,000,000 of amortization expense during the year to account for the reduction in value of intangible assets. And just like depreciation expense, amortization expense is not a cash outlay in the year recorded, and therefore is a positive adjustment to determine cash flow from profit-making activities. (See the second adjustment in the cash flow statement.)

The depreciation and amortization add-backs to net income can be explained another way. For the sake of argument here, assume all sales revenue had been collected in cash during the year. Part of this cash inflow from customers pays the company for the use of its long-term operating assets during the year. In setting its sales prices, a business includes depreciation and amortization as a cost of doing business.

In this sense, the business sells a fraction of its fixed and intangible assets to its customers each year. As a result, each year, a business recovers part of the capital invested in its fixed and intangible assets in cash flow from sales revenue. In short, the company in this example recaptured $1,643,000 of the investment in its property, machinery, and equipment assets and intangible assets, which is a significant source of cash flow.

5. ***Accounts payable:*** The ending balance in the company's accounts payable liability reveals that manufacturing costs, product purchases, costs of sales revenue, and operating expenses were not fully paid during the year. The ending balance in this liability relieved the company of making cash payments of $1,459,000 (Exhibit 3.1). Not paying these costs avoids cash outflow. Consider the other side of the coin, as well. The company started the year with $1,405,000 in accounts payable. These liabilities were paid during the year. The $1,459,000 not paid minus $1,405,000 paid has a net $54,000 positive impact on cash flow. See the sixth adjustment in the cash flow statement.

6. ***Accrued expenses payable:*** This liability works the same way as accounts payable. The company did not pay $1,258,000 of its expenses during the year, which is the balance in this liability at the end of the year. However, the company did pay the $1,084,000 beginning amount of this liability. The $1,258,000 not paid minus $1,084,000 paid has a net $174,000 positive impact on cash flow. See the seventh adjustment in the cash flow statement.

7. ***Other current liabilities:*** At the start of the year, the company had other current liabilities of $1,011,000, which were primarily related to advance payments or deposits received from customers. At the end of the year, the balance in other current liabilities had increased to $1,348,000, resulting in a net increase of $337,000. By receiving additional deposits or advance payments from customers for future sales, the company generated a positive benefit to cash flow of $337,000. See the eighth adjustment in the cash flow statement.

Summing up the eight cash flow adjustments to net income:

- Increases in operating assets cause decreases in cash flow from profit, and decreases in operating assets result in increases in cash flow from profit.
- Increases in operating liabilities help cash flow from profit, and decreases in operating liabilities result in decreases in cash flow from profit.

See in Exhibit 3.1 that the combined net effect of the eight adjustments is that cash flow from profit is $3,879,000, which is $3,066,000 more than profit for the year. This difference between cash flow and bottom-line profit is due to the changes in the company's operating assets and liabilities. In summary, the business realized $3,879,000 cash flow from its operating activities during the year. This source of cash flow is vital to every business.

Completing the Statement of Cash Flows with Investing and Financing Activities

Please refer to Exhibit 3.2. The preceding section of this chapter explains the first of the three sections in the statement of cash flows. This section of the chapter explains the statement's other two sections, which, by comparison, are a piece of cake to understand.

The second section of the statement of cash flows (Exhibit 3.2) summarizes the *investment* activities of the business during the year in long-term operating assets. In the example, QW Example Tech, Inc. spent $500,000 on new fixed assets (tangible long-term operating assets) and $5,000,000 on intangible assets (e.g., software development, goodwill, patents, etc.). See the lines extending from these expenditures in the statement of cash flows to the property, machinery, and equipment asset account and intangible asset account in the balance sheet.

The investing activities section includes proceeds from disposals of investments (net of tax) if there are any such disposals during the period. In our example, the business did not dispose of any of its long-term operating assets, tangible or intangible, during the year. An ongoing business typically makes some disposals of fixed assets during the year.

The third section of the statement of cash flows (refer to Exhibit 3.2 again) reports the cash flows of *financing* activities. The term *financing* refers to dealings between the business and its sources of capital (i.e., its lenders and its stockholders). The company in our example increased its long-term loans during the year by $3,000,000. It also repaid $1,250,000 of long-term loans during the year (more than likely, when the company secured the new $3,000,000 long-term loan, it was required to pay off any outstanding balances from loans secured in previous years). Short-term loans were paid down by $990,000 during the year as the company had excess cash to reduce outstanding debt and lower interest expense. Further, the company raised $2,500,000 from issuing new capital stock shares (to existing investors and key business partners). See the lines of connection from the statement of cash flows to the corresponding balance sheet accounts in Exhibit 3.2.

The business distributed $250,000 in cash dividends from profit to its shareowners during the year. Cash dividends are included in the financing activities section of the cash flow statement. Why not put cash dividends next to cash flow from profit (i.e., from operating activities)? I say more about the placement of cash dividends later in the chapter. Its $813,000 net income for the year increases the company's retained earnings account, and the $250,000 cash dividends decrease this shareholders' equity account. Therefore, the net increase in retained earnings during the year is $563,000 (see Exhibit 3.2 to check this).

The bottom line of the statement of cash flows is the $1,389,000 increase in cash during the year (see Exhibit 3.2).

EXHIBIT 3.2—CASH FLOW FROM INVESTING & FINANCING ACTIVITIES, BASE CASE (SEB)

Dollar Amounts in Thousands

BALANCE SHEET	12/31/2022	12/31/2023	Change
Assets			
Cash & Equivalents	$ 775	$ 2,164	$ 1,389
Accounts Receivable	$ 6,776	$ 8,009	$ 1,233
Inventory	$ 3,822	$ 1,706	$(2,116)
Prepaid Expenses	$ 600	$ 625	$ 25
Property, Machinery, & Equipment	$ 4,000	$ 4,500	$ 500
Less: Accumulated Depreciation	$ (1,571)	$ (2,214)	$ (643)
Intangible Assets, Net	$ 2,000	$ 6,000	$ 4,000
Other Assets	$ 100	$ 100	$ 0
Total Assets	$16,502	$20,889	
Liabilities			
Accounts Payable	$ 1,405	$ 1,459	$ 54
Accrued Liabilities Payable	$ 1,084	$ 1,258	$ 174
Other Current Liabilities & Deferred Revenue	$ 1,011	$ 1,348	$ 337
Short-Term Loans Payable	$ 3,390	$ 2,400	$ (990)
Loans Payable & Other Long-Term Debt, Less ST Loans	$ 750	$ 2,500	$ 1,750
Total Liabilities	$ 7,640	$ 8,965	
			$ 2,500
Stockholders' Equity			$ 563
Capital Stock	$ 7,500	$10,000	
Retained Earnings	$ 1,362	$ 1,924	
Total Liabilities & Stockholders' Equity	$16,502	$20,889	

STATEMENT OF CASH FLOWS FOR YEAR	12/31/2023	
Net Income (Loss) after Income Taxes (Exhibit 2.1)	$ 813	
Operating Activities, Cash Provided (Used):		
Depreciation & Amortization		
for Depreciation Expense	$ 643	
for Amortization Expense	$ 1,000	
Decrease (increase) in Accounts Receivables	$(1,233)	
Decrease (increase) in Inventory	$ 2,116	
Decrease (increase) in Other Current Assets	$ (25)	
Increase (decrease) in Accounts Payables	$ 54	
Increase (decrease) in Accrued Liabilities	$ 174	
Increase (decrease) in Other Liabilities	$ 337	
Net Cash Flow from Operating Activities		$ 3,879
Investing Activities, Cash Provided (Used):		
Capital Expenditures	$ (500)	
Investments in Intangible & Other Assets	$(5,000)	
Net Cash Flow from Investing Activities		$(5,500)
Financing Activities, Cash Provided (Used):		
Dividends or Distributions Paid	$ (250)	
Sale (Repurchase) of Equity	$ 2,500	
Proceeds from Issuance of Loans (i.e., Debt)	$ 3,000	
Repayments of Long-Term Loans	$(1,250)	
Net Borrowings (Repayments) of Short-Term Loans	$ (990)	
Net Cash Flow from Financing Activities		$ 3,010
Net Increase (Decrease) in Cash During the Year		$ 1,389

Well, perhaps I shouldn't call the change in cash the *bottom line*. The term *bottom line* is more or less reserved for the last line of the income statement, but I see nothing wrong with using it here to refer to the bottom line of the cash flow statement. That line is the final, net result of all three types of activities that determine the increase or decrease in cash during the year.

Seeing the Big Picture of Cash Flows

Earning profit is a vital source of cash inflow to every business. Profit is the *internal* source of cash flow—money generated by the business itself without going outside the company to secure external sources of capital. The first section of this chapter explains that the company generated $3,879,000 cash flow during the year just ended from its operating activities. Profit provided almost $4 million for the business—and that isn't chicken feed.

The obvious question is: What did the business do with its cash flow from profit? The remainder of the cash flow statement answers this important question. The rest of the cash flow statement reports other sources of cash that were tapped by the business during the year that provided additional capital to the business. And, most important, the statement of cash flows reveals what the business did with this money.

The company generated $3,879,000 cash from its profit-making activities during the year. What *could* it do with this money? One option is simply to increase its cash balance—just let the money pile up in its checking account. This is not a productive use of the cash unless the business is on the ragged edge and desperately needs to increase its day-to-day working cash balance. The business could also pay down some of its liabilities. Or, the company could use some of the money to pay cash dividends to its stockholders.

In fact, the business did pay $250,000 in cash dividends to its stockholders during the year. The amount of cash dividends to shareholders is one of the key items reported in the statement of cash flows—see the third section of the cash flow statement in Exhibit 3.2. After subtracting $250,000 cash dividends from the $3,879,000 cash flow from profit, the company had $3,629,000 cash flow remaining from operating activities. You may ask: What did the business do with this cash?

To modernize and expand its production and sales capacity, and obtain the rights to sell new technology (i.e., software), during the year the business invested $5,500,000 in new long-term operating assets, including tangible and intangible assets. These cash outlays are called *capital expenditures*, which emphasizes the long-term nature of investing capital in these assets. You may have noticed that the total amount of capital expenditures was considerably more than cash flow from profit net of cash dividends ($5,500,000 capital expenditures less $3,629,000 cash flow from profit net of cash dividends equals $1,871,000 shortfall). This money had to come from somewhere.

A business has three sources to cover such a cash shortfall: (1) borrow more money on short-term and long-term loans (that it repays), (2) secure additional capital from shareowners by issuing new capital stock shares, and (3) spend down its cash balance. QW Example Tech, Inc. did not spend down its cash balance and, in fact, actually increased it by $1,389,000. Rather, our example company elected to raise cash from increasing net borrowings from short-term and long-term loans and through selling capital stock to shareholders (amounts from Exhibit 3.2), as summarized in Exhibit 3.3.

When a business grows year over year (as measured by increased sales revenue), its cash flow from profit net of cash dividends typically only provides some of the cash it needs for its capital expenditures. Therefore, the business has to expand its debt and equity capital, which it did in our example.

Business managers, lenders, and investors closely monitor capital expenditures. These cash outlays are a bet on the future by the company. The business is saying, in effect, that it needs the new long-term assets (both tangible and intangible) to maintain or improve its competitive position or to expand its facilities for future growth. These are some of the most critical decisions business managers make.

Making capital investments is always risky. On the one hand, who knows what will happen in the future? On the other hand, not making such investments may sign the death warrant of a business. By not making such investments, the company may fall behind its competition and lose market share that would be impossible to regain. Then again, being overinvested and having excess capacity can be an albatross around the neck of a business.

EXHIBIT 3.3—CASH FLOW RECONCILIATION, BASE CASE (SEB)

Dollar Amounts in Thousands

Cash Flow Reconciliation, FYE:	31-Dec-2023
Cash Shortfall Before Financing Activities	$(1,871)
Proceeds from Issuance of Loans (i.e., debt)	$ 3,000
Sale (repurchase) of Equity	$ 2,500
Repayments of Long-Term Loans	$(1,250)
Net Borrowings (Repayments) of Short-Term Loans	$ (990)
Net Increase in Cash	$ 1,389

In any case, the business laid out $5,500,000 during the year for new assets (see Exhibit 3.2 again). In doing so, the business had to make key financing decisions—where to get the money for the asset purchases, which it did by securing new long-term debt and selling capital stock. This left the company's ending cash balance at $2,164,000, which, relative to its $59,494,000 annual sales revenue, equals about two weeks of sales revenue.

I should point out that there are no general standards or guidelines regarding how large a company's working cash balance should be. Most business managers would view the company's cash balance in this example as adequate, I think. How much cash cushion does a business need as a safety reserve to protect against unfavorable developments? Opinions differ on this question, but one item I would like to mention involves the company's available borrowing capital on its working capital line of credit (covered at length in Chapter 14 of *How to Read a Financial Report*, 10th Edition). As summarized in this chapter, QW Example Tech, Inc. can borrow up to $5,760,000 on its working capital line of credit, of which it has only borrowed $1,900,000 as of the FYE 12/31/23. This leaves $3,860,000 of borrowing capacity available. So, in addition to the $2,164,000 of available cash, the company has another $3,860,000 of borrowing capacity, which in total provides roughly $6,000,000 of available liquid resources to operate the business. This is an important concept to understand as a company's total available liquidity does not only include available cash, but also the ability to borrow and raise cash within 24 to 48 hours. At QW Example Tech, Inc., the management team has done a good job of structuring loan facilities from lenders to support its cash operating needs.

What if the economy takes a nosedive, or what if the company has a serious falloff in sales? What if some of its accounts receivable are not collected on time? What if the company cannot sell its inventory soon enough to keep the cash flow cycle in motion? What if it doesn't have enough money to pay its employees on time? There are no easy answers to these cash dilemmas, but having available loans to access at a moment's notice certainly helps.

The business could have forgone cash dividends to keep its working cash balance at a higher level. In all likelihood, its stockholders want a cash dividend on their investments in the business. The board of directors might have been under pressure to deliver cash dividends. In any case, QW Example Tech, Inc. distributed $250,000 cash dividends, which are reported in the financing activities section in the cash flow statement (Exhibit 3.2).

In summary, the cash flow statement deserves as much attention and scrutiny as the income statement and balance sheet. Though unlikely, a company making a profit could be headed for liquidity problems (having too little ready cash) or solvency problems (not being able to pay liabilities on time). Making profit does not guarantee liquidity and solvency. The cash flow statement should be read carefully to see if there are any danger signs or red flags.

I would also like to mention that statements of cash flows reported by most public corporations are cluttered with a lot of detail—often far too much detail, in my opinion. My advice is to focus mainly on the big-ticket items and skip the minor details in reading a statement of cash flows. Stand back and try to see the big picture. The income statements reported by most public corporations have far fewer lines of information than cash flow statements and are generally much easier to understand. This is an odd state of affairs, indeed.

A Few Final Words on Cash Flow

Most financial statement readers have a good intuitive understanding of a balance sheet (assets, liabilities, and shareholders' equity) and that profit equals sales revenue minus expenses. In contrast, most financial statement readers seem confused about cash flow from profit. They think that making profit means making money, and that cash increases the same amount as bottom-line profit. This is not true. Profit and cash flow are two different numbers, both of which are important in their own right.

I remind you that accountants are accrual-basis people, not cash-basis people. To most accountants, accrual basis is second nature. Indeed, I've met accountants who have trouble understanding cash flow because they are so submerged in the accrual basis. As a matter of fact, I've seen CPAs who have difficulty preparing a statement of cash flows.

In preparing financial reports, accountants should keep in mind that readers generally have more difficulty understanding the statement of cash flows (particularly the first section) than the balance sheet and income statement. But I see little evidence of this in the actual reporting of cash flow statements. I have read countless statements of cash flows and found that many are exceedingly complicated. It's not unusual to see a statement of cash flows of a public company that reports 30, 40, or more lines of information. Furthermore, it is impossible to reconcile all the items reported in the statement of cash flows with their corresponding assets and liabilities in the balance sheet.

Businesses should provide a readable statement of cash flows. It would be helpful if management provided a summary and discussion of the company's cash flows for the year. Instead, most businesses offer little or no comment regarding their cash flows, making it difficult to interpret them. Even CPAs would have trouble doing a complete and thorough analysis of the cash flow statements of many companies.

Also, there are several technical accounting problems in reporting cash flows. For example, should the cash flows connected with the discontinued operations of a business be reported separately from its ongoing, recurring cash flows? Should cash flows of certain short-term activities be reported gross or net? These cash flow issues are beyond the scope of this book. (I can almost hear you breathing easier here.)

One thing is evident in the authoritative pronouncement on reporting cash flows. A business should refrain from including cash flow per share in its financial reports. In particular, a business should not report cash flow from operating activities per share. Public companies are required to report earnings (net income) per share (EPS). The accounting authorities do not want financial statement readers to confuse EPS with cash flow.

One of my criticisms of the statement of cash flows—aside from the huge number of lines reported by most companies—is the placement of cash dividends in the financing activities section. Instead, I favor placing cash dividends immediately under cash flow from operating activities. Deducting from operating activities the amount of cash dividends that result from cash flow would highlight the amount of cash flow the company had available for general business purposes.

The purpose is to show more clearly how much cash flow from profit was available to the business after cash dividends. The financial statement reader could easily size up dividends against the amount of cash flow from profit, and see the amount of cash remaining for other needs of the business. But the current standard is to put dividends in the financing activities section of the cash flow statement. My view is that businesses should have more options regarding where to place cash dividends in their statements of cash flows.

4

CONNECTING THE FINANCIAL STATEMENTS BY BUSINESS CYCLE

The concept of accounting cycles and connections between the financial statements is covered at length in our book *How to Read a Financial Report* (now in its 10th edition). This book dedicates 10 chapters in Part Two to providing detailed explanations of how the financial information presented in an income statement is linked or connected to the balance sheet and how financial information presented in the balance sheet is linked or connected to the statement of cash flows. For those of you who would like to dig deeper into understanding accounting connections at a more granular, step-by-step level, I would encourage you to read (or reread) *How to Read a Financial Report*, with a specific focus on Chapters 7 through 16.

In this chapter, I will cover how financial statements are connected but will approach the subject differently. *How to Read a Financial Report* explains financial information connections from a more technical accounting viewpoint or based on when an actual financial transaction has taken place between two primary accounts (such as a sale of products or services to a customer that impacts both sales revenue in the income statement and accounts receivable in the balance sheet). The discussion on financial statement connections is broken down into far more detail, with individual chapters dedicated to specific topics and relationships.

In this chapter, I will expand on financial statement connections by summarizing related financial transactions associated with a specific business cycle, from soup to nuts (i.e., the entire selling cycle). Second, I will expand our discussion on financial statement connections by taking it up a notch to help you understand the flow of financial information transactions from start to finish for a specific cycle. My goal is to expand and enhance your knowledge of financial transactions and information from the basics (e.g., a sale of a product to a customer on credit creates revenue for the company as well as a trade receivable) so you are slightly more sophisticated at understanding a business cycle from birth to death.

I will limit our discussion to covering four primary financial business cycles: the sales cycle, the purchasing cycle, the operating expense cycle, and the investment and financing cycle (which are closely related). Other financial business cycles exist, but for most companies, the four cycles overviewed in this chapter cover the bulk of financial transactions and will help you understand how financial information moves inside a company and where it originates. I should also note that the exhibits presented in this chapter will be more detailed as they relate to documenting the flow of transactions for an entire business cycle. Four to five financial connections (referred to as *financial flows*) are presented to account for a business cycle rather than a single accounting transaction. So be patient with the presentation, and review the material as needed to enhance your knowledge of these critical business cycles.

The Sales Cycle

The entire purpose of a business is to develop a plan that offers a product or service to the market that customers value, and that will allow the business to earn a profit. This process starts at the top of the income statement, where sales revenue is reported. But the selling process or cycle is far more complex than the top line of the income statement would lead you to believe, as before any company makes a sale, it must create a business plan, raise capital to execute the business plan, invest in infrastructure to implement the business plan, develop products or services the market will place a value on, market or promote these products or services to potential customers, then actually complete or close a sale with the customer (triggering sales revenue in the income statement), and finally properly support and service the customer (ensuring they become repeat customers, which in the business world is often referred to as being "sticky"). The concept of customer retention is extremely important for all companies. I am unaware of any successful business that does not sell products or services over and over to the same customer. Just think about Apple, Inc. for a moment and their ability to sell new versions of the iPhone to existing customers year after year. Without dedicated and loyal (i.e., sticky) customers, Apple would have been out of business decades ago.

This is what I mean by the *sales cycle*, as companies will incur numerous operating expenses both before a sale is made (e.g., spending money on advertising) and after it is completed (e.g., investing in a service center to respond to customer questions, technical support needs, etc.). Exhibit 4.1 helps visualize the entire sales cycle from the perspective of accounting connections between the income statement and the balance sheet. I have compressed the financial statements further to keep the presentation on one page for ease of review, highlighting four primary information flows.

1. The first financial information flow captures the various operating expenses incurred to support the direct selling, marketing, and promotional efforts prior to a sale being made or with customer service costs after the sale. These expenses would generally first be captured as a trade payable (e.g., advertising spends with a social media company to be paid in 30 days) or an accrued liability (e.g., employee wages payable) until a cash payment is made per the terms established by the supplier or the company policy established to pay employees (e.g., employees are paid every two weeks, in arrears).
2. The second financial information flow captures a simple sale between the company and a customer for the delivery of products and services. In this case, the company provides 30-day payment terms to the customer so the sale would be captured as a trade accounts receivable until the customer pays.

3. The third financial information flow is a bit different as it captures an advance billing to a customer for a software service to be provided over the next 12 months (e.g., a SaaS sale). The customer is billed for the software service in advance, which is recorded as accounts receivable, but not GAAP sales revenue, as the company must defer recognizing the earned revenue over a 12-month period. Rather, the billing is captured in other current liabilities or deferred revenue on the balance sheet. The customer would eventually remit payment just like in flow 2.

4. The fourth financial information flow is presented to reflect the fact that, over a period of 12 months, the other current liability or deferred revenue would be reduced, and sales revenue increased as the company fulfills its obligation for the advance billing and earns a prorated portion of the software service sale. What is interesting about this transaction is that (unlike the other three) cash will not be impacted, as the customer should have paid the advance billing long ago.

5. Finally, I place the number 5 in a box at the end of the reference to "Cash & Equivalents." I elected not to include additional connecting lines and arrows to avoid creating too much clutter in Exhibit 4.1, but the general idea is that eventually, all transactions lead to the cash accounts. That is, when customers pay, the accounts receivable balance would be reduced, and the cash accounts increased. Likewise, when accounts payable and accrued liabilities are paid, these account balances would decrease as would the cash balance. As the old saying goes, "all roads lead to Rome," which in the business world means, "all financial transactions eventually lead to cash."

I have highlighted and bolded the cash account to emphasize that for financial information flows 1, 2, and 3, the result of the transactions will always clear through cash (as vendors are paid and customers remit payments). Financial flow 4 helps explain how sales revenue is earned from a different type of customer billing that is based on establishing an accounting policy to recognize earned sales revenue over an appropriate period properly.

Exhibit 4.1 is presented to help you understand that recording sales revenue in the income statement is more complex than billing a customer for the delivery of a product or service (and waiting to get paid). Revenue recognition represents a hot issue when issuing GAAP financial statements. It is something all companies must clearly understand and proactively manage to ensure that external and internal parties are not misled (a concept that will be emphasized in Chapter 6). This goes back to why I emphasized understanding the entire sales cycle (and not just connections) from an accounting perspective, as it is not always black and white (gray, as in a gray area, would be our favorite choice of color here). It should also be noted that for most companies, the selling cycle (from conceptualizing a product or service for sale to turning customers into repeat buyers) is almost always longer than anticipated and requires more management attention and financial capital to support. So, plan accordingly and make sure you have plenty of capital, as there is nothing worse than almost reaching the promised land and then having the door slammed shut.

EXHIBIT 4.1—FINANCIAL STATEMENT CONNECTIONS—THE SALES CYCLE, BASE CASE (SEB)

Dollar Amounts in Thousands

Income Statement For the Fiscal Year Ending	12/31/2023
Sales Revenue, Net	$ 59,494
Costs of Sales Revenue	$(21,766)
Gross Profit	$ 37,728
Operating Expenses:	
Selling, Marketing, & Promotional	$ 18,518
Corporate General & Administrative	$ 6,771
Research, Development, & Design	$ 7,139
Depreciation & Amortization Expense	$ 1,643
Operating Income (Loss) EBITDA	$ 3,658
Other Expenses (Income):	
Other Expenses, Income, & Discon. Ops	$ 2,000
Interest Expense	$ 407
Income Tax Expense (Benefit)	$ 438
Net Profit (Loss)	$ 813

Balance Sheet as of the Period Ending	12/31/2023
Assets:	
Cash & Equivalents	*$ 2,164*
Accounts Receivable, Net	$ 8,009
Inventory	$ 1,706
Prepaid Expenses	$ 625
Property, Machinery, & Equipment	$ 4,500
Accumulated Depreciation	$ (2,214)
Intangible Assets & Goodwill, Net	$ 6,000
Other Assets	$ 100
Total Assets	$20,889
Liabilities:	
Accounts Payable	$ 1,459
Accrued Liabilities & Other	$ 1,258
Current Portion of Debt	$ 2,400
Other Current Lia. & Deferred Rev.	$ 1,348
Notes Payable & Other Long-Term Debt	$ 2,500
Total Liabilities	$ 8,965
Stockholders' Equity:	
Capital Stock	$10,000
Dividends	$ (250)
Retained Earnings	$ 2,174
Total Stockholders' Equity	$11,924
Total Liabilities & Stockholders' Equity	$20,889

Confidential—Property of QW Example Tech, Inc.

The Purchasing Cycle

My focus on the purchasing cycle will be geared toward costs of goods sold (for product-related companies) or costs of sales revenue (for service-based companies). And like the sales cycle, the purchasing cycle is much more complex than simply buying or manufacturing products and selling them to the customer. You cannot understand the purchasing cycle without some background information about developing and managing the supply chain. Both product- and service-driven companies must manage supply chains that can be extraordinarily complex and far-reaching in terms of coordinating a vast pool of suppliers, vendors, staff, and other third parties to ensure that the right product or service is available for sale to the right parties at the right time. Speak to anyone involved with the supply chain, and you will quickly understand just how much effort and resources it takes for even a small company selling 30 different products to manage effectively. Compounding management of the supply chain is that in today's global economy, companies have to coordinate vendors, suppliers, and employees that span the globe. This is why the purchasing cycle and supply chain incur significant operating expenses, both before receiving the product and long after it has been sold.

Exhibit 4.2 presents the purchasing cycle and the accounting connections more completely. I have compressed the financial statements further to keep the presentation on one page for ease of review, highlighting four primary information flows.

1. The first financial information flow captures the various operating expenses incurred to support any product research and development costs, management team expenses related to managing the supply chain, and so on, before a product or service being made available for sale or subsequent vendor management expenses. These expenses would generally first be captured as a trade payable (e.g., trial product sample order with a vendor to be paid in 30 days) or an accrued liability (e.g., employee wages payable) until a cash payment is made per the terms established by the supplier or the company policy established to pay employees (e.g., employees are paid every two weeks, in arrears).

2. The second financial information flow is between balance sheet accounts only, as before a product can be sold, it must be purchased (or manufactured internally), which is often done on supplier-provided terms. For example, if a company purchases 10,000 units of a product, which are received and made available for sale, the inventory account would increase along with a trade account payable to the supplier (which may provide payment terms of 30 or 60 days). There is no impact on the income statement because, until a product is sold, it will not be recorded as a cost of goods sold.

3. Two financial information flows are captured in our third connection. These are the actual cost of a product being sold

EXHIBIT 4.2—FINANCIAL STATEMENT CONNECTIONS—THE PURCHASING CYCLE, BASE CASE (SEB)

Dollar Amounts in Thousands

Income Statement For the Fiscal Year Ending	12/31/2023
Sales Revenue, Net	$ 59,494
Costs of Sales Revenue	$(21,766)
Gross Profit	$ 37,728
Operating Expenses:	
Selling, Marketing, & Promotional	$ 18,518
Corporate General & Administrative	$ 6,771
Research, Development, & Design	$ 7,139
Depreciation & Amortization Expense	$ 1,643
Operating Income (Loss) EBITDA	$ 3,658
Other Expenses (Income):	
Other Expenses, Income, & Discon. Ops	$ 2,000
Interest Expense	$ 407
Income Tax Expense (Benefit)	$ 438
Net Profit (Loss)	$ 813

Balance Sheet as of the Period Ending	12/31/2023
Assets:	
Cash & Equivalents	***$ 2,164***
Accounts Receivable, Net	$ 8,009
Inventory	$ 1,706
Prepaid Expenses	$ 625
Property, Machinery, & Equipment	$ 4,500
Accumulated Depreciation	$ (2,214)
Intangible Assets & Goodwill, Net	$ 6,000
Other Assets	$ 100
Total Assets	$ 20,889
Liabilities	
Accounts Payable	$ 1,459
Accrued Liabilities & Other	$ 1,258
Current Portion of Debt	$ 2,400
Other Current Lia. & Deferred Rev.	$ 1,348
Notes Payable & Other Long-Term Debt	$ 2,500
Total Liabilities	$ 8,965
Stockholders' Equity:	
Capital Stock	$ 10,000
Dividends	$ (250)
Retained Earnings	$ 2,174
Total Stockholders' Equity	$ 11,924
Total Liabilities & Stockholders' Equity	$ 20,889

Confidential—Property of QW Example Tech, Inc.

(which would reduce the value in inventory and increase the costs of goods sold) as well as any other direct costs of sales that might be incurred, such as rent on a building used to produce the products, or staff wages and burden for employees who are involved with producing the products or delivering services (to the customer). This is why I referenced two connections: while selling a product reduces inventory, costs of sales may also increase trade accounts payable or accrued liabilities.

4. Next up, I could not resist including a fourth connection that specifically relates to our example company. I cover this topic in more depth in Chapter 7, but what our example company elected to do was to write off certain inventory that was deemed to be worthless. Rather than record this inventory write-off as costs of goods sold, the company elected to reflect the write-off as a one-time nonrecurring expense and record it as other expenses (so that its gross profit and gross margin were not adversely affected). This write-off represents a noncash expense from a time in the past when the company had to use cash to purchase the inventory (flow 2 in Exhibit 4.2), when the election to write off the inventory represented an accounting entry (to reduce inventory and increase other expenses).
5. Similarly to the sales cycle, a reference is made to the number 5 in a box at the end of "Cash & Equivalents." This indicates that, eventually, all inventory purchases, operating expenses, employee wages and compensation, and related expenses will need to be paid and flow through the cash accounts.

Exhibit 4.2 aims to help you understand that purchasing or making products for sale (or delivering services to the customer) is not as simple as placing an order for the product or service (and waiting for a customer to purchase it). The entire purchasing and supply chain cycle is complex, expensive to manage, and requires a great deal of coordination between multiple parties. Bearing this in mind, I can offer two pieces of advice about the purchasing cycle and supply chain better. First, disruptions to the supply chain are the rule rather than the exception. It is inevitable that somewhere along the line, an adverse event will occur that requires responsive management actions. Second, if there has ever been an area in a business that relies on clear and concise communication skills, this is it. Technology is not a cure-all or replacement for a function that lives and dies on being able to communicate effectively.

The Operating Expense Cycle

The operating expense cycle has been touched on with our discussions on the sales and purchasing cycles, so I won't spend much additional time on this cycle. If you refer to Exhibits 4.1 and 4.2, the first financial information flow captures the essence of operating expenses relating to the impact on the current liabilities section of the balance sheet (including trade accounts payable and accrued liabilities). Most, but not all, operating expenses tend to flow through a company's financial statements in this fashion, where the expense is incurred during a period but paid later.

Operating expenses capture a wide range of business expenses that companies incur to support ongoing operations and include the following items (in no specific order):

- Wages, salaries, commissions, bonuses, and other compensation paid to managers, office staff, salespersons, warehouse workers, security guards, and other employees. (Compensation of production employees and associated benefits such as payroll taxes are included in the costs of goods manufactured and become part of inventory cost.)
- Payroll taxes and fringe benefit costs of labor, such as health and medical plan contributions by the employer and the cost of employee retirement plans (associated with nonproductive staff).
- Professional fees for legal, accounting, human resources, and so on.
- Office and data processing supplies, telecommunication expenses, Internet, and website costs.
- Rental of office buildings, copiers, trucks and autos, telephone system equipment, computers, and other assets.
- Utility costs of electricity, water, sewage, and so on.
- Dues and subscriptions, such as software platform expenses.
- Liability, fire, accident, and other insurance costs.
- Marketing, advertising, and sales promotion costs, which are major expenditures of many businesses.
- Travel, meals, lodging, and entertainment costs.

This list is not all-inclusive. I'm sure you could think of many more expenses related to business operation. Even relatively small businesses keep 100 or more separate accounts for specific operating expenses. Large corporations keep thousands of specific expense accounts. In their external financial reports, however, most publicly owned corporations report only one, two, or three operating expense categories.

From an accounting perspective, some operating expenses are recorded when they are paid, not before or after. An example of this relates to companies that remit payments daily to social media advertising platforms such as Facebook. Each day, the company spends a certain amount on advertising, which is paid via a direct payment from their bank account to Facebook. (This payment is usually via an electronic remittance, such as ACH.) It would be convenient if every dollar of operating expenses were a dollar paid out in the same period, but running a business is not so simple. For many operating expenses, a business cannot wait to record the expense until it pays the expense. As soon as a liability is incurred, the amount of expense should be recorded. The term *incurred* means that the business has a definite responsibility to pay a third party with a legal claim against the business.

A liability is incurred when a company takes on an obligation to make future payment and has received the economic benefit of the cost of operating the business. Recording the liability for an unpaid expense is one fundamental aspect of *accrual-basis accounting*. Expenses are *accrued* (i.e., recorded before they are paid) so that the amount of each expense is deducted from sales revenue to measure profit correctly for the period.

Two final thoughts related to the operating expense cycle: First, certain operating expenses may be prepaid for an operating period. For example, general liability insurance coverage is often paid up front for the entire year the policy covers. Per GAAP, this expense should be recorded as a prepaid asset (under the classification of prepaid expenses in the current asset section of the balance sheet) and amortized or expensed over the appropriate period (e.g., 12 months if the insurance policy covers a one year period). This is the opposite of most operating expenses as it is paid in advance (before it was incurred) instead of being incurred and then paid later.

Second, strong accounting policies, procedures, and internal controls must be established by a company to ensure that not only are all expenses accounted for in the correct period (whether paid or not) but just as importantly, the expenses are properly recorded to the correct account in the accounting system. There is nothing worse than having to sort through financial information that is polluted with the incorrect coding of expenses.

The Investment and Financing Cycles

Our final stop with business cycles lands us with the investment and financing cycles. I have combined our discussion on these two subjects given their close association (e.g., to make a large investment in assets, the company must be able to finance the investment) and importance. Like our discussions on the sales and purchasing cycles, it will quickly become apparent that the investment and financing cycle is both complex and time-consuming, dependent on a strong business foundation and plan to support or justify the economic feasibility of the investment and that the required financial capital is appropriate to support the investment.

The start of the investment and financing cycle begins with a plan. It does not matter if the plan has been prepared to launch a new business or is associated with a large company looking to invest in a new manufacturing facility. A well-developed plan must be supported at multiple levels, including market feasibility, operational effectiveness, environmental and legal compliance, and economic justification, just to highlight some major components. Developing a plan takes a significant amount of time, resources, and management attention, which again brings us to the start of the process in that operating expenses will be incurred well before any investment decision is made and financial capital pursued. Then, only if it is deemed economically justifiable to proceed will investment and financing decisions be made.

Exhibit 4.3 summarizes the primary financial flows related to the investment and financing cycle. Please keep in mind that unlike the sales and purchasing cycles presented earlier, the investment and financing cycle overview and related connections have occurred over several years and represent the cumulative effect of multiple capital asset purchases and efforts to secure capital from debt and equity sources (some going back to the first year of operations for our example company). I have compressed the financial statements further to keep the presentation on one page for ease of review, highlighting four primary information flows.

1. The first financial information flow captures the various operating expenses incurred to develop the investment plan, including management team expenses, professional fees incurred to help build the plan, and so on. These expenses would generally first be captured as a trade payable (e.g., a marketing consulting company that completed a feasibility study providing 90-day payment terms) or an accrued liability (e.g., employee wages payable) until a cash payment is made per the terms established by the supplier or the company policy established to pay employees (e.g., employees are paid every two weeks, in arrears).
2. Second, the financial information flow highlights that QW Example Tech, Inc. raised financial capital (and received cash) in the form of debt and equity to support the proposed investments (over several years of operations). Although

EXHIBIT 4.3—FINANCIAL STATEMENT CONNECTIONS—INVESTMENT & FINANCING CYCLE, BASE CASE (SEB)

Dollar Amounts in Thousands

Income Statement For the Fiscal Year Ending	12/31/2023
Sales Revenue, Net	$ 59,494
Costs of Sales Revenue	$(21,766)
Gross Profit	$ 37,728
Operating Expenses:	
Selling, Marketing, & Promotional	$ 18,518
Corporate General & Administrative	$ 6,771
Research, Development, & Design	$ 7,139
Depreciation & Amortization Expense	$ 1,643
Operating Income (Loss) EBITDA	$ 3,658
Other Expenses (Income):	
Other Expenses, Income, & Discon. Ops	$ 2,000
Interest Expense	$ 407
Income Tax Expense (Benefit)	$ 438
Net Profit (Loss)	$ 813

Balance Sheet as of the Period Ending	12/31/2023
Assets:	
Cash & Equivalents	***$ 2,164***
Accounts Receivable, Net	$ 8,009
Inventory	$ 1,706
Prepaid Expenses	$ 625
Property, Machinery, & Equipment	$ 4,500
Accumulated Depreciation	$ (2,214)
Intangible Assets & Goodwill, Net	$ 6,000
Other Assets	$ 100
Total Assets	$ 20,889
Liabilities:	
Accounts Payable	$ 1,459
Accrued Liabilities & Other	$ 1,258
Current Portion of Debt	$ 2,400
Other Current Lia. & Deferred Rev.	$ 1,348
Notes Payable & Other Long-Term Debt	$ 2,500
Total Liabilities	$ 8,965
Stockholders' Equity:	
Capital Stock	$ 10,000
Dividends	$ (250)
Retained Earnings	$ 2,174
Total Stockholders' Equity	$ 11,924
Total Liabilities & Stockholders' Equity	$ 20,889

Confidential—Property of QW Example Tech, Inc.

possible, it is highly unlikely that an investment in an asset will be made if the proper financial capital has not been secured. At this point, the only impact is on the balance sheet, as cash, notes payable, and stockholders' balances all increased.

3. Third, our flow captures that, with cash in hand, the company has made a significant investment in an intangible asset during the FYE 12/31/23 to support their aggressive business plan and drive to increase software sales. Again, only a balance sheet impact is present, as the cash that was raised was used to make a significant purchase of $5,000,000 in intangible assets during the FYE 12/31/23. The reason the ending balance is $6,000,000 is due to the fact that an intangible asset balance of $1,000,000 was carried forward from a prior year (a $2,000,000 balance as of the FYE 12/31/22 less $1,000,000 of current year amortization expense).

4. Fourth, you finally see a financial information flow that connects the balance sheet with the income statement in the form of depreciation and amortization expense. When companies invest in either tangible (e.g., machinery or equipment) or intangible (e.g., patents or trade secrets) assets, it is assumed that, over a period of time, these assets will be consumed and lose value. For tangible assets, businesses must record depreciation expense on a periodic basis to recognize the reduction in value (as the asset is consumed). For intangible assets, businesses generally record amortization expense (for the same purpose) over an appropriate period to recognize the decrease in value. In our example company, depreciation expense increases the total amount of accumulated depreciation (since inception), which is reported on a separate line item. For intangible assets, amortization expense is reflected as a net reduction to the asset value. This is why you see *net* after intangible assets and goodwill.

5. Our fifth and final financial flow or connection ties interest expense to the current and long-term debt our example company has outstanding. Loans carry interest rates and associated interest expense, so the connection between company debt or loans and interest expense should be logical.

Chapter 15 provides additional information related to raising capital from equity sources, but I would like to close our discussion on the investing and financing cycle with two critical thoughts. First, the financing cycle is usually an extremely intensive process that is time-consuming, exhausting, frustrating, and stressful. It is one thing to produce a plan and get in front of the right financing source, hoping that they display some level of interest; it is entirely different to convince the financing source to write the check and commit real capital to the investment opportunity.

Second, be prepared for rejection, which you should not take personally. Securing financing, whether for a new start-up company or for an internal business expansion, is one of the most challenging aspects of operating a business and one of the primary reasons there are so few real entrepreneurs in relation to the number of people working in the marketplace. If it were easy, everyone would be doing it. Trust me when I say securing financing is anything but easy.

Part Two

DIVING DEEPER INTO OUR CASE STUDY

5

OUR CASE STUDY—SAME BUSINESS, THREE DIFFERENT PICTURES

The past four chapters have provided either an introduction on how to read a financial report and financial statements or a refresher course on how to read a financial report and financial statements (if you have read *How to Read a Financial Report*). At this point, if you feel your accounting and financial skill sets are beyond basic or introductory levels, then it makes sense to dive headfirst into the rest of this book. However, if this is your first time learning about financial reports and financial statements, and you would like to strengthen your knowledge base, then I suggest re-reading Chapters 1 through 4, or better yet, reading *How to Read a Financial Report*, 10th Edition. This suggestion might come across as a blatant attempt to increase my book sales, but in all honesty, taking the opportunity to strengthen your core knowledge of financial reports and financial statements will not only improve your comprehension of the material presented in this book, but should also better equip and arm you with invaluable knowledge for real-world financial and accounting encounters. Conversely, my job with all the "How To" books I've written is to make sure you can swim with the sharks instead of being the chum and get eaten alive.

Starting with Chapter 5 and extending through Chapter 10, my focus is going to pivot and emphasize what accountants and financial types like best, good old-fashioned number crunching. To support expanding your knowledge of reading and understanding financial reports and financial statements, I will present three case study companies for comparison. The companies are essentially the same because they are technology-based businesses selling tech products, services, and software (i.e., SaaS, which stands for "software as a service"). The only difference between our case study companies will be centered on the executive management teams and the accounting policies and procedures that have been established and applied.

Our first case study company is a simple family-operated business (referred to as FB throughout the remainder of this book) that has been owned and managed by the same family for decades. Our second case study company (referred to as SEB throughout the remainder of this book) is a conservative "Steady Eddy" business that was introduced in Chapters 1 through 4. Our third case study company is an aggressively managed business (referred to as PEB throughout the remainder of this book) owned by a private equity firm that recently acquired the business from the previous owners. I selected these case studies based on 30+ years of providing accounting and financial consulting services to businesses. Rest assured, they are very real indeed, as in my consulting business travels I've seen just about everything you can imagine on the accounting and financial fronts. So, with this said, let's not waste any more time and learn more about our three case study companies.

The Family Business (FB): Our Simple Case

For hundreds of years, family-owned and operated businesses have represented one of the mainstays of the USA capitalist economy. Family businesses are very real and particularly important with some estimates placing family-owned businesses contributing to roughly 57 percent of the USA's GDP and 63 percent of the workforce. These are big numbers. Countless family-owned businesses operate across the country, spanning decades of family ownership and having representation in just about every industry you can imagine. Significant characteristics of family-owned businesses include the importance of carrying on the mission established at the company's founding and maintaining its culture and traditions. If you need any further proof, consider the family business I've been entrusted with continuing, which my father started over 40 years ago while teaching at the University of Colorado. His passion for teaching accounting and finance evolved into authoring countless books that have been published and distributed around the world for over 40 years. (This is now in my hands, lord help us all, and it will eventually pass to my oldest son.) One thing I can assure you of is the importance of carrying on my father's legacy and continuing to educate people who have an appetite for the material presented in our books.

Our family-owned business has been operated and controlled by the same family for the past 50 years. It has successfully evolved and adapted to the challenges of operating a technology-based company that is always subject to rapidly changing innovations, but FB has retained some old-school management strategies, especially within its accounting and finance functions. These include:

- FB maintains a simple relationship with the same accounting firm it has used for the past 30 years, Dick & Jane Smith ABT Services, LLC (accounting, bookkeeping, and taxation). The company uses this firm to prepare periodic income tax returns, produce compiled financial statements (as audited financial statements are not prepared), and provide other financial and accounting services as needed.
- FB raised $2.5 million of equity capital in 2023, which was secured from a family trust in the form of selling common stock. No outside money is allowed in, never has been, and never will be.
- The company's lending relationship has been in place for over a decade, including the same bank and loan officers. To support the loans provided to the company, PGs are present (i.e., personal guarantees by the majority owners) with second secured interests established in various real estate owned by family members. This may not be wise, but it is how business with the bank has been done for years, and the family doesn't know any better. The family's willingness to stand behind the loans reflects their belief in the business.

- The accounting and finance team is solid but has limited experience outside of the family-owned business. They're not overly savvy, knowledgeable, and experienced in complex business and financial transactions. Honest but inexperienced, they tend to focus on processing transactions to ensure accuracy and compliance reporting rather than completing more complex financial analyses.
- The board of directors (BOD) comprises family members and close business associates, including one member from the bank. As always, outside involvement is limited because family dynamics and politics play an outsized role in the BOD.
- Currently, FB has no real interest in selling the company, in part or in whole, because the current majority owners envision the family will continue its ownership for years to come. However, as the next and younger generation establishes their relevance in the company, an eventual exit or liquidity event (terms used to indicate a company may be sold and generate a significant cash windfall) may occur sooner rather than later.

Now, refer to Exhibits 5.1 through 5.3, which provide the financial statements for FB, including the income statement in Exhibit 5.1, the balance sheet in Exhibit 5.2, and the statement of cash flows in Exhibit 5.3.

EXHIBIT 5.1—COMPILED FINANCIAL STATEMENTS—INCOME STATEMENT, SIMPLE CASE (FB)

Dollar Amounts in Thousands

Income Statement

For the Fiscal Years Ending	12/31/2022	12/31/2023
Sales Revenue, Net	$ 54,474	$ 59,806
Costs of Sales Revenue, Service	$(12,882)	$(14,374)
Costs of Sales Revenue, Products	$(11,048)	$ (7,245)
Gross Profit (aka Gross Margin)	$ 30,544	$ 38,188
Operating Expenses:		
Selling, General, & Administrative	$ 22,525	$ 25,045
Research & Development	$ 5,692	$ 7,139
Depreciation & Amortization	$ 905	$ 976
Total Operating Expenses	$ 29,122	$ 33,160
Operating Income (Loss)	$ 1,421	$ 5,027
Other Expenses (Income):		
Other Expenses or (Income)	$ 0	$ 0
Interest Expense	$ 339	$ 407
Total Other Expenses (Income)	$ 339	$ 407
Net Income (Loss) before Income Taxes	$ 1,082	$ 4,620
Income Tax Expense (Benefit)	$ 41	$ 438
Net Income (Loss) after Income Taxes	$ 1,041	$ 4,182

See Accompanying Schedules

EXHIBIT 5.2—COMPILED FINANCIAL STATEMENTS—BALANCE SHEET, SIMPLE CASE (FB)

Dollar Amounts in Thousands

Balance Sheet as of the Fiscal Year Ending	12/31/2022	12/31/2023
Assets		
Current Assets:		
Cash & Equivalents	$ 775	$ 2,164
Accounts Receivable	$ 6,803	$ 8,229
Inventory	$ 3,913	$ 3,944
Prepaid Expenses	$ 600	$ 625
Total Current Assets	$12,091	$14,963
Long-Term Operating & Other Assets:		
Property, Machinery, & Equipment	$ 4,000	$ 4,500
Less: Accumulated Depreciation	$ (1,571)	$ (2,214)
Net Property, Machinery, & Equipment	$ 2,429	$ 2,286
Other Assets:		
Intangible Assets, Net	$ 4,000	$ 8,667
Other Assets	$ 100	$ 100
Total Long-Term Operating & Other Assets	$ 6,529	$11,052
Total Assets	$18,619	$26,015

Balance Sheet as of the Fiscal Year Ending	12/31/2022	12/31/2023
Liabilities		
Current Liabilities:		
Accounts Payable	$ 1,405	$ 1,459
Accrued Liabilities Payable	$ 734	$ 858
Short-Term Loans Payable	$ 3,390	$ 2,400
Other Current Liabilities & Deferred Revenue	$ 300	$ 325
Total Current Liabilities	$ 5,829	$ 5,042
Long-Term Liabilities:		
Loans Payable & Other Long-Term Debt, Less ST Loans	$ 750	$ 2,500
Total Liabilities	$ 6,579	$ 7,542
Stockholders' Equity		
Capital Stock	$ 7,500	$10,000
Retained Earnings	$ 4,540	$ 8,473
Total Stockholders' Equity	$12,040	$18,473
Total Liabilities & Stockholders' Equity	$18,619	$26,015

See Accompanying Schedules

EXHIBIT 5.3—COMPILED FINANCIAL STATEMENTS—STATEMENT OF CASH FLOWS, SIMPLE CASE (FB)

Dollar Amounts in Thousands

Statement of Cash Flows For the Fiscal Years Ending	12/31/2022	12/31/2023
Net Income (Loss) after Income Taxes	$ 1,041	$ 4,182
Operating Activities, Cash provided (used):		
Depreciation & Amortization	$ 905	$ 976
Decrease (increase) in accounts receivables	$(1,114)	$(1,427)
Decrease (increase) in inventory	$ (325)	$ (31)
Decrease (increase) in other current assets	$ (50)	$ (25)
Increase (decrease) in accounts payables	$ 155	$ 54
Increase (decrease) in accrued liabilities	$ 68	$ (8)
Increase (decrease) in other liabilities	$ (47)	$ 157
Net Cash Flow from Operating Activities	$ 634	$ 3,879
Investing Activities, Cash provided (used):		
Capital Expenditures	$ (250)	$ (500)
Investments in Intangible & Other Assets	$ 0	$(5,000)
Net Cash Flow from Investing Activities	$ (250)	$(5,500)

Statement of Cash Flows For the Fiscal Years Ending	12/31/2022	12/31/2023
Financing Activities, Cash provided (used):		
Dividends or Distributions Paid	$ 0	$ (250)
Sale (repurchase) of Equity	$ 0	$ 2,500
Proceeds from Issuance of Loans (i.e., debt)	$ 0	$ 3,000
Repayments of Long-Term Loans	$(750)	$(1,250)
Net Borrowings (Repayments) of Short-Term Loans	$ 560	$ (990)
Other Financing Activities	$ 0	$ 0
Net Cash Flow from Financing Activities	$(190)	$ 3,010
Net Increase (decrease) in Cash & Equivalents	$ 194	$ 1,389
Beginning Cash & Equivalents Balance	$ 581	$ 775
Ending Cash & Equivalents Balance	$ 775	$ 2,164

See Accompanying Schedules

In Chapters 6 through 10, we'll spend plenty of time crunching the numbers, but I would like to point out something important in the financial statements. That is, FB does not have audited financial statements prepared, but instead uses their accounting firm to prepare compiled financial statements. For a detailed understanding of the difference between audited, reviewed, and compiled financial statements, please refer to *How to Read a Financial Report*. In a nutshell, the difference is significant. With audited financial statements, a qualified and independent third party attests that the financial statements have been prepared in accordance with GAAP (generally accepted accounting principles). Compiled financial statements mean that a third party has taken the company's internally prepared financial statements and compiled them in a format suitable for external presentation. There were no audit procedures or analytical analysis, just limited oversight from an external party. This is why external parties, such as lenders, investors, and analysts, prioritize audited financial statements, which are deemed much more reliable and credible than compiled or reviewed financial statements.

The Steady Eddy Business (SEB): Our Base Case

In Chapters 1 through 4, I provided multiple exhibits that presented financial statements and information for our second case study company, SEB. This represents a very common and prevalent type of company that operates throughout the United States. SEB has evolved smoothly since its founding years ago. Launched by a passionate but somewhat undisciplined entrepreneur, it was acquired by a group of more seasoned, sophisticated, and experienced owners that also have instilled a deep management team that is very astute and understands the importance of building a business over a long period. At a macro level, please note the following strategies and resources utilized by SEB:

- SEB utilizes the accounting CPA firm of Kleen, Kneet, and Tidey, LLC. This firm completes an annual audit of the company's financial statements accompanied by what is often referred to as a clean audit opinion (i.e., everything looks good, no major GAAP or operating exceptions identified). Further, this CPA also prepares all required income tax returns and other required compliance filings.
- The capital raised in 2023 was secured from company insiders, accredited investors, and parties or close business associates familiar with its business model and industry. Not only did these parties provide fresh capital but also they represent a great resource and knowledge bank to lean on. They also understand that an exit from their investment will take time.
- The loans provided to SEB were secured from private credit markets (often referred to as non-bank or non-traditional sources). The loans have been properly structured for the company, do not carry PGs (i.e., personal guarantees), and will provide flexibility for long-term growth.
- The accounting and finance team are seasoned professionals, relatively sophisticated, experienced, and have a deep bench (i.e., significant team members to support the company's operating needs). In addition, the executive leading the accounting and finance team (often carrying the title of CFO or chief financial officer) tends to be conservative and plays it relatively close to the vest when it comes to accounting and financial reporting matters.
- The BOD is well rounded with both extensive industry and business experience and is comprised of both in-house executives, current company owners, and external independent parties. This type of mix is always a welcome sign.
- SEB has no immediate plans for an exit or liquidity event and is anticipating executing a long-term business plan to position the company for a sale in 7 to 10 years. However, the owners and BOD are always sensitive to market conditions, and if an opportunity is presented to exit, it will be considered.

Well, what a difference from FB in terms of management experience, planning, focus, and strategy. This is not to say SEB is better or worse managed than FB, but different (based on culture, history, etc.). Let's take a look at SEB's financial statements (which were presented in Chapter 2) as presented again in Exhibits 5.4 through 5.6.

Here, please direct your attention to two items. First, we have audited financial statements, always a welcome sign. Second, notice the significant difference between FB's and SEB's net bottom line (aka net profit or net income) for both 2022 and 2023 (comparing Exhibits 5.1 and 5.4), yet when you look at the balance sheet (comparing Exhibits 5.2 and 5.5), both companies have the exact same cash balances (at the end of each year). How is this possible? Through the magic of accounting and financial statement reporting, this question will be answered by the end of the book.

EXHIBIT 5.4—AUDITED FINANCIAL STATEMENTS—INCOME STATEMENT, BASE CASE (SEB)

Dollar Amounts in Thousands

Income Statement		
For the Fiscal Years Ending	12/31/2022	12/31/2023
Sales Revenue, Net	$ 54,210	$ 59,494
Costs of Sales Revenue, Service	$(12,882)	$(14,374)
Costs of Sales Revenue, Products	$(11,040)	$ (7,392)
Gross Profit (aka Gross Margin)	$ 30,288	$ 37,728
Operating Expenses:		
Selling, General, & Administrative	$ 22,567	$ 25,289
Research & Development	$ 5,692	$ 7,139
Depreciation & Amortization	$ 1,571	$ 1,643
Total Operating Expenses	$ 29,831	$ 34,071
Operating Income (Loss)	$ 457	$ 3,658
Other Expenses (Income):		
Other Expenses or (Income)	$ 0	$ 2,000
Interest Expense	$ 339	$ 407
Total Other Expenses (Income)	$ 339	$ 2,407
Net Income (Loss) before Income Taxes	$ 118	$ 1,251
Income Tax Expense (benefit)	$ 41	$ 438
Net Income (Loss) after Income Taxes	$ 77	$ 813

See Notes to Financial Statements

EXHIBIT 5.5—AUDITED FINANCIAL STATEMENTS—BALANCE SHEET, BASE CASE (SEB)

Dollar Amounts in Thousands

Balance Sheet as of the Fiscal Year Ending	12/31/2022	12/31/2023
Assets		
Current Assets:		
Cash & Equivalents	$ 775	$ 2,164
Accounts Receivable	$ 6,776	$ 8,009
Inventory	$ 3,822	$ 1,706
Prepaid Expenses	$ 600	$ 625
Total Current Assets	$11,973	$12,504
Long-Term Operating & Other Assets:		
Property, Machinery, & Equipment	$ 4,000	$ 4,500
Less: Accumulated Depreciation	$ (1,571)	$ (2,214)
Net Property, Machinery, & Equipment	$ 2,429	$ 2,286
Other Assets:		
Intangible Assets, Net	$ 2,000	$ 6,000
Other Assets	$ 100	$ 100
Total Long-Term Operating & Other Assets	$ 4,529	$ 8,386
Total Assets	$16,502	$20,889

Balance Sheet as of the Fiscal Year Ending	12/31/2022	12/31/2023
Liabilities		
Current Liabilities:		
Accounts Payable	$ 1,405	$ 1,459
Accrued Liabilities Payable	$ 1,084	$ 1,258
Short-Term Loans Payable	$ 3,390	$ 2,400
Other Current Liabilities & Deferred Revenue	$ 1,011	$ 1,348
Total Current Liabilities	$ 6,890	$ 6,465
Long-Term Liabilities:		
Loans Payable & Other Long-Term Debt, Less ST Loans	$ 750	$ 2,500
Total Liabilities	$ 7,640	$ 8,965
Stockholders' Equity		
Capital Stock	$ 7,500	$10,000
Retained Earnings	$ 1,362	$ 1,924
Total Stockholders' Equity	$ 8,862	$11,924
Total Liabilities & Stockholders' Equity	$16,502	$20,889

See Notes to Financial Statements

EXHIBIT 5.6—AUDITED FINANCIAL STATEMENTS—STATEMENT OF CASH FLOWS, BASE CASE (SEB)

Dollar Amounts in Thousands

Statement of Cash Flows For the Fiscal Years Ending	12/31/2022	12/31/2023
Net Income (Loss) after Income Taxes	$ 77	$ 813
Operating Activities, Cash provided (used):		
Depreciation & Amortization	$ 1,571	$ 1,643
Decrease (increase) in accounts receivables	$(1,122)	$(1,233)
Decrease (increase) in inventory	$ (333)	$ 2,116
Decrease (increase) in other current assets	$ (50)	$ (25)
Increase (decrease) in accounts payables	$ 155	$ 54
Increase (decrease) in accrued liabilities	$ 118	$ 42
Increase (decrease) in other liabilities	$ 217	$ 469
Net Cash Flow from Operating Activities	$ 634	$ 3,879
Investing Activities, Cash provided (used):		
Capital Expenditures	$ (250)	$ (500)
Investments in Intangible & Other Assets	$ 0	$(5,000)
Net Cash Flow from Investing Activities	$ (250)	$(5,500)

Statement of Cash Flows For the Fiscal Years Ending	12/31/2022	12/31/2023
Financing Activities, Cash provided (used):		
Dividends or Distributions Paid	$ 0	$ (250)
Sale (repurchase) of Equity	$ 0	$ 2,500
Proceeds from Issuance of Loans (i.e., debt)	$ 0	$ 3,000
Repayments of Long-Term Loans	$(750)	$(1,250)
Net Borrowings (Repayments) of Short-Term Loans	$ 560	$ (990)
Other Financing Activities	$ 0	$ 0
Net Cash Flow from Financing Activities	$(190)	$ 3,010
Net Increase (decrease) in Cash & Equivalents	$ 194	$ 1,389
Beginning Cash & Equivalents Balance	$ 581	$ 775
Ending Cash & Equivalents Balance	$ 775	$ 2,164

See Notes to Financial Statements

The PE Business (PEB): Our Aggressive Case

Finally, we land in our last business case study, which represents a company that was recently acquired by a private equity group, the BB&DD fund (which stands for Barbarossa Brothers, famous pirates, and Duke & Duke Commodity Brokers, a fictional finance company from the movie *Trading Places*). Private equity (aka PE) groups tend to be very large, well-capitalized, and sophisticated investment funds that search out value opportunities in companies that have significant growth potential and value upside. If you ever want to experience getting into the ocean with sharks, working with PE firms might be a good place to start as these parties are generally very sophisticated, slick, intelligent, and polished when it comes to identifying businesses with significant upside value potential. At a macro level, here again, please note the following strategies and resources utilized by PEB:

- PEB utilizes the accounting CPA firm of Dewey, Fixim, & Howe, LLC, a rapidly growing and aggressive CPA firm that specializes in working with private equity firms. This firm completes an annual audit of the company's financial statements accompanied by a clean audit opinion (i.e., everything looks good, no major GAAP or operating exceptions identified). This CPA also prepares all required income tax returns and other required compliance filings.
- PEB also raised $2,500,000 of capital during 2023 using a structure of stock referred to as preferred equity. I explain capital structures and preferred equity in Chapter 15 along with the pros and cons of using different types of capital stock, such as common versus preferred. The $2,500,000 of capital was secured from a specific fund used by the private equity group to invest in these types of business opportunities.
- PEB's lending facilities have been secured from an associated group that BB&DD utilizes to provide loans to portfolio companies (another term for a company that is owned and managed by the private equity group as part of a portfolio of businesses). The loans do not require any PGs and carry reasonable interest rates, but they are structured to have a first secured or senior credit position in PEB's assets. This may present a hidden risk to PEB, as if a speedbump or pothole is hit down the road and PEB's performance is substandard, the senior lender may become more aggressive to protect its financial position within the company.
- The accounting and finance team are seasoned professionals, very sophisticated, and have extensive experience with building a company and selling it for a profit. Here, the CFO is well versed in the financial markets and has over 15 years of experience buying and selling companies. The CFO has built a team that is focused on achieving rapid growth and using more aggressive accounting policies and strategies to achieve high-reaching growth goals.

- The BOD is demanding, well connected to the financial markets and industry, has deep contacts in the industry, and is experienced with managing investments within a private equity environment. The BOD contains both internal company executives and has a heavy influence from the private equity group that owns the company.
- PEB has an internal goal to build and sell the business within the next 3 to 5 years, as this time frame fits within the investment fund strategy developed by BB&DD. The goal is to grow quickly, drive earnings, and exit during a window that should provide a premium value for PEB.

I'm intentionally changing the ownership and management dynamics of PEB to emphasize just how influential these business elements can be when preparing financial statements and reports. Let's take a look at our PEB financial statements as presented in Exhibits 5.7 through 5.9.

The management team and ownership group of PEB must really know what they're doing! Look at the operating performance and profits generated compared to the FB and SEB. Quite impressive, but the question is whether the operating profits generated are real or imaginary (a topic I save until Chapter 14).

EXHIBIT 5.7—AUDITED FINANCIAL STATEMENTS—INCOME STATEMENT, AGGRESSIVE CASE (PEB)

Dollar Amounts in Thousands

Income Statement		
For the Fiscal Years Ending	**12/31/2022**	**12/31/2023**
Sales Revenue, Net	$ 54,342	$ 60,650
Costs of Sales Revenue, Service	$(12,882)	$(14,624)
Costs of Sales Revenue, Products	$(11,040)	$ (7,392)
Gross Profit (aka Gross Margin)	$ 30,420	$ 38,634
Operating Expenses:		
Selling, General, & Administrative	$ 22,567	$ 25,089
Research & Development	$ 4,192	$ 4,639
Depreciation & Amortization	$ 1,205	$ 1,776
Total Operating Expenses	$ 27,964	$ 31,504
Operating Income (Loss)	$ 2,456	$ 7,130
Other Expenses (Income):		
Other Expenses or (Income)	$ 0	$ 0
Interest Expense	$ 339	$ 407
Total Other Expenses (Income)	$ 339	$ 407
Net Income (Loss) before Income Taxes	$ 2,117	$ 6,723
Income Tax Expense (benefit)	$ 41	$ 438
Net Income (Loss) after Income Taxes	$ 2,076	$ 6,285

See Notes to Financial Statements

EXHIBIT 5.8—AUDITED FINANCIAL STATEMENTS—BALANCE SHEET, AGGRESSIVE CASE (PEB)

Dollar Amounts in Thousands

Balance Sheet as of the Fiscal Year Ending	12/31/2022	12/31/2023
Assets		
Current Assets:		
Cash & Equivalents	$ 775	$ 2,164
Accounts Receivable	$ 6,776	$ 9,209
Inventory	$ 3,822	$ 3,706
Prepaid Expenses	$ 600	$ 625
Total Current Assets	$11,973	$15,704
Long-Term Operating & Other Assets:		
Property, Machinery, & Equipment	$ 4,000	$ 4,500
Less: Accumulated Depreciation	$ (1,571)	$ (2,214)
Net Property, Machinery, & Equipment	$ 2,429	$ 2,286
Other Assets:		
Intangible Assets, Net	$ 5,200	$11,567
Other Assets	$ 100	$ 100
Total Long-Term Operating & Other Assets	$ 7,729	$13,952
Total Assets	$19,702	$29,656

Balance Sheet as of the Fiscal Year Ending	12/31/2022	12/31/2023
Liabilities		
Current Liabilities:		
Accounts Payable	$ 1,405	$ 1,459
Accrued Liabilities Payable	$ 1,084	$ 1,508
Short-Term Loans Payable	$ 3,390	$ 2,400
Other Current Liabilities & Deferred Revenue	$ 656	$ 837
Total Current Liabilities	$ 6,535	$ 6,204
Long-Term Liabilities:		
Loans Payable & Other Long-Term Debt, Less ST Loans	$ 750	$ 2,500
Total Liabilities	$ 7,285	$ 8,704
Stockholders' Equity		
Capital Stock	$ 7,500	$10,000
Retained Earnings	$ 4,917	$10,953
Total Stockholders' Equity	$12,417	$20,953
Total Liabilities & Stockholders' Equity	$19,702	$29,656

See Notes to Financial Statements

EXHIBIT 5.9—AUDITED FINANCIAL STATEMENTS—STATEMENT OF CASH FLOWS, AGGRESSIVE CASE (PEB)

Dollar Amounts in Thousands

Statement of Cash Flows For the Fiscal Years Ending	12/31/2022	12/31/2023
Net Income (Loss) after Income Taxes	$ 2,076	$ 6,285
Operating Activities, Cash provided (used):		
Depreciation & Amortization	$ 1,205	$ 1,776
Decrease (increase) in accounts receivables	$(1,122)	$(2,433)
Decrease (increase) in inventory	$ (333)	$ 116
Decrease (increase) in other current assets	$ (50)	$ (25)
Increase (decrease) in accounts payables	$ 155	$ 54
Increase (decrease) in accrued liabilities	$ 118	$ 292
Increase (decrease) in other liabilities	$ 85	$ 313
Net Cash Flow from Operating Activities	$ 2,134	$ 6,379
Investing Activities, Cash provided (used):		
Capital Expenditures	$ (250)	$ (500)
Investments in Intangible & Other Assets	$(1,500)	$(7,500)
Net Cash Flow from Investing Activities	$(1,750)	$(8,000)

Statement of Cash Flows For the Fiscal Years Ending	12/31/2022	12/31/2023
Financing Activities, Cash provided (used):		
Dividends or Distributions Paid	$ 0	$ (250)
Sale (repurchase) of Equity	$ 0	$ 2,500
Proceeds from Issuance of Loans (i.e., debt)	$ 0	$ 3,000
Repayments of Long-Term Loans	$(750)	$(1,250)
Net Borrowings (Repayments) of Short-Term Loans	$ 560	$ (990)
Other Financing Activities	$ 0	$ 0
Net Cash Flow from Financing Activities	$(190)	$ 3,010
Net Increase (decrease) in Cash & Equivalents	$ 194	$ 1,389
Beginning Cash & Equivalents Balance	$ 581	$ 775
Ending Cash & Equivalents Balance	$ 775	$ 2,164

See Notes to Financial Statements

Before You Dive In, Remember These Helpful Hints

As you push forward in the book and begin to dig into Chapters 6 through 10 (where some serious number crunching takes place), I would offer these hints to help prepare you to digest the concepts and information in the most efficient manner possible:

- First, this book represents an evolution and continuation of *How to Read a Financial Report* (now in its 10th edition). It is designed to elevate your understanding of financial reports and financial statements by delivering the content in a workbook formal (e.g., hands-on approach; more exhibits, calculations, examples; etc.). Translation: Don't be afraid to actively engage with the concepts, take notes, recalculate figures directly in the book and so on.
- Second, you will notice that in each of our case studies, I kept income tax expense constant. In theory, income tax expense should vary with each company based on the net income generated before income taxes. However, I kept income tax expense constant to drive home a key point related to cash and the cash flow statement, which will be expanded upon through the remainder of the book. Don't worry; the income tax expense figures are left constant for a specific reason.
- Third, it never hurts to have a calculator standing ready, either on your phone or using an old-fashioned HP12C (I'm referring to myself, a relic and traditionalist.) Given that we're going to be completing additional calculations along the way, having a readily available and reliable calculator is highly recommended.
- Fourth, the exhibits used in this book are free to all customers. I strongly suggest you request the Excel workbook file (which I will forward to you) to assist with your reading.
- Fifth and finally, I hope you enjoy the material. Please remember that there's a reason I summarized the management and ownership structure of each of our case study companies in the manner presented in this chapter. The background provided on each case study company was not completed in an arbitrary fashion, but it comes from real-life experiences of working with these types of businesses and seeing the influence ownership, management, and lending sources can have on implementing accounting policies and preparing financial statements and reports (to achieve specific objectives). At various points in the book, this will make more sense as I specifically highlight financial information that may be produced with different pressures being exerted.

6

ACCOUNTS RECEIVABLE: A CLOSER EXAMINATION

Starting with Chapter 6 and continuing through Chapter 10, we will shift our focus from reviewing summary-level content to diving deeper into our three case studies and examining four different balance sheet accounts and their associated relationship and impact on the income statement. For each of the four balance sheet accounts, a summary of the different accounting policies and procedures used by each of our three case study companies will be provided that clearly explains the basis, reasoning, and logic behind the amounts presented. The purpose of providing this level of detail is twofold:

- First, I want to make sure a clear path or audit trail is established to help you understand the source of the exact figures of how a change in a balance sheet account will impact the income statement (either in a positive or negative fashion). When possible, additional exhibits and calculations will be provided to assist with auditing the figures presented.
- Second, quite often the accounting function is often viewed with the blinders on, only from the perspective of crunching numbers. This is far from the truth as accounting policies and procedures are often characterized by intense analyses, discussions, the application of different perspectives, company politics, and so on. Hence, by providing a summary of the logic used to set an accounting policy, you will gain further insight as to just how varied accounting policies can be and more thoroughly understand the statement I've made over and over that accounting is just as much an art form as a science.

The four balance sheet accounts I've chosen will be accounts receivable (Chapter 6), inventory (Chapter 7), long-term intangible assets (Chapter 8), and other current liabilities including deferred revenue (Chapter 9). In actuality, I could have presented far more than these balance sheet account examples, however, the four accounts I've chosen were intentionally selected because they relate to accounting areas that are more prone to applying different accounting policies and are relatively hot topics in today's business world.

I should also note that the structure of Chapters 6 through 9 will remain the same. After a brief introduction is provided as to why the balance sheet account was selected (highlighting why it is a focal point), each chapter will contain the following sections:

1. First, a brief (and expanded overview) refresher will be provided on the connection between the balance sheet account and the income statement. The connection refresher exhibit is only provided for our base case company operating scenario as it is not necessary to provide a new exhibit for each case study scenario (as the same logic applies). I should also note that in this book, I take the discussion of connections up a notch by explaining additional connections between the balance sheet and income statement.
2. Second, a summary of the accounting policy and procedures (along with the reasoning) will be provided for each of our three case studies. This will be accompanied by an expanded or exploded account analysis that breaks down the primary account (e.g., accounts receivable) into multiple subaccounts that comprise the primary account balance.
3. Third, financial analyses will be applied to the numbers to compare and contrast our three case studies. This section in each chapter is referred to as "crunching numbers" and will focus on key operating metrics, performance indicators, etc. that are relevant for the balance sheet account selected.

4. Fourth and finally, I close with a brief overview of the key accounting issues associated with the primary topics covered in the chapter. The accounting issues overview is not designed to be all inclusive of every topic impacting the selected balance sheet account but rather is offered to provide you with a small "taste" of just how many accounting issues are present, for just one balance sheet account.

Finally, in Chapter 10, I bring it all together as I present a summary of our three case study companies in a side by side fashion to compare and contrast the income statements, the balance sheets, and the statements of cash flow. Chapter 10 also includes a running total or score card that has been prepared and presented for each case study to keep track of the differences in the accounting figures (on a balance sheet account basis), both individually and cumulatively, to reconcile the financial statements between each case study company. Chapter 10 then closes with, what else (which I'm sure you've guessed by now), tying everything together by reconciling the cash flows generated by each of our case study companies.

Note: Starting in Exhibit 6.1, the income statement and balance sheet have been compressed and are stripped of various subtotals. (The same is true of all exhibits in the coming chapters.) For example, the income statement has been simplified, meaning that it does not contain lines displaying total operating expenses and other intermediate measures of profit. Likewise, in the balance sheet, no subtotals are shown for current assets and current liabilities and for the amount of property, machinery, and equipment that has less accumulated depreciation. Excluding subtotals gives us lean and mean financial statements to work with. Furthermore, Exhibit 6.1 does not include the company's statement of cash flows for the year. The connections between changes in the balance sheet accounts and the cash flow statement are explained in Chapter 3. The cash flow statement would be a distraction at this point.

So, with the ground rules laid out, let's attack the first accounting topic beast, which has been on everyone's radar for the past 10+ years: recognizing sales revenue and the associated accounts receivable. There is no better place to start than the top of the income statement, which is the first place most parties begin when reviewing a company's financial statements.

Almost all external parties hone in on and pay close attention to a company's top-line sales revenue performance, as just about everyone makes an effort to calculate the year-over-year sales revenue increase for a business. The faster a company's sales revenue grows, the more valuable the company becomes. (A faster growth in net profits should occur as well.) Hence, there is a strong motivation for companies to drive top-line sales revenue growth as it indicates management is performing well, profits should be improving, and the value of the business should be increasing.

These are great signs, but I offer this critical bit of advice. The most important financial data points (including top-line sales revenue growth) are the ones that tend to be the most susceptible to misreporting, massaging, and outright abuse (for lack of a better term). Further, companies have gotten very aggressive and creative when billing customers for the sale of products or services (e.g., selling software as a service, or SaaS, in advance for an entire year), and over the past decades have taken upon themselves to interpret when actual sales revenue is earned (which does not mean invoicing the customer for the sale of products or services).

This trend has not gone unnoticed by authoritative bodies. As a result, a rather complex and lengthy (but very logical) regulatory guideline titled ASC 606 was developed and required of all companies starting in late 2017. For those of you who are accounting junkies or maybe for anyone that simply needs some reading material to assist with falling asleep at night, I would encourage you to review ASC 606, which spells out the framework for when and how sales revenue should be recognized.

EXHIBIT 6.1—SALES REVENUE, ACCOUNTS RECEIVABLE, AND EXPENSES—BASE CASE (SEB)

Dollar Amounts in Thousands

INCOME STATEMENT

Sales Revenue, Net	$ 59,494
Costs of Sales Revenue, Service	$(14,374)
Costs of Sales Revenue, Products	$ (7,392)
Gross Profit (aka Gross Margin)	$ 37,728
Expenses:	
Selling, General, & Administrative	$(25,289)
Research & Development	$ (7,139)
Depreciation & Amortization	$ (1,643)
Operating Income (Loss)	$ 3,658
Other Expenses or (Income)	$ (2,000)
Interest Expense	$ (407)
Net Income (Loss) before Income Taxes	$ 1,251
Income Tax Expense (Benefit)	$ (438)
Net Income (Loss) after Income Taxes	$ 813

BALANCE SHEET

ASSETS	
Cash & Equivalents	$ 2,164
Accounts Receivable	$ 8,009
Inventory	$ 1,706
Prepaid Expenses	$ 625
Property, Machinery, & Equipment	$ 4,500
Less: Accumulated Depreciation	$ (2,214)
Intangible Assets, Net	$ 6,000
Other Assets	$ 100
Total Assets	$20,889
LIABILITIES	
Accounts Payable	$ 1,459
Accrued Liabilities Payable	$ 1,112
Income Taxes Payable	$ 146
Other Current Liabilities & Deferred Revenue	$ 1,348
Short-Term Loans Payable	$ 2,400
Loans Payable & Other Long-Term Debt, Less ST Loans	$ 2,500
Total Liabilities	$ 8,965
STOCKHOLDERS' EQUITY	
Capital Stock	$10,000
Retained Earnings	$ 1,924
Total Liabilities and Stockholders' Equity	$20,889

My goal with this chapter is to start our detailed case study analysis by focusing on the start of the income statement food chain, sales revenue. This will help you understand key relationships and connections between sales revenue, accounts receivable, and bad debt expense.

Refresher Connection: Accounts Receivable, Sales Revenue, and Expenses

Please refer to Exhibit 6.1, which presents two connections between accounts receivable in the balance sheet and sales revenue and operating expenses in the income statement.

a. Connection number one shows the connection between *sales revenue* in the income statement and the *accounts receivable* asset account in the balance sheet. The central idea here is that the profit-making activities reported in the income statement drive or determine an asset or a liability. However, assets and liabilities can also impact the income statement. In our business example, the company's sales revenue for the FYE 12/31/23 just ended was \$59,494,000. Of this total sales revenue, \$8,009,000 is in the accounts receivable asset account at the end of the year. The \$8,009,000 is the portion of annual sales that has not yet been collected at the end of the year.

b. Connection number two may not be as direct or visible as connection number one, but it is still important to understand. This connection presents a relationship between a company's reserve for bad debts (a contra account or offset to the accounts receivable balance) and selling, general, and administrative (SG&A) expenses. When a company incurs bad debts from customers who cannot pay their outstanding invoices, an expense must be recorded in the income statement. For the most part, bad debt expense should be relatively immaterial and, as such, is not reflected as a separate line item in the income statement but rather is most often grouped or consolidated within a general expense account such as SG&A expense.

In our base case business example, the company generated \$59,494,000 of total sales revenue during the year. This is a sizable amount, equal to an average weekly sales revenue of \$1,144,000. When making a sale, the total sale amount (for products or services) is recorded in the *sales revenue* account. This account accumulates all sales made during the year starting on 1/1/23 and ending on 12/31/23. On the first day of the year (in our business example, 1/1/23), it starts with a zero balance; at the end of the last day of the year (i.e., 12/31/23), it has a \$59,494,000 balance. In short, the balance in this account at year-end is the cumulative sum of all sales for the entire year (assuming all sales are recorded).

In our example, the business makes all its sales on credit, which means that cash is not received until sometime after the time of sale. This company sells to other businesses that demand credit. (Many retailers, such as supermarkets and gas stations, make all sales for cash, or accept credit cards that are converted into cash immediately.) The amount owed to the company from making a sale on credit is immediately recorded in the accounts receivable asset account for the amount of each sale. Sometime later, when cash is collected from customers, the cash account is increased, and the accounts receivable account is decreased.

Extending credit to customers creates a cash inflow lag. The accounts receivable balance is the amount of this lag. At year-end, the balance in this asset account is the amount of uncollected sales revenue. Most of the sales made on credit during the year have been converted into cash by the end of the year. Also, the accounts receivable balance at the start of the year from credit sales made last year was collected. But many sales made during the latter part of the year have not yet been collected by the end of the year. The total amount of these uncollected sales is found in the ending balance of accounts receivable.

Some of the company's customers pay quickly to take advantage of prompt payment discounts. (These discounts on list prices reduce sale prices, but speed up cash receipts.) However, the average customer waits six to seven weeks to pay the company and forgoes the prompt payment discount. Some customers even wait 12 weeks or more to pay the company, despite the company's efforts to encourage them to pay sooner. The company puts up with these slow payers because they generate many repeat sales.

Accounting Policies and Procedures Summary

I'm going to summarize each of our three case study companies' accounting policies and procedures applied and then provide an exhibit that compares and contrasts each one.

- Base Case: Our Steady Eddy Business (SEB) scenario has implemented the bad debt allowance method to account for anticipated bad debts. On a periodic basis, SEB analyzes collection trends and the state of its business operating environment and calculates an estimated exposure or risk of potential future uncollectible accounts receivables. For the most recent FYE 12/31/23, SEB increased its reserve for potential bad debts based on assessing the macroeconomic environment and perceived increased risks associated with customers not being able to pay.
- Simple Case: Our Family Business (FB) scenario has elected to use the direct write-off method to account for bad debts. Bad debts are written off only when an actual customer account receivable is deemed uncollectible after all collection efforts have been exhausted. This policy has been in place since the company's formation and is based on the advice received from the company's external CPA firm that prepares its annual income tax returns.
- Aggressive Case: Our Aggressive Business (PEB) scenario has elected to use the same accounting policy as SEB and has established a reserve for potential future uncollectible accounts receivables. However, for the most recent FYE 12/31/23, it elected to maintain its estimated bad debt reserve ratio as the company sees no significant potential economic headwinds that may result in increased bad debts.

Now, let's visualize our three case studies in Exhibit 6.2 based on the described accounting policies and provide some additional commentary.

EXHIBIT 6.2—ACCOUNTS RECEIVABLE COMPARISON—THREE CASE STUDIES
Dollar Amounts in Thousands

Amounts—as of the FYE 12/31/22	SEB Base Case	FB Simple Case	PEB Aggressive Case
Gross Accounts Receivable	$6,878	$6,803	$6,878
Earned Revenue, Unbilled	$0	$ 0	$ 0
Less: Allowance for Doubtful Accounts	$ (102)	$ 0	$ (102)
Net Accounts Receivable	$6,776	$6,803	$6,776

Amounts—as of the FYE 12/31/23	SEB Base Case	FB Simple Case	PEB Aggressive Case
Gross Accounts Receivable	$8,329	$8,229	$8,329
Earned Revenue, Unbilled	$ 0	$ 0	$1,000
Less: Allowance for Doubtful Accounts	$ (320)	$ 0	$ (120)
Net Accounts Receivable	$8,009	$8,229	$9,209

The key takeaways from Exhibit 6.2 are as follows:

- First, the net accounts receivable balances agree to the accounts receivable balances presented in Chapter 5 for each respective case study's balance sheet (as it should).
- Second, our FB case study has a zero balance in the allowance for doubtful accounts, which is consistent with its accounting policy of realizing bad debts only when a customer account is deemed 100% worthless (and written off). This explains why the gross accounts receivable balance is lower for the FB case study than the SEB and PEB case studies as the allowance for doubtful accounts is an estimate of customer bad debts that may need to be written off down the road.
- Third, for our SEB case study, a significant increase in the allowance for doubtful accounts balance occurred between the FYE 12/31/22 and FYE 12/31/23 (from $102,000 to $320,000, an increase of $218,000). This was the result of SEB taking a more conservative approach and realizing additional risks may be present with their customers' ability to pay during a challenging economic environment. On the other hand, PEB felt it is basically business as usual and did not feel an additional reserve for bad debts was needed as of the FYE

12/31/23 (and kept their reserve relatively consistent with future years).

- Fourth, did you notice a new line item in our PEB case study? If not, please take another look as PEB has elected to take a fairly aggressive position and record $1,000,000 of additional revenue and accounts receivable for special software project sales that the company deemed to be basically complete and legitimately earned (at least in the eyes of management) as of the FYE 12/31/23 even though it wasn't technically invoiced to the customer as of the end of the year (but rather formally invoiced to the customer in January of 2024). You may ask, "How is this possible?" The answer lies in the interpretation of accounting rules, regulations, and guidelines. In the case of PEB, the company's management, along with their CPA firm, have taken the position that this sales revenue was constructively earned as of the FYE 12/31/23 as the earnings process, as measured by their internal standards and policies, was complete. *Voila*, PEB found another $1,000,000 of sales revenue for the FYE 12/31/23 that pushed its total sales just north of $60,000,000, an important sales revenue metric for PEB.

My goal in presenting Exhibit 6.2 and summarizing the accounting policies for each case study company is not to confuse you but rather to have you focus on a critical concept. As you dig into the financial reports and financial statements presented by companies, especially with financial disclosures and information presented in financial footnotes (refer to Chapter 17 in *How to Read a Financial Statement*, 10th Edition), you will be provided an opportunity to gain much more insight as to management's thinking on how to present financial reports and financial statements, and what type of accounting policies are being implemented, whether conservative or aggressive. Remember the phrase often used by top business and financial analysts: *The devil's in the details.* While something may appear reasonable on the surface, once you dig deeper, hidden information may become apparent that can greatly assist with your financial assessment.

Let's Crunch Some Numbers

In sum and for the case studies presented, it should be noted that each company has a mix of quick, regular, and slow-paying customers. Each of our case study customers extends 30-day or one-month payment terms to its customers. With this said, I have never worked with a company that achieves a 100 percent payment success rate within the terms provided. (If I did, it would represent a major flag that something is amiss.) Some customers may pay in two weeks, others may take four weeks to pay, still others may push the envelope a bit and pay in six weeks, and finally, we have those customers that know they can take advantage of their size and basically pay when they want to (e.g., at 60 days instead of the 30 days outlined in the terms). When customer account receivables start to age past 60 days, management should pay close attention because this may indicate the customer is in financial distress and cannot pay their outstanding obligation.

Now, let's crunch some numbers by first calculating a critical ratio referred to as the DSO (i.e., days sales outstanding in accounts receivable). Refer to Exhibit 6.3, which calculates the DSO for each of our case study companies using the following formula:

$$\left(\text{Total Accounts Receivable} / \left(\text{Total Sales} / 12\right)\right) * 30 = \text{DSO}$$

EXHIBIT 6.3—ACCOUNTS RECEIVABLE DAYS SALES OUTSTANDING & TURNOVER RATIO—THREE CASE STUDIES

Dollar Amounts in Thousands

Amounts—as of the FYE 12/31/22	SEB Base Case	FB Simple Case	PEB Aggressive Case
Net Sales Revenue	$54,210	$54,474	$54,342
Average Monthly Sales	$ 4,518	$ 4,539	$ 4,528
Net Accounts Receivable	$ 6,776	$ 6,803	$ 6,776
Average Days Sales Outstanding Accounts Receivable	45.00	44.96	44.89
Accounts Receivable Turnover Ratio	8.00	8.01	8.02

Amounts—as of the FYE 12/31/23	SEB Base Case	FB Simple Case	PEB Aggressive Case
Net Sales Revenue	$59,494	$59,806	$60,650
Average Monthly Sales	$ 4,958	$ 4,984	$ 5,054
Net Accounts Receivable	$ 8,009	$ 8,229	$ 9,209
Average Days Sales Outstanding Accounts Receivable	48.46	49.54	54.66
DSO Change from Prior Year, %	7.70%	10.19%	21.77%
Accounts Receivable Turnover Ratio	7.43	7.27	6.59
AR Turnover Ratio Change from Prior Year, %	–7.15%	–9.25%	–17.88%

What-if Analysis Alternative Amounts—as of the FYE 12/31/23	SEB Base Case	FB Simple Case	PEB Aggressive Case
Adjusted Days Sales Outstanding Figure	41.46	42.54	47.66
Revised Net Accounts Receivable Balance	$ 6,777	$ 6,989	$ 7,941
Net Increase in Cash from Lower DSO	$ 1,232	$ 1,241	$ 1,268
Average Interest Rate on Debt	8.00%	8.00%	8.00%
Potential Interest Expense Savings	$ 99	$ 99	$ 101

Next, I also present the accounts receivable turnover ratio in Exhibit 6.3 using the following formula:

$$\frac{\text{Net Sales Revenue}}{\text{Net Accounts Receivable}} = \text{Accounts Receivable Turnover Ratio}$$

So, great, what do these two calculations tell us about our case study companies to which I offer the following responses?

- As you see in Exhibit 6.3, the ending balance of accounts receivable in SEB is $8,009,000 as of the FYE 12/31/23; this amount equals 48.46 days' worth of annual sales revenue, which has increased from 45 days as of the FYE 12/31/22 (a 7.7 percent increase). The key point is that the average sales credit period determines the size of accounts receivable. The longer the average sales credit period, the larger the accounts receivable amount, which means that more cash is tied up in financing accounts receivables.
- For all three case studies, the average DSO for the FYE 12/31/22 is approximately 45 days or roughly 6.4 weeks. This tells us that the average customer pays their invoices within 6 to 7 weeks of the invoice date. But notice that for each of our case study companies, the average DSO for the FYE 12/31/23 has increased, and for our PEB case study company, it has increased by a whopping 10 days (from 45 DSO as of 12/31/22 to almost 55 DSO as of 12/31/23). Wow, that's a significant increase of almost 22 percent in one year and would warrant additional review to determine if the increase is associated with: (a) problem customers that are in financial distress and can't pay, (b) large customers that are taking longer to pay and skewing the calculation, (c) seasonal sales occurred late in the year and skewed the year-end accounts receivable balance, (d) a change in the composition of the accounts receivable balance (which occurred with our PEB case study as noted with the added $1,000,000 of receivables recorded), and/or (e) some other factor is present.
- Looking at the calculations from a different perspective, the accounts receivable turnover ratio for each of our case study companies amounted to roughly 8x as of the FYE 12/31/22. If the figure were 12x, it would mean that, on average, accounts receivables are turning over once a month during the year. If the figure were 6x, it would mean that, on average, accounts receivables are turning over every two months during the year. The key concept is that the lower the accounts receivable turnover ratio, the higher the accounts receivable balance (indicating more capital is being consumed in financing accounts receivable). Let's take a look at the FYE 12/31/23, as for each of our case study companies the turnover ratio decreased from the prior year with PEB being the poster child for potential problems (with its accounts receivable turnover ratio decreasing from 8x as of the FYE 12/31/22 to 6.59 as of the FYE 12/31/23, a 17.88% decrease). We have already discussed potential causes for the deterioration of this ratio in the previous bullet point. Still, general relationship to remember is as accounts receivable DSO increases, the accounts receivable turnover ratio decreases.
- Finally, I would point your attention to a "what-if" calculation at the bottom of Exhibit 6.3, which estimates just how much cash (and potential interest expense savings) could be generated if each of our case study companies was able to decrease their respective accounts receivable DSO by just one week or seven days. As you can see, each case study company could possibly free up over $1,200,000 of cash, which is not chump change.

In summary, one key concept holds true for all businesses and is based on one of the oldest sayings out there—Time is Money. What this means is that time is the essence of the matter. What interests' the business manager, and the company's creditors and investors as well, is how long it takes on average to turn accounts receivable into cash. I think the accounts receivable turnover ratio is most meaningful when it is used to determine the number of weeks (or days, if you like) it takes a company to convert its accounts receivable into cash.

You may argue that 48.46 days for SEB is too long an average sales credit period for the company. This is precisely the point: What should it be? The manager in charge has to decide whether the average credit period is getting out of hand. The manager can shorten credit terms, shut off credit to slow payers, or step up collection efforts. This isn't the place to discuss customer credit policies relative to marketing strategies and customer relations, which would take us far beyond the field of accounting. But there is an important point to make here.

Assume that, without losing any sales, each of our case study company's average sales credit period can be reduced by one week or seven days, which for SEB would reduce the accounts receivable DSO to 41.46 days for the FYE 12/31/23. In this alternative scenario (again refer to Exhibit 6.3), the company's ending accounts receivable balance would have been $1,232,000 lower. The company would have collected $1,232,000 more cash during the year. With this additional cash, the company could have borrowed $1,232,000 less. At an annual 8 percent interest rate, this would have saved the business approximately $99,000 in interest before income tax. Or the owners could have invested $1,232,000 less in the business and put their money elsewhere.

The main point is that capital has a cost. Excess accounts receivable means that excess debt or excess owners' equity capital is being used by the business. Our case study businesses are not as capital efficient as they should be. A slowdown in collecting customers' receivables or a deliberate shift in business policy allowing longer credit terms causes accounts receivable to increase. Additional capital would have to be secured, or the company would have to attempt to get by on a smaller cash balance.

If you were the business manager in this example, you should decide whether the size of accounts receivable is consistent with your company's sales credit terms and your collection policies. Perhaps 48.46 days for SEB is too long, and you must act. If you were a creditor or an investor, you should pay attention to whether the manager is allowing the average sales credit period to get out of control. A major change in the average credit period may signal a significant change in the company's policies.

Accounting Issues

The following short discussion of accounting issues related to sales revenue recognition and realizing expenses barely scratch the surface. Nevertheless, you should be aware that the numbers you see in financial statements depend on the exact accounting methods used to recognize and record those numbers. The chief accounting or CFO of every business must decide which accounting methods to use to record sales revenue and expenses. These accounting decisions often require tough and somewhat arbitrary choices between alternative methods.

You may be unaware that accounting decisions are not entirely obvious and clear-cut in most situations. In fact, they are quite arbitrary to one degree or another in most cases. The choice of particular accounting methods makes profit lower or higher and also makes the amounts of assets and liabilities lower or higher. Revenue is either an increase in an asset or a decrease in a liability. An expense is either a decrease in an asset or an increase in a liability.

Revenue accounting has become a hot issue in recent years—indeed, it may be the number-one issue in financial accounting and reporting. (If you are a glutton for punishment, I recommend you research ASC 606, which represents the new revenue recognition standard that impacts all businesses engaging with customers for the transfer of goods or services.) What are the main issues in accounting for sales and accounts receivable? The main accounting problem in recording sales is *timing*. It's not always clear exactly when a sale is completed and all terms are final and definite. For instance, customers may have the right to return products they have purchased or to take discounts from sales prices after the point of sale. Sales prices may still be negotiable even after the point of sale. Then, there are the costs of product warranties and guarantees to consider.

The asset generated by credit sales (i.e., accounts receivable) may be partially or fully uncollectible. When should the business record the expense for uncollectible receivables (called *bad debts*)?

As you can see, there are several serious problems surrounding accounting for sales. Therefore, a business should make clear in the footnotes to its financial statements the basic accounting method it uses for recording sales revenue.

7

INVENTORY: AN ASSET RIPE FOR ERRORS

Business inventories (i.e., tangible products awaiting sale to the final customer) come in all sizes, shapes, forms, and dollar amounts, ranging from a loaf of bread sold at a grocery store to lumber sold to a home builder to a laptop computer awaiting sale at a retail store to a new car on sale at a dealer's lot. In some cases, like business-to-business (B2B) sales, inventory is sold from a manufacturer to a wholesaler, while in other cases, inventory is sold from the manufacturer to a retailer that eventually sells the products to a consumer. (In this situation, a B2B transaction leads to a business-to-consumer [B2C] transaction).

To help visualize the flow of inventory, think of a large auto manufacturer, such as Ford or General Motors. You can imagine just how complex their manufacturing processes are, given the sheer volume of cars produced annually. Each automobile encompasses thousands of individual parts that must be assembled into a finished product. In another example, imagine how many different finished products Amazon purchases from its suppliers and, subsequently, makes available for sale to its customers. A retailer as large as Amazon has millions of products held for sale in inventory worth billions of dollars. Technology and automated inventory management systems make managing this type of business assets possible, but it requires significant resources, experience, infrastructure, personnel, and insight.

I've elected to focus on inventory as our second accounting topic and balance sheet account because it is an asset that is vital to countless businesses around the world. It also carries significant financial risks that must constantly be managed to ensure that the inventory value stated in the balance sheet is accurate. To further expand on just how challenging it can be to manage and value inventory, consider these business and economic risks:

- Obsolescence: Anybody operating in the tech industry can attest to just how fast inventory can become obsolete, in some cases, literally overnight. The longer you hold inventory without selling it, the greater the risk of obsolescence.
- Theft, shrinkage, and damage: Inventory is a tangible asset that, if not properly safeguarded and stored, can be easily stolen, damaged, or lost. Just imagine how much inventory was destroyed when Hurricane Katrina struck New Orleans in 2005.
- Spoilage: This is a very significant risk in industries like restaurants and grocery stores. Inventory spoilage occurs when products are no longer suitable for sale or public consumption.
- Valuation basis: Per generally accepted accounting principles (GAAP), businesses can value inventory using different methods, including FIFO (first-in, first-out), LIFO (last-in, first-out), average cost, or other accepted methods. I won't bore you with the intricacies of valuing inventory but let's just say that setting inventory values is equal parts fact (i.e., hard numbers) and art (via using estimates to value inventory).
- Technical ownership: In some business models, inventory is not technically owned but rather held on consignment for the legal owner, who will receive payment for the products (less some type of a commission or brokerage fee) after they are sold. You can imagine the accounting nightmare associated with a company that sells both owned and consigned inventory.

This list is not all-inclusive, but it offers a glimpse into why inventory is ripe for potential valuation errors and, in some cases, outright misrepresentation in the financial statements. This is why I've selected inventory as the second balance sheet account for a deeper dive into financial reports and financial statements.

For our case study presentations, I provide an expanded version of costs of sales revenue, which allocates the total expense between expenses incurred as a result of selling services (e.g., direct personnel time and costs incurred to deliver a service to the customer) and expenses incurred as a result of selling products. As you work through this chapter and the remainder of the book, it should become clear why this distinction is required.

Refresher Connection: Costs of Sales Revenue, Inventory, Accounts Payable, and Other Expenses

Our case study companies purchase the majority of the products they sell from third-party suppliers, but they manufacture some products. To begin the manufacturing process, each company purchases the raw materials needed in its production process. These purchases are made on credit; the company doesn't pay for them immediately. Also, other production inputs are bought on credit. For example, once a month, the public utility sends a bill for the gas and electricity used during the month, and the company takes several weeks to pay it. The company also purchases several manufacturing inputs on credit. Finally, the company sells products that it purchases from other manufacturers, and it buys these on credit. As you probably know, a business has to maintain its credit reputation and good standing to continue buying materials, manufacturing inputs, and products on credit.

Retailers and wholesalers don't make the products they sell; they buy products and resell them. The products they buy are usually in a condition ready for resale. Unless they have a lousy reputation or a poor credit history, retailers and wholesalers buy on credit, and they have accounts payable from inventory purchases. Technically speaking, our case study companies manufacture some products and purchase and resell others. Please refer to Exhibit 7.1, which presents connections between specific balance sheet and income statement accounts that are highly associated with one another: inventory (a current asset in the balance sheet), costs of sales revenue expense (an expense in the income statement), and accounts payable (a current liability in the balance sheet). As a reminder, Exhibit 7.1 is presented just for our base case company, SEB.

EXHIBIT 7.1—COSTS OF SALES REVENUE, INVENTORY, ACCOUNTS PAYABLE, AND OTHER EXPENSES—BASE CASE (SEB)

Dollar Amounts in Thousands

INCOME STATEMENT	
Sales Revenue, Net	$ 59,494
Costs of Sales Revenue, Service	$(14,374)
Costs of Sales Revenue, Products	$ (7,392)
Gross Profit (aka Gross Margin)	$ 37,728
Expenses:	
Selling, General, & Administrative	$(25,289)
Research & Development	$ (7,139)
Depreciation & Amortization	$ (1,643)
Operating Income (Loss)	$ 3,658
Other Expenses or (Income)	$ (2,000)
Interest Expense	$ (407)
Net Income (Loss) before Income Taxes	$ 1,251
Income Tax Expense (Benefit)	$ (438)
Net Income (Loss) after Income Taxes	$ 813

BALANCE SHEET	
ASSETS	
Cash & Equivalents	$ 2,164
Accounts Receivable	$ 8,009
Inventory	$ 1,706
Prepaid Expenses	$ 625
Property, Machinery, & Equipment	$ 4,500
Less: Accumulated Depreciation	$ (2,214)
Intangible Assets, Net	$ 6,000
Other Assets	$ 100
Total Assets	$20,889
LIABILITIES	
Accounts Payable	
for Product Inventory	$ 711
for Services & Operating Expenses	$ 748
Accrued Liabilities Payable	$ 1,112
Income Taxes Payable	$ 146
Other Current Liabilities & Deferred Revenue	$ 1,348
Short-Term Loans Payable	$ 2,400
Loans Payable & Other Long-Term Debt, Less ST Loans	$ 2,500
Total Liabilities	$ 8,965
STOCKHOLDERS' EQUITY	
Capital Stock	$10,000
Retained Earnings	$ 1,924
Total Liabilities and Stockholders' Equity	$20,889

Here I provide a summary of how these connections generally function in a business:

1. Inventory and accounts payable: In our case study companies, various technology products (i.e., inventory) are acquired for resale from different suppliers. When the inventory is acquired, our case study companies are provided credit from the suppliers (before payment is due) that range from 30 to 60 days from the date the products are received. In this situation, the inventory asset and the accounts payable liability, both balance sheet accounts, would increase.

   This should be logical because a business can't (or at least shouldn't) sell products held in inventory before they own them. Thus, the business must purchase the products (or make them) before reselling them to customers. Virtually every company reports accounts payable in its balance sheet. Accounts payable is a short-term, non-interest-bearing liability arising from buying services, supplies, materials, and products on credit.

   One primary source of accounts payable is making *inventory* purchases on credit. A second source of accounts payable is from *expenses* that are not paid immediately. At this point, I divide the total balance of the company's accounts payable liability into two parts, one for each source (refer to Exhibit 7.1 again).

2. Inventory and costs of sales revenue expense: When the products (i.e., inventory) are resold to our case study companies' customers, the direct connection is that the inventory asset balance would decrease (as products are shipped/delivered to customers), and the costs of sales revenue expense account in the income statement would increase.

Costs of sales revenue expense (for products) means just that: The cost of all products sold to customers during the year. Revenue from sales is recorded in the sales revenue account, which could be called the top line of the income statement (see Exhibit 7.1). The costs of sales revenue expense is reported in the income statement just below sales revenue, as you can see. Costs of sales revenue expense is one of the largest expenses in the company's income statement, being almost as large as selling, general, and administrative expenses for the year.

Putting costs of sales revenue expense first, at the head of the expenses, is logical because it's the most direct and immediate cost of selling products and services. Please recall that costs of sales revenue expense is deducted from sales revenue in income statements so that *gross margin* can be reported. I can't emphasize enough the importance of gross margin (also called *gross profit*), so I will explore the topic a bit more here.

The word *gross* emphasizes that only direct costs of sales revenue expense (for products and services sold), and *no other expenses*, have been deducted from sales revenue. Understanding gross margin is the starting point for earning an adequate net income for the period. (Remember that net income is the final, bottom-line profit.) In other words, the first step is to sell products and services for enough gross margin so that all other expenses can be covered and the business can also earn a profit. I discuss the company's other expenses throughout this book.

You can do the arithmetic and determine that costs of sales revenue expense in our business example equals 36.6 percent of sales revenue. Therefore, gross margin equals 63.4 percent of sales revenue. The business sells many assorted products and services, some for more than 63.4 percent gross margin and some for less. In total, for all products and services the business sold during the year, the average gross margin is 63.4 percent—which isn't unreasonable for a diversified technology-based business. I would offer a word of caution here: Different companies operating in different industries can have vastly different gross margins. They can range from over 70 percent to as little as 30 percent.

To sell products, most businesses must keep a stock of products on hand, which is called *inventory*. If a company sells products, it would be a real shock to see no inventory in its balance sheet. Notice in Exhibit 7.1 that the line of connection is not between *sales revenue* and *inventory*, but between *costs of sales revenue expense* and *inventory*. In the balance sheet, the inventory asset is reported at cost, not at its sales value.

The inventory asset account accumulates the cost of the products purchased or manufactured. Acquisition cost stays in an inventory asset account until the products are sold to customers. At the time of sale, the cost of the products is removed from inventory and charged out to costs of sales revenue expense. (Products may become nonsalable or may be stolen or damaged, in which case their cost is written down or removed from inventory, and the amount is charged to costs of sales revenue or some other expense, which I discuss at the end of the chapter.)

3. Inventory and other expenses: This connection is new and only applies to our case study business SEB (as you will see below) and provides a connection between writing off $2,000,000 of inventory that is deemed worthless and recording the write-off as an *other expense*. Rather than reflect the $2,000,000 write-off or loss as *costs of sales revenue—products*, management elected to reflect this loss as an other expense. It appears below the operating income based on the fact pattern present. First, the write-off represents a one-time, nonrecurring expense that was unique to older products and inventory that will not be restocked. Second, the write-off did not reflect a typical customer sale; rather it was sold for scrap value to a third party that specializes in liquidating worthless inventory. Third, SEB did not want to distort its net operating income and bury the loss in the income statement where it may not be visible to external parties.

This summary of connections is presented deliberately. First, inventory must be acquired (either purchased or manufactured), which usually involves buying the product from a supplier. Thus, the inventory balance and accounts payable increase. Second, most inventory is then sold to customers, which reduces the inventory balance and increases the costs of sales revenue for products. Third, I have yet to see a company that has been able to sell all of its inventory as, at some point, various products become obsolete, damaged, stolen, or just plain lost. This results in companies having to perform periodic inventory assessments and realizing expenses, in one form or another, for the reduction in inventory value associated with non-customer sale transactions.

Accounting Policies and Procedures Summary

To continue our fun from the previous chapter, I will summarize each of our three case study companies' accounting policies and procedures applied to inventory and then provide an exhibit that compares and contrasts each one.

- Base case: SEB utilizes proactive accounting policies and procedures to ensure inventory is properly valued at the end of each period. SEB conducts physical inventory procedures similar to FB and PEB to validate the physical existence of the inventory. In addition, SEB performs a detailed inventory market valuation analysis (performed by an independent third party) at the end of each year to assess the risk associated with holding inventory that has no viable market remaining and has lost its value. Based on SEB's business model pivot (focused on selling technology services and software, and moving away from selling products) and the results of the market valuation analysis, SEB elected to increase its reserve for obsolete and slow-moving inventory by $2,000,000 as of the FYE 12/31/23.
- Simple case: FB does a good job of tracking inventory and making sure it is physically accounted for at the end of each accounting period. Physical inventories are performed at each quarter end by qualified staff and management to ensure the items listed as owned in the automated accounting inventory tracking system are physically present in the company's warehouse. When inventory discrepancies are present, if the missing inventory cannot be located, FB writes off the missing inventory at its last value and records the write-off as direct costs of product sales. FB does not perform extensive reviews and evaluations related to obsolete, slow-moving, or similar inventory, as the company's management team feels that no matter for what inventory, the company can always sell the inventory for a price above the current value. Thus, FB does not maintain inventory valuation, obsolescence, or similar reserve.
- Aggressive case: Finally, we reach PEB, which uses similar accounting policies and procedures to SEB but with one significant difference. PEB elected not to engage an independent third-party inventory valuation specialty firm to assess if elevated risks were present with products held in inventory as of the FYE 12/31/23. Rather, the company conducted its own internal detailed analysis of inventory valuation risks and came to the conclusion that viable external markets were still present to sell aging finished goods inventory over the next 6 to 18 months. As a result, the reserve for obsolete and slow-moving inventory was increased as of the FYE 12/31/23 (to account for some limited risk). Still, a large inventory write-off was not deemed necessary (which PEB's accounting firm agreed with and accepted the results).

Now, let's visualize our three case studies in Exhibit 7.2 based on the accounting policies summarized previously and provide some additional commentary.

EXHIBIT 7.2—INVENTORY COMPARISON—THREE CASE STUDIES

Dollar Amounts in Thousands

Amounts—as of the FYE 12/31/22	SEB Base Case	FB Simple Case	PEB Aggressive Case
Inventory:			
Raw Material	$ 382	$ 382	$ 382
Work In Process	$ 191	$ 191	$ 191
Finished Goods	$ 3,440	$3,340	$3,440
Less: Reserve for Slow-Moving & Obsolete	$ (191)	$ 0	$ (191)
Total Inventory	$ 3,822	$3,913	$3,822

Amounts—as of the FYE 12/31/23	SEB Base Case	FB Simple Case	PEB Aggressive Case
Inventory:			
Raw Material	$ 171	$ 171	$ 171
Work In Process	$ 85	$ 85	$ 85
Finished Goods	$ 3,839	$3,689	$3,839
Less: Reserve for Slow-Moving & Obsolete	$(2,388)	$ 0	$ (388)
Total Inventory	$ 1,706	$3,944	$3,706

The key takeaways from Exhibit 7.2 are as follows:

- First, the total inventory valuation figures were relatively consistent as of the FYE 12/31/22 between each case study company. You will notice that FB does not have an inventory reserve (based on its accounting policy) but directly reduces the value of finished goods for any year-end physical inventory discrepancy.
- Second, notice the significant differences in the total inventory values for each case study company as of the FYE 12/31/23. FB is carrying the highest inventory valuation balance, followed closely by PEB. Then, SEB's total inventory value comes in well below FB and PEB, given the large write-off of $2,000,000 it took during the FYE 12/31/23 to account for obsolete inventory.

- Third, each of our case study companies carries a large amount of finished goods inventory, ranging from $3,689,000 for the FB to $3,839,000 for SEB and PEB. If you compare this figure (without accounting for the reserve established for obsolete inventory), it would amount to approximately 50% of the costs of sales revenue—products for the FYE 12/31/23 (refer to Exhibit 7.1 to compare these figures against costs of sales revenue—products from the income statement). We'll see when we do some number crunching below why this is such an important figure.

My goal in presenting Exhibit 7.2, along with summarizing the accounting policies for each case study company, is not to confuse you but rather to have you focus on a critical concept. That is, as you dig into the financial reports and financial statements presented by companies, especially with financial disclosures and information presented in financial footnotes (refer to Chapter 17 in *HTRFR*, 10th Edition), you will be provided an opportunity to gain much more insight as to management's thinking on how to present financial reports and financial statements, and what type of accounting policies are being implemented, whether conservative or aggressive.

Let's Crunch Some Numbers

Moving on to crunching the numbers, here is where we're going to see some significant variances and red flags pop up with our case study companies. First, let's calculate a critical ratio referred to as the DSI (i.e., days sales outstanding in inventory). Refer to Exhibit 7.3, which calculates the DSI for each of our case study companies using the following formula:

(Total Inventory / (Total Costs of Sales Revenue – Products / 12)) * 30 = DSI

Next, I also present the inventory turnover ratio in Exhibit 7.3 using the following formula:

(Total Costs of Sales Revenue – Products / Total Inventory) = Inventory Turnover Ratio

We have to ask the question: What do these two calculations tell us about our case study companies? I offer the following responses.

- As of the FYE 12/31/22, each case study company has approximately 125 days of inventory on hand to support product sales and is turning over its inventory a little less than three times per year. Not great or terrible numbers but these calculations do indicate excess inventory is building, as keeping the figures closer to 90 days and four times (respectively and our internal benchmarks) would be more comfortable.
- However, for the FYE 12/31/23, the real action begins as the calculations for our case study companies begin to separate significantly. SEB's inventory KPIs (key performance indicators) look solid and have improved from the prior year, as the DSI is now down to 83 days, and the inventory turnover ratio stands at 4.33. Both are better than the internal target benchmarks set above. However, FB and PEB seem to have some real troubles brewing with their inventory, as each company now has over 180 days of inventory in DSI, and their respective inventory turnover ratios have decreased to less than two times per year. These calculations are heading in the wrong direction and warrant close attention as the results indicate inventory valuation issues may be present.
- The key issue that needs to be asked of FB and PEB is simple—is the total inventory value as presented accurate? What is clear is that both of these companies have excessive inventory on hand, as instead of having 90 days of inventory available for sale, both have closer to 180 days of inventory available for sale (per the DSI) and are turning over their inventory not even twice per year. These calculations indicate both companies are sitting on excessive inventory levels that may not be saleable, at least not at a price that matches the

EXHIBIT 7.3—INVENTORY DAYS SALES OUTSTANDING & TURNOVER RATIO—THREE CASE STUDIES

Dollar Amounts in Thousands

Amounts—as of the FYE 12/31/22	SEB Base Case	FB Simple Case	PEB Aggressive Case
Costs of Sales Revenue—Products Only	$11,040	$11,048	$11,040
Average Costs of Sales Revenue—Products, Monthly	$ 920	$ 921	$ 920
Total Inventory	$ 3,822	$ 3,913	$ 3,822
Average Days Sales Outstanding Inventory	124.63	127.50	124.63
Inventory Turnover Ratio	2.89	2.82	2.89

Amounts—as of the FYE 12/31/23	SEB Base Case	FB Simple Case	PEB Aggressive Case
Costs of Sales Revenue—Products Only	$ 7,392	$ 7,245	$ 7,392
Average Costs of Sales Revenue—Products, Monthly	$ 616	$ 604	$ 616
Total Inventory	$ 1,706	$ 3,944	$ 3,706
Average Days Sales Outstanding Inventory	83.08	196.00	180.49
DSI Change from Prior Year, %	–33.34%	53.72%	44.82%
Inventory Turnover Ratio	4.33	1.84	1.99
Inventory Turnover Ratio Change, Prior Year, %	50.00%	–34.95%	–30.95%

What-if Analysis Alternative Amounts—as of the FYE 12/31/23	SEB Base Case
Costs of Sales Revenue—Products Only	$ 7,392
Average Costs of Sales Revenue—Products, Monthly	$ 616
Average Days Sales Outstanding Inventory	70.00
Total Adjusted Inventory Value	$ 1,422
Difference—Increase in Cash	$ 284

established value. This represents a perfect situation where digging further into the details is warranted, given the significance of inventory KPI trends and the potential negative impact on net income.

When discussing the balance sheet in Chapter 2, I referred to the fact that the balance sheet is where losses go to hide, cash goes to die, and the bullshit goes to lie. FB and PEB offer perfect examples. As losses sit in inventory, which neither company has fully recognized, cash dies as the inventory purchased a year or two ago is now worthless. Finally, the bullshit goes to lie in the case of PEB, which has convinced the external auditors that the inventory owned by the company can not only be sold but, just as importantly, can bring in an amount above the cost value of the inventory. Will PEB's management team be proven right? Only time will tell, but it's safe to say that more than a few companies have been caught in the inventory valuation trap, where they convince themselves that their inventory has a viable market and value (and can eventually be recouped). Such inventory is often sold at a deep discount.

Inventory Control and Management

In our base case business, SEB's *average* inventory holding period for all products for the FYE 12/31/23 is roughly 12 weeks or 84 days, a little less than three months on average. This time interval includes the production process time and the warehouse storage time. For example, a product may take three weeks to manufacture and then be held in storage for 10 weeks, or vice versa. Internally, manufacturers separate *raw material* and *work-in-process* inventory (products being manufactured) from *finished goods* (completed inventory ready for delivery to customers). The business does not need a work-in-process account for any products it buys from other companies in a condition ready for resale. Usually, only one combined inventory account is reported in externally reported balance sheets, as shown in Exhibit 7.1. Internally, many separate inventory accounts are reported to managers, as displayed in Exhibit 7.2.

The main point is that the average inventory holding period determines the size of inventory relative to annual costs of sales revenue sold expense (for products). The longer the manufacturing and warehouse holding period is, the larger the inventory amount. Business managers prefer to operate with the lowest level of inventory possible without causing lost sales due to out-of-stock products. A business invests substantial capital in inventory.

Time is the essence of the matter, as with the average sales credit period extended to customers. What interests the managers, as well as the company's creditors and investors, is how long the company holds inventory before products are sold. The inventory turnover ratio is most meaningful when used to determine the number of weeks (or days, if you prefer) to sell products. This has been calculated in Exhibit 7.3.

Is 12 weeks too long? Should the company's average inventory holding period be shorter? These are precisely the key questions business managers, creditors, and investors should get answers to. If the holding period is longer than necessary, too much capital is tied up in inventory (see our case study companies FB and PEB). Or, the company may be cash-poor because it keeps too much money in inventory and not enough in the bank.

To demonstrate this point, with better inventory management SEB could have reduced its average inventory holding period to 10 weeks or 70 days. This would have been a rather dramatic improvement. But modern inventory management techniques such as supply-chain management promise such improvement. If the company had reduced its average inventory holding period to just 10 weeks, its ending inventory would have been:

In this scenario, ending inventory would be $284,000 smaller ($1,706,000 versus $1,422,000). SEB would have needed $284,000 less capital or would have had this much more cash balance at its disposal (refer to Exhibit 7.3).

But a word of caution is warranted here. With only 10 weeks' inventory, SEB may be unable to make some sales because certain products might not be available for immediate customer delivery. In other words, if overall inventory is too low, stock-outs may occur. Nothing is more frustrating, especially to the sales staff, than having willing customers but no products to deliver to them. The cost of carrying inventory has to be balanced against the profit opportunities lost by not having products on hand ready for sale.

In summary, business managers, creditors, and investors should watch that the inventory holding period is neither too long nor too short. Call this the Goldilocks test. If too long, capital is being wasted; if too short, profit opportunities are missed. Comparisons of a company's inventory holding period with those of its competitors and with historical trends provide useful benchmarks.

Accounting Issues

Several serious accounting issues concerning inventory are discussed in this section, but I want to make note of accounting issues that are associated with accounts payable (our first connection discussed in Exhibit 7.1). In sharp contrast to inventory accounting issues related to sales, expenses, and valuation concerns, there are relatively few accounting problems concerning the accounts payable liability. The main financial reporting issue concerns the *disclosure* of relevant information about this liability.

Readers of financial statements are entitled to assume that the amount reported for accounts payable is the amount that will be paid in the near future. However, suppose the business is in the middle of negotiations with one or more of its accounts payable creditors regarding prices and other terms. Suppose that these disagreements involve material (significant) amounts. In this situation, the business should disclose these negotiations in the footnotes to its financial statements.

Readers of financial statements are also entitled to assume that the company's accounts payable creditors (the parties to whom it owes money) do *not* have senior or prior claims ahead of other creditors and debtholders of the business. In other words, the accounts payable creditors are assumed to be *general* creditors of the business, with no special claims on the business's assets. If the accounts payable creditors do have unusual rights for payment against the business, these abnormal claims should be disclosed in the footnotes to its financial statements.

Here is another key point: Financial statement readers are entitled to assume that the accounts payable are *current*, which means that the liabilities are not seriously overdue (i.e., way beyond their due dates for payment). Suppose, for instance, that half of the company's accounts payable are two or three months overdue. In this situation, the business should disclose the overdue amount in the footnotes to its financial statements.

I may not need to emphasize this, but accounts payable are noninterest-bearing and should not be intermingled with the interest-bearing debts of the business. As you see in Exhibit 7.1, interest-bearing liabilities (notes payable) are reported in separate liability accounts. By the way, long-overdue accounts payable may begin to accrue interest at the creditor's option.

The disclosure standards discussed here for accounts payable are not necessarily complied within actual financial reports. You don't see much disclosure about accounts payable in business financial statements. I think a business should make full disclosure in its financial reports. But companies are cut a lot of slack in the area of accounts payable. You won't find detailed information about a company's accounts payable liability in its financial statements, even though it may be more than 10 percent of its total assets and larger than its cash balance at the balance sheet date.

Accounting for costs of sales revenue expense and inventory cost is another matter altogether and is beset with many problems.

First, businesses that manufacture their products have serious problems determining the total cost per unit of their products. This is no walk in the park.

College and university accounting programs offer an entire course on this topic (usually called *cost accounting*). One main problem is allocating *indirect* production costs to the different products that benefit from the cost. For example, how should you allocate the cost of security guards who patrol many production departments or the depreciation on the production plant in which hundreds of different products are manufactured?

Retailers and wholesalers (distributors) buy products in a condition ready for resale. Compared with manufacturers, resellers have a much easier time determining the cost of their products—although there are a few thorny problems. In any case, once acquisition costs have been recorded (for manufacturers and resellers), another problem rears its ugly head: Product costs fluctuate over time. From period to period, product costs move up or down.

Suppose a business has acquired two units of a product, the first for \$100 and the second for \$104. The business sells one unit of the product. What is the correct cost to remove from the inventory asset account and to record in the cost of goods sold expense? Accountants have come up with three different ways to answer this question: \$100 (first-in, first-out), \$102 (average cost), and \$104 (last-in, first-out). All three methods are acceptable. Different businesses use different methods.

You might think that a business would select the method that best matches its sales revenue to get the best measure of gross margin. Generally speaking, the best method would be the one most consistent with how the business sets its sales prices. But this logic does not always prevail. A business selects a cost of goods sold method for other reasons, and the method may or may not jibe with its sales pricing policies.

The inventory asset account is written down to record losses from falling sales prices, lower replacement costs, damage and spoilage, and shrinkage (shoplifting and employee theft). The losses may be recorded in the costs of sales revenue expense account or be put in another expense account. Companies may or may not disclose where the losses from these write-downs are recorded, so I want to let you in on a little secret with our example business.

As you recall, our base case company, SEB, is a diversified technology company selling products, services, and software. This company operates in the tech industry, which is notorious for rapid change, given the industry's speed. Products considered advanced or cutting-edge one year may be obsolete the following year. This is where SEB has a secret, which it has elected to disclose, albeit not in a 100 percent clear fashion, in its current year financial statements as follows:

- First, if you refer to Exhibit 5.5, you will notice that the inventory balance at the end of the previous FYE 12/31/22 amounted to \$3,822,000. Fast forward to the FYE 12/31/23 inventory balance, which stood at \$1,706,000, a decrease of \$2,116,000. Wow! What a decrease during a year when the company grew its top-line revenue from \$54,210,000 to \$59,494,000 (Exhibit 5.4). Is something else going on here?
- Second, please note that during the FYE 12/31/23, SEB incurred a one-time expense or loss of \$2,000,000, which is reflected as an "other expense" in the income statement (refer to Exhibit 5.4). What this \$2,000,000 of other expenses represents should be disclosed in the financial statement footnotes. In this example, it is the company writing off worthless, obsolete, and damaged inventory that has no remaining value. Now, the decrease in inventory value begins to make sense

because the company didn't sell this inventory but decided to take a one-time charge (i.e., other, non-recurring expense) of $2,000,000 during the FYE 12/31/23 to account for this lost value. But why take the hit (a one-time expense) in 2023 and report it as other expenses, below operating income? The answer to this question will be presented in Chapter 14, when I discuss how companies use financial engineering to present financial operating results in a specific format that may be considered more reader or market friendly (for lack of a better term).

I want to close this chapter with an additional observation on valuing inventory. Because a business has a choice of accounting methods, it should reveal its costs of sales revenue expense method in the footnotes to its financial statements. If the business uses the last-in, first-out (LIFO) method, it should disclose in the footnote the approximate current cost value of its inventory as if it had been using the first-in, first-out (FIFO) method. Other unusual events, such as a major inventory write-down, should also be disclosed in the footnote. Unfortunately, many, if not most, inventory footnotes are fairly technical and difficult to understand.

8

LONG-TERM ASSETS, USEFUL LIVES, AND NON-CASH EXPENSES

Before plowing into the nature of long-term capital assets, their respectful useful lives, and depreciation and amortization expenses (which both represent non-cash expenses), I offer a general review of expenses. Financial statement accounting is especially concerned with the timing of recording expenses. The main goal is to record expenses in the correct period, neither too soon nor too late, so that profit for the period is as accurate as possible.

The two guiding principles for recording expenses are:

1. Match expenses with sales revenue: Costs of sales revenue expense, sales commissions expense, and any other expense directly connected with making particular sales are recorded in the same period as the sales revenue. This is relatively straightforward; all direct expenses of making sales should be matched against sales revenue. It would be foolish to put revenue in one period and the expenses of that revenue in another period.
2. Match other expenses with the period benefited: Many expenses are not directly identifiable with particular sales. Such *nondirect expenses* include office employees' salaries, rental of warehouse space, computer processing and accounting costs, legal and audit fees, interest on borrowed money, and others. Nondirect expenses are just as necessary as direct expenses, but they cannot be matched to particular sales. Therefore, nondirect expenses are recorded in the period in which the benefit to the business occurs.

This chapter explains that the costs of the long-lived operating assets (including both tangible and intangible assets) of a business, in theory, should be recorded to expense over the span of their useful lives. These assets (with the exception of land) gradually lose their usefulness and business value over time. The allocation of the cost of a long-term tangible operating asset (e.g., manufacturing equipment that may have a useful life of 10 years) to expense over the useful life of the asset is called *depreciation*. Allocation of the cost of a long-term intangible operating asset (e.g., a patent that may have a useful life of fifteen years) is called *amortization*. In accounting, depreciation and amortization facilitate the multiyear *allocation* of the costs of long-term assets.

As we work our way down the asset side of the balance sheet, we will turn our attention to long-term capital assets and, more specifically, intangible assets. As a quick refresher, the two most common types of long-term capital assets are tangible assets (items with a physical presence) such as business equipment, machinery, buildings, furniture, fixtures, computers, autos, and the like and intangible assets (items that do not have a physical presence) such as patents, trademarks, tradenames, trade secrets, computer software, goodwill, copyrights, and general intellectual property.

For example, a GM auto manufacturing plant comprises many tangible assets. This facility likely includes a building to house the operation, land on which the building is located, machinery and equipment required to manufacture autos, and so on. By contrast, a large pharmaceutical company such as Pfizer owns and controls countless patents related to drug discovery efforts. Those patents represent intangible assets on Pfizer's balance sheet. GM and Pfizer are very different companies with very different long-term capital assets that are essential to the financial and economic success of each respective enterprise.

In today's technology- and information-based economy, the value of intangible assets, such as patents, software development code, and proprietary algorithms, are just as valuable to an organization as tangible assets like equipment and buildings. In this chapter, I focus on the long-term balance sheet account for intangible assets and the associated accounting for the following reasons:

1. Over the past 50-plus years, the US economy has gravitated toward a technology- and service-based economy (one that is more reliant on intangible assets) compared to a manufacturing-based economy (one that tends to require heavy investments in tangible assets). Proprietary assets such as software code, algorithms, and artificial intelligence (AI) applications are now more important and valuable than ever before, especially for technology companies.
2. When a tangible fixed asset, such as machinery used to help manufacture a car, is depreciated (i.e., a portion of the asset is expensed each year to account for the loss of its value), the rules are straightforward. If the machinery has a useful life of 10 years, the company that owns the machinery depreciates it over a 10-year period (using an accepted GAAP depreciation method). The value of intangible assets is amortized over the period of their useful life. Amortization is the same concept as depreciation expense, but it is generally used to account for an intangible asset's loss of value. Determining an intangible asset's useful life is not always clear or consistent. In some cases, a company may amortize an intangible asset, such as a patent that was internally developed and issued over a 15-year period starting with the date of issuance. In other cases, goodwill or secret computer code may not be amortized at all because the company that owns these assets has determined that no impairment to the value of these assets has occurred, and they remain as valuable as ever. The point is that the amortization of intangible assets is more subjective and arbitrary than the depreciation of tangible assets.
3. The determination of the value assigned to an intangible asset, such as new computer software that has been developed internally (in a company), may differ between businesses. Some companies may take a more conservative approach and assign little or no value to the development of new computer software as its future sales potential and market acceptance is relatively unknown. As such, these companies may realize higher research and development expenses as the costs to develop the computer software are expensed in the income statement. By contrast, other companies may have more confidence in the value of the internally developed computer software and elect to capitalize (i.e., record the costs associated with developing the computer software as an asset) the costs incurred to develop the computer software as a long-term capital asset using the account title "Capitalized Software Development Costs." This asset would be amortized over a period that represents the useful life of the computer software as determined by the company's management team.

In this chapter, you will see how impactful capitalizing computer software development costs is when comparing our case study company PEB with SEB and FB.

Intangible Assets Basics

Many businesses invest in *intangible* assets, which have no physical existence. You can't see or touch these assets. For example, a business may purchase a valuable patent that it will use in its production process over many years or invest in software development code that represents a trade secret to the company. Or a business may buy an established trademark that is well-known among consumers. When a business buys patents or trademarks or invests in other intangible assets, the costs of these particular assets are recorded in long-term asset accounts called Intangible assets, net (and general holding account for all intangible assets).

Another example of intangible assets is based in the concept of goodwill. When one company buys another business and pays more than the sum of its identifiable assets (minus its liabilities), the resulting difference is referred to as goodwill. Often, the company to be acquired has been in business for many years, and it has built up a trusted name and reputation. It may have a large list of loyal customers who will continue to buy the company's products in the future. The experience and loyalty of the acquired company's employees may be the main reason to pay for more than the identifiable assets being acquired. Or the business being bought out may have secret processes and product formulas that give it a strong competitive advantage.

There are many reasons to pay more for an established, going-concern business than just the sum of its identifiable assets (minus the liabilities being assumed when buying the business). When the acquiring company pays more than the sum of the acquisition's specific assets (less liabilities), the excess is generally recorded in the asset account called *goodwill*. (Whether to systematically charge off the cost of goodwill and other intangible assets is a vexing issue beyond this book's scope.)

Exhibit 8.1 also reveals another reporting matter related to accumulated depreciation and amortization expense in the balance sheet. Notice that an accumulated depreciation balance is present in the balance sheet that represents the sum of all depreciation expense taken over the years for the various fixed assets. As you can see, this amounts to $2,214,000 as of 12/31/23.

When reporting intangible assets, there is no such similar account for accumulated amortization reported in the balance sheet, but rather a reference is made to "Intangible Assets, Net." The key word here is *net*, which indicates that the total original cost of the intangible assets represents the gross original cost less any amortization expense taken over the years. Exhibit 8.2 provides a detailed accounting and reconciliation of how the intangible net asset balance is calculated for each of our case study companies.

Refresher Connection: Long-Term Capital Assets and Depreciation and Amortization Expense

To properly illustrate the relevant connections, I've elected to present our PEB case study (instead of SEB) as it will better reflect the various connections present. Please refer to Exhibit 8.1, which presents three connections between the income statement and the balance sheet as follows:

1. The first connection is between the costs of long-term tangible assets, including property, machinery, and equipment (except land) allocated to depreciation expense over their estimated useful lives. The amount of depreciation expense is not recorded as a decrease in the asset account. Instead, it is accumulated in a *contra* or *offset* account, called "Accumulated Depreciation."
2. For intangible assets, the amortization expense connections are often reported as a net decrease to the gross cost, which is reflected as "Intangible Assets, Net." As a reminder, amortization expense is similar to depreciation expense but with more subjective estimates of useful lives.
3. Finally, I present a third connection between "Research and Development Expense" and "Intangible Assets, Net." Per our PEB case study company, the management team elected to capitalize $2,500,000 of computer software development costs as an asset rather than an expense as it was determined that the value of the newly developed computer software was sufficient to warrant recording the expenditures as an asset.

I do not want to downplay the importance of the relationship and connections between long-term tangible capital assets (commonly referred to as fixed assets), depreciation expense, and accumulated depreciation. There is no question that these connections are important (see Chapter 10 of *How to Read a Financial Report*, 10th Edition). Rather, the goal of this chapter is to highlight the role intangible assets and amortization expense play in the financial statements. The connections between the balance sheet and income statement, while similar to fixed assets and depreciation expense, can be even more impactful and volatile when preparing financial reports and financial statements.

EXHIBIT 8.1—DEPRECIATION & AMORTIZATION EXPENSE, LONG-TERM CAPITAL ASSETS, AND RESEARCH & DEVELOPMENT EXPENSE—AGGRESSIVE CASE (PEB)

Dollar Amounts in Thousands

INCOME STATEMENT

Sales Revenue, Net	$ 60,650
Costs of Sales Revenue, Service	$(14,624)
Costs of Sales Revenue, Products	$ (7,392)
Gross Profit (aka Gross Margin)	$ 38,634
Expenses:	
Selling, General, & Administrative	$(25,089)
Research & Development	$ (4,639)
Depreciation & Amortization	
for Depreciation Expense	$ (643)
for Amortization Expense	$ (1,133)
Operating Income (Loss)	$ 7,130
Other Expenses or (Income)	$ 0
Interest Expense	$ (407)
Net Income (Loss) before Income Taxes	$ 6,723
Income Tax Expense (Benefit)	$ (438)
Net Income (Loss) after Income Taxes	$ 6,285

BALANCE SHEET

ASSETS	
Cash & Equivalents	$ 2,164
Accounts Receivable	$ 9,209
Inventory	$ 3,706
Prepaid Expenses	$ 625
Property, Machinery, & Equipment	$ 4,500
Less: Accumulated Depreciation	$ (2,214)
Book Value of Fixed Assets	$ 2,286
Intangible Assets, Net	$11,567
Other Assets	$ 100
Total Assets	$29,656
LIABILITIES	
Accounts Payable	
for Product Inventory	$ 711
for Services & Operating Expenses	$ 748
Accrued Liabilities Payable	$ 1,362
Income Taxes Payable	$ 146
Other Current Liabilities & Deferred Revenue	$ 837
Short-Term Loans Payable	$ 2,400
Loans Payable & Other Long-Term Debt, Less ST Loans	$ 2,500
Total Liabilities	$ 8,704
STOCKHOLDERS' EQUITY	
Capital Stock	$10,000
Retained Earnings	$10,953
Total Liabilities and Stockholders' Equity	$29,656

Accounting Policies and Procedures Summary

The accounting policies and procedures used by each of our case study companies, to account for intangible assets, amortization expense, and research and development expenses are vastly different and represent a reflection of the management and ownership team of each case study company.

- Base case (SEB): The purchase of intangible assets are recorded at the cost of the acquisition, which during the FYE 12/31/23, amounted to $5,000,000. No amortization expense has been recorded on the current year's intangible asset purchase of $5,000,000, as the company's management has determined that this intangible asset value has not changed. The company has elected to amortize the previous purchase of intangible assets (that occurred four years ago) over a five-year period and records $1,000,000 of amortization expense per year. All research and development costs are expensed as incurred in the income statement, as FB has elected not to capitalize any of these expenses during the year due to the uncertainty of realizing any future value from the development of new computer software.
- Simple case (FB): The purchase of intangible assets is recorded at the cost of the acquisition, which during the FYE 12/31/23, amounted to $5,000,000. FB relies on its external accounting firm to provide guidance on amortizing intangible assets, which follow general rules as established by the IRS. That is, intangible assets such as goodwill are amortized on a straight-line basis over 15 years. All research and development costs are expensed as incurred in the income statement, as FB has elected not to capitalize any of these expenses during the year (which has been the company's accounting policy for years). Further, no amortization expense has been recorded on the current year's intangible asset purchase of $5,000,000 as the external accounting firm has advised that amortization of this intangible asset should not begin until the FYE 12/31/24.
- Aggressive case (PEB): The purchase of intangible assets is recorded at the cost of the acquisition, which, during the FYE 12/31/23, amounted to $5,000,000. No amortization expense has been recorded on the current year's intangible asset purchase of $5,000,000, as the company's management has determined that this intangible asset value has not changed. For previously purchased intangible assets, PEB has elected to amortize the original cost of these purchases over a straight-line period of 15 years (based on the IRS regulations). Finally, PEB has elected to capitalize $1,500,000 of research and development expenses incurred in the FYE 12/31/22 as software development costs and capitalize another $2,500,000 of research and development costs incurred in the FYE 12/31/23 under the same intangible asset account. PEB's management

felt that there was sufficient value and market viability for the new computer software to justify capitalizing these costs. The company estimates the useful life of the internally developed computer software is five years and is amortizing these capitalized costs over this five-year period.

That's a lot of information to digest related to the accounting for various intangible assets, so let's visualize our three case studies based on the accounting policies summarized to this point and provide some additional commentary (Exhibit 8.2).

The three key takeaways from Exhibit 8.2 are as follows:

1. Notice the different ending balance amounts in the "Intangible Assets, Net" account between each of our case studies for the FYE 12/31/23. For SEB, the balance is $6,000,000 compared to $8,667,000 for FB and $11,567,000 for PEB. Does this mean SEB's value is more accurate than PEB or FB? This is for the reader of the financial statements to interpret. However, it highlights just how significant an impact utilizing different accounting policies can have on the perceived value of an asset, as reported in the balance sheet.
2. Focus on the expense summary, which reflects how applying different accounting policies allows PEB to generate $2,367,000 of additional income (or in this case, an expense reduction) compared to SEB. The impact of this difference will be more fully explored in Chapter 10. The point is that PEB is managed by an aggressive ownership group that has an incentive to drive up sales and net income to achieve a more favorable purchase price when the company is sold. Is this fair and reasonable? Their CPA firm has attested that PEB's audited financial statements comply with GAAP, so who's to challenge the financial results?
3. The first two items in this list demonstrate that the accounting policies between our three case study companies have zero impact on cash balance. (Spoiler alert: I will prove this statement in Chapter 10.) It is important to understand two concepts as they relate to our three case study companies. First, as previously discussed, depreciation and amortization expenses represent non-cash expenses. The original purchase price of a long-term capital asset is when cash changed hands. The periodic expensing of long-term capital assets, whether via depreciation or amortization, represents an estimate of how much a realized asset's value decreases during that period. Second, whether a company expenses all research and development costs as they are incurred (such as FB and SEB) or capitalizes a portion of them as a long-term capital asset (such as PEB), the same amount of cash was used. The only difference relates to how the cash was recorded in the financial statements, as an expense in the income statement or partly as a long-term capital asset in the balance sheet.

Currently, accounting standards do not require the intangible asset's cost to be systematically allocated to expense, but companies can elect to establish set amortization periods (called *amortization* expense). Instead, when an intangible asset suffers an observable loss of value, a business makes an entry to *write down* the recorded value of the intangible asset. Companies assess periodically (and at least annually) whether their intangible assets have been impaired. If they have, the company records an expense for the effect of the impairment. In our case study examples, the companies elected to implement set amortization periods to recognize the reduction in the intangible assets' values. I provided this hypothetical example to highlight the impact of non-cash expenses (such as amortization and depreciation) on the balance sheet and income statement and explain why it is so critical to understand these concepts.

EXHIBIT 8.2—INTANGIBLE ASSETS & RELATED EXPENSE COMPARISON—THREE CASE STUDIES
Dollar Amounts in Thousands

Amounts—as of the FYE 12/31/22	SEB Base Case	FB Simple Case	PEB Aggressive Case
Intangible Assets Summary:			
Previous Cost of Intangible Assets, Goodwill	$ 5,000	$ 5,000	$ 5,000
Accumulated Amortization, Previously Acquired	$(3,000)	$(1,000)	$(1,000)
Newly Acquired Intangible Assets, Software	$ 0	$ 0	$ 0
Accumulated Amortization, Newly Acquired	$ 0	$ 0	$ 0
Internally Capitalized Software Development Costs	$ 0	$ 0	$ 1,500
Accumulated Amortization, Software Dev. Costs	$ 0	$ 0	$ (300)
Intangible Assets, Net	$ 2,000	$ 4,000	$ 5,200
Expense Summary (Impacted Expenses Only):			
Depreciation & Amortization Expense	$ 1,571	$ 905	$ 1,205
Research & Development Expense	$ 5,692	$ 5,692	$ 4,192
Subtotal of Impacted Expenses	$ 7,263	$ 6,597	$ 5,397
Difference from SEB Base Case	n/a	$ 667	$ 1,867

Amounts—as of the FYE 12/31/23	SEB Base Case	FB Simple Case	PEB Aggressive Case
Intangible Assets Summary:			
Previous Cost of Intangible Assets, Goodwill	$ 5,000	$ 5,000	$ 5,000
Accumulated Amortization, Previously Acquired	$(4,000)	$(1,333)	$ (1,333)
Newly Acquired Intangible Assets, Software	$ 5,000	$ 5,000	$ 5,000
Accumulated Amortization, Newly Acquired	$ 0	$ 0	$ 0
Internally Capitalized Software Development Costs	$ 0	$ 0	$ 4,000
Accumulated Amortization, Software Dev. Costs	$ 0	$ 0	$ (1,100)
Intangible Assets, Net	$ 6,000	$ 8,667	$11,567
Expense Summary (Impacted Expenses Only):			
Depreciation & Amortization Expense	$ 1,643	$ 976	$ 1,776
Research & Development Expense	$ 7,139	$ 7,139	$ 4,639
Subtotal of Impacted Expenses	$ 8,782	$ 8,115	$ 6,415
Difference from SEB Base Case	n/a	$ 667	$ 2,367

Let's Crunch Some Numbers

Unlike the number crunching in Chapter 6 (accounts receivable) and Chapter 7 (inventory), analysis of long-term capital assets does not use similar calculations for days sales. Rather, Exhibit 8.3 applies some financial statement ratio analysis concepts (a sneak peek of a Chapter 12 topic) and showcases how much impact the difference in expenses between our three case study companies has on basic financial statement ratio analysis related to key performance measurements including return on sales, return on assets, and return on stockholders' equity.

For a detailed explanation of these ratio analyses, refer to Chapter 12. For now, the point of this number crunching is to quantify the impact the difference expense figures have on critical financial ratio analysis. For example, PEB's total depreciation and amortization expense and research and development expense are lower than SEB's by approximately $2,367,000 for the FYE 12/31/23. When comparing this figure to PEB's total stockholders' equity as of the FYE 12/31/23, the impact provides the illusion that PEB generated an incremental improvement of 11.3 percent on the return on stockholders' equity. The same calculations and logic apply to the other ratio analyses for return on sales and return on assets, with the key issue remaining the same. By implementing different accounting policies related to amortization expense and capitalizing research and development costs as an asset, PEB's financial reports (as measured by certain key ratios) give the appearance that the company is performing much better than SEB and FB. Is this really the case? That is up to the reader of the financial reports and statements to determine, but one thing is certain: By arming yourself with more knowledge of where financial information comes from and how the financial statements are connected, you will be able to analyze a company's financial performance with more confidence and clarity.

EXHIBIT 8.3—FINANCIAL RETURN ANALYSIS—THREE CASE STUDIES

Dollar Amounts in Thousands

Amounts—as of the FYE 12/31/22	SEB Base Case	FB Simple Case	PEB Aggressive Case
Expense Summary (Impacted Expenses Only):			
Depreciation & Amortization Expense	$ 1,571	$ 905	$ 1,205
Research & Development Expense	$ 5,692	$ 5,692	$ 4,192
Subtotal of Impacted Expenses	$ 7,263	$ 6,597	$ 5,397
Difference from SEB Base Case	n/a	$ 667	$ 1,867
Financial Return Analysis:			
Return on Sales			
- Total Sales	$54,210	$54,474	$54,342
- Increase in Net Income from Reduced Expense	$ 0	$ 667	$ 1,867
- % Increase	0.00%	1.22%	3.44%
Return on Stockholders' Equity			
- Total Stockholders' Equity	$ 8,862	$12,040	$12,417
- Increase in Net Income from Reduced Expense	$ 0	$ 667	$ 1,867
- % Increase	0.00%	5.54%	15.03%
Return on Assets			
- Total Assets	$16,502	$18,619	$19,702
- Increase in Net Income from Reduced Expense	$ 0	$ 667	$ 1,867
- % Increase	0.00%	3.58%	9.47%

EXHIBIT 8.3—(CONTINUED)

Amounts—as of the FYE 12/31/23	SEB Base Case	FB Simple Case	PEB Aggressive Case
Expense Summary (Impacted Expenses Only):			
Depreciation & Amortization Expense	$ 1,643	$ 976	$ 1,776
Research & Development Expense	$ 7,139	$ 7,139	$ 4,639
Subtotal of Impacted Expenses	$ 8,782	$ 8,115	$ 6,415
Difference from SEB Base Case	n/a	$ 667	$ 2,367
Financial Return Analysis:			
Return on Sales			
- Total Sales	$59,494	$59,806	$60,650
- Increase in Net Income from Reduced Expense	$ 0	$ 667	$ 2,367
- % Increase	0.00%	1.11%	3.90%
Return on Stockholders' Equity			
- Total Stockholders' Equity	$11,924	$18,473	$20,953
- Increase in Net Income from Reduced Expense	$ 0	$ 667	$ 2,367
- % Increase	0.00%	3.61%	11.30%
Return on Assets			
- Total Assets	$20,889	$26,015	$29,656
- Increase in Net Income from Reduced Expense	$ 0	$ 667	$ 2,367
- % Increase	0.00%	2.56%	7.98%

Accounting Issues

There's a multitude of accounting problems regarding the depreciation and amortization of long-term operating assets (i.e., fixed and intangible assets). A company's fixed and intangible assets are typically a sizable part of its total assets, so these accounting problems are important.

Many books have been written on the theory of depreciation and amortization, arguing the merits of different methods. Most businesses resort to the income tax ground rules for depreciating their fixed assets because it is a practical and expedient way to depreciation accounting questions.

Another common issue with fixed and intangible assets is impairment. A business should write down a fixed or intangible asset if its economic value has become *impaired.* This can occur when an asset's value declines unexpectedly so that the cost of acquiring it will not be recovered. An airline, for example, could have surplus jets that it no longer needs, or a manufacturer may shut down an entire plant because of a fall-off in demand for the products made there. When a business has excess capacity, it should take a hard look at whether its fixed assets should be written down, even though the loss of economic value can put a big dent in profit.

There are also accounting problems that emerge when distinguishing the costs of routine maintenance of fixed assets and major outlays that extend their life or improve their appearance or efficiency. Routine maintenance costs should be expensed as they occur. The costs of major improvements should be recorded in the fixed asset account and depreciated over future years.

Insurance can pose another complication. A business may self-insure some of its fixed and intangible assets instead of buying casualty insurance coverage. But this makes the business vulnerable to huge write-offs if it suffers an actual loss. When a business self-insures its fixed assets, should it record an estimated expense each year for a future loss that hasn't yet happened and may never happen? Most businesses do not.

There are many serious accounting problems surrounding fixed and intangible assets, so a business should explain its depreciation and amortization and other fixed and intangible asset accounting policies in the footnotes to its financial statements. Also, a company should disclose how it accounts for its intangible assets, especially when it makes a major write-down in one or more of them during the year.

In Chapter 7, I argue that the company's cost of sales revenue expense accounting method should be consistent with how the business sets sales prices. Likewise, I would argue that the primary factor in choosing the depreciation and amortization expense methods should be the number of years over which the business plans to recoup the costs invested in its fixed and intangible assets through sales revenue. Suppose the business adopts a sales pricing policy for recapturing the cost of a fixed or intangible asset over 20 years. I would argue that a 20-year depreciation or amortization life should be used. However, it may be preferable to depreciate or amortize the cost over 10 years, as permitted by the income tax law. Talk about a mismatch between sales revenue and expenses!

9

OTHER CURRENT LIABILITIES: A BREEDING GROUND FOR ABUSE

We have reached the last of our four chapters dedicated to providing a deeper understanding of financial statement account balances, connections, and their respective impact on the income statement and balance sheet. Chapter 6 focuses on accounts receivable; Chapter 7 addresses the sticky issue involving inventory and the risks it presents; and Chapter 8 provides a thorough discussion of accounting for intangible assets. In this chapter, we examine other current liabilities, a group of accounts that may seem innocent, but can be a breeding ground for abuse.

To start, let's clarify what I mean by other current liabilities. What I'm not referring to is accounts payable, income taxes payable, and short-term loans payable. Generally, these balance sheet accounts are straightforward and supported by reliable quantitative calculations or third-party documentation. They are often less susceptible to accounting policy variations between different companies. I'm going to focus on two accounts: (1) accrued liabilities and (2) other current liabilities, (including accounting for deferred revenue), both of which can become an accounting "dumping ground."

The reason I've elected to dedicate Chapter 9 to these two buckets of other current liabilities is for the following primary reasons:

Accrued liabilities can be a very broad account that includes estimates of outstanding obligations related to employee compensation that is earned but not yet paid (as of the balance sheet date), any direct burden associated with employee compensation (e.g., employer payroll taxes, workers' compensation insurance, and the like), sales commissions due on sales revenue recorded in the income statement but not paid until a later date, services rendered from third parties during the period that has not been billed, potential legal or litigation settlements that are outstanding that are known or likely to occur (and need to be estimated and recorded), future warranty claims due for products previously sold (think of Tesla and the warrant reserve it needs to set aside for product recalls), property taxes billed in arrears, interest due on outstanding debt, and related obligations. The key takeaway is my reference to the word *estimate*. Accrued liabilities are often heavily based on estimates to accrue for an obligation that is technically outstanding at the end of a period and for which the ultimate payment amount, timing, and payee are unknown.

Deferred revenue (which is often referred to as unearned revenue) represents invoices forwarded to customers for goods and services that technically have not been fully delivered as of the date of the balance sheet. If a customer prepays for products that the company will ship in 30 days, the company should not technically record the sale until the products have been shipped, received, and accepted. This seems logical enough, but when a service is purchased, let's say that provides a business the right to use a software product over the course of one year, and the customer is invoiced for the entire year up front, the company that sold the software is required to recognize the sales revenue from the sale over the relevant 12-month period (and should not record 100 percent of the sale at the point of invoicing the customer). Again, this seems logical, but you would be amazed at how often this situation occurs and is subject to accounting abuse by a company selling the software or service.

The connection between operating expenses and accrued liabilities is based on the same general idea as accounts payable: Unpaid expenses at year-end are recorded so that the full, correct amount of expense is recognized in the proper period to ensure profit is measured correctly for the year. In Chapter 11 of *How to Read a Financial Report*, 10th Edition, I explain that a business records certain expenses as operating costs as soon as the invoices are received, even though it doesn't pay them until weeks later. When dealing with accrued liabilities, a business has to look for certain unpaid expenses (or understand that these expenses exist and need to be estimated) at the end of the period, even if the expenses may not be able to be substantiated until well down the road. No bills or invoices are received for these expenses; they build up, or *accrue*, over time.

Refresher Connection: Accrued Liabilities, Other Current Liabilities, Sales Revenue, and Expenses

Exhibit 9.1 presents two primary connections between the income statement and the balance sheet.

1. The first connection highlights the relationship between accruing for payroll costs, commissions, and associated payroll burden such as PTO or paid time off and different expenses in the income statement. The reason there are multiple expense connections to accrued liabilities for payroll is that the accrual for payroll and associated costs may relate to one of the following:

    a. employees that support the research and development function,

    b. employees that are part of the general and administration functions of PEB, or

    c. employees that are directly associated with the generating service or software revenue for PEB.

2. The second connection is something that was not directly addressed in *How to Read a Financial Report*. It highlights the relationship between billing customers in advance for services and software purchased (e.g., for a 12-month software license) that is first recorded as deferred revenue but then on a periodic basis (usually monthly), a portion of the advanced billing is realized as sales revenue. For example, if a customer purchased a software license for $12,000 covering the period of 10/1/23 through 9/30/24, a typical accounting policy would be to realize 1/12 of the $12,000 advance billing, or $1,000, on a monthly basis. Based on this accounting policy, the company would realize $3,000 of sales revenue for the period of 10/1/23 through 12/31/23 (three months at $1,000 per month) with the remaining $9,000 recorded as deferred or unearned revenue as of 12/31/23.

While these connections may seem simple, I would recommend you proceed with an abundance of caution. Why? Because different companies complete different financial analyses that can result in different calculations being generated with different estimates and results. Furthermore, when it comes to deferred or unearned revenue, one company may take a simple approach and realize revenue equally in prorated monthly amounts over the period of the contract (e.g., $1,000 per month, as in our example). However, another company may interpret the earnings process and costs incurred to generate the $12,000 software sale in a different light and conclude that 40 percent of the costs have been incurred to secure and finalize the sale in the month the customer is invoiced, with the remaining 60 percent being earned over the final 11 months. Same sale, same product, different accounting policy.

EXHIBIT 9.1—ACCRUED LIABILITIES & OPERATING EXPENSES AND DEFERRED REVENUE & SALES REVENUE—AGGRESSIVE CASE (PEB)

Dollar Amounts in Thousands

INCOME STATEMENT

Sales Revenue, Net	$ 60,650
Costs of Sales Revenue, Service	$(14,624)
Costs of Sales Revenue, Products	$ (7,392)
Gross Profit (aka Gross Margin)	$ 38,634
Expenses:	
Selling, General, & Administrative	$(25,089)
Research & Development	$ (4,639)
Depreciation & Amortization	
for Depreciation Expense	$ (643)
for Amortization Expense	$ (1,133)
Operating Income (Loss)	$ 7,130
Other Expenses or (Income)	$ 0
Interest Expense	$ (407)
Net Income (Loss) before Income Taxes	$ 6,723
Income Tax Expense (Benefit)	$ (438)
Net Income (Loss) after Income Taxes	$ 6,285

BALANCE SHEET

ASSETS	
Cash & Equivalents	$ 2,164
Accounts Receivable	$ 9,209
Inventory	$ 3,706
Prepaid Expenses	$ 625
Property, Machinery, & Equipment	$ 4,500
Less: Accumulated Depreciation	$ (2,214)
Book Value of Fixed Assets	$ 2,286
Intangible Assets, Net	$11,567
Other Assets	$ 100
Total Assets	$29,656
LIABILITIES	
Accounts Payable	$ 1,459
Accrued Liabilities Payable	
for Payroll, Wages, Commissions, & PTO	$ 1,240
for Interest Payable	$ 122
Income Taxes Payable	$ 146
Other Current Liabilities & Deferred Revenue	$ 837
Short-Term Loans Payable	$ 2,400
Loans Payable & Other Long-Term Debt, Less ST Loans	$ 2,500
Total Liabilities	$ 8,704
STOCKHOLDERS' EQUITY	
Capital Stock	$10,000
Retained Earnings	$10,953
Total Liabilities and Stockholders' Equity	$29,656

As for accrued liabilities, accountants as well as business managers should know which expenses accumulate over time and make the appropriate calculations for these unpaid amounts at year-end. A business does not receive an invoice (bill) for these expenses from an outside vendor or supplier. A business has to generate its own internal invoices for itself, as it were. Its accounting department must be especially alert to which specific expenses need to be accrued.

In some cases, the calculations used to support accruing liabilities and recording the expense is well known. For example, employee sales commissions that are due on sales recorded in the month of December 2023, but paid one month in arrears (i.e., in January 2024) should be relatively easy to calculate. However, calculating potential obligations and other types of accrued liabilities are much more difficult to estimate. For example, the final settlement of a lawsuit may be difficult to determine both in relation to the likelihood of losing the lawsuit and what the ultimate settlement may look like. Another example would be establishing a warranty reserve for a series of new products developed, manufactured, and sold by a company. Without having a history of prior customer warranty claims (along with having limited quality and reliability data), the company may have to base the warranty estimate on a rather broad range of factors.

Here is where sometimes you may come across a reference to the terms BOTE, WAG, and SWAG that are used in the finance and accounting world. BOTE stands for "back of the envelope," WAG stands for "wild-ass guess," and SWAG stands for "scientific wild-ass guess." You would be amazed at how often these concepts are applied by companies that are attempting to forecast, whether it relates to preparing an estimate for future product warranty claims or completing a five-year financial projection model. In some cases, the calculation of amounts recorded as accrued liabilities is based on solid and reliable data. In other cases, the accrued liability balance may be nothing more than a WAG. This is why understanding the nature of accrued liabilities compared to total liabilities is important. The larger and more uncertain the balances recorded in accrued liabilities, the greater likelihood errors are present in the financial statements.

Failure to record accrued liabilities for unpaid expenses could cause serious errors in a company's annual financial statements. For example, liabilities could be understated in its balance sheet, and expenses could be understated in its income statement for the year. A business should identify which expenses accumulate over time and record the appropriate amounts of these liabilities at the end of the year.

Accounting Policies and Procedures Summary

For ease of understanding, I've summarized the accounting policies for each case study company on an individual basis, explaining their policies for accruing employee compensation and for recording advanced customer billings.

- Base Case (SEB):
  - Accrued Payroll & Burden: All payroll, employee compensation, commissions, and direct burden (including vacation and paid time off) owed as of the end of a period is calculated and recorded as accrued payroll and burden.
  - Advance Billings: SEB records all software sales that are billed in advance for the next 12 months as deferred revenue. SEB then records 1/12 of the deferred revenue as earned on an equal monthly basis over a 12-month period.
- Simple Case (FB):
  - Accrued Payroll & Burden: FB accrues for payroll, employee compensation, and commissions owed as of the end of period but does not record any obligation due for vacation, paid time off, and similar wage-direct burden expenses. These are recorded in the financial statements when paid to the employee.
  - Advance Billings: Historically, FB has not generated a significant amount of advanced or pre-billings to their customers and has viewed accounting for these advanced billings as immaterial (i.e., deemed to not have a significant impact on FB's financial statements). As such, FB realizes the sales revenue generated from advanced billings as 100 percent earned in the period billed, which is also consistent with how FB reports these sales for tax purposes.
- Aggressive Case (PEB):
  - Accrued Payroll & Burden: All payroll, employee compensation, commissions, and direct burden (including vacation and paid time off) owed as of the end of a period is calculated and recorded as accrued payroll and burden. Further, PEB has recorded an additional $250,000 accrued wage and burden obligation as accrued liabilities to account for additional expenses that are anticipated related to the $1,000,000 of earned but not billed revenue recognized during the FYE 12/31/23.
  - Advance Billings: PEB records all software sales that are billed in advance for the next twelve months as deferred revenue. PEB then records 1/3 of the advanced billings as earned during the month the software sale occurred and recognizes the remaining 2/3 of revenue in equal amounts over the remaining 11 months of the contract period. PEB has determined that in order to properly match earned revenue with the expenses incurred, this accelerated earnings policy is appropriate.

Now, let's visualize our three case studies in Exhibit 9.2 based on the accounting policies summarized above and provide some additional commentary.

EXHIBIT 9.2—ACCRUED LIABILITIES & OPERATING EXPENSES AND DEFERRED REVENUE & SALES REVENUE—THREE CASE STUDIES

Dollar Amounts in Thousands

Amounts—as of the FYE 12/31/22	SEB Base Case	FB Simple Case	PEB Aggressive Case
Accrued Liabilities:			
for Payroll, Wages, Commissions, & PTO	$ 955	$ 605	$ 955
for Interest Payable	$ 115	$ 115	$ 115
Total Accrued Liabilities	$1,070	$ 720	$1,070
Deferred Revenue & Other Current Liabilities:			
Customer Advanced Billings & Deposits	$ 711	$ 0	$ 356
Other Current Liabilities	$ 300	$ 300	$ 300
Total Deferred Revenue & Other Current Liabilities	$1,011	$ 300	$ 656
Total for Both Accrued Liabilities & Deferred Revenue	$2,081	$1,020	$1,726
Difference with Base Case Company, SEB	n/a	$1,061	$ 356

Amounts—as of the FYE 12/31/23	SEB Base Case	FB Simple Case	PEB Aggressive Case
Accrued Liabilities:			
for Payroll, Wages, Commissions, & PTO	$ 990	$ 590	$1,240
for Interest Payable	$ 122	$ 122	$ 122
Total Accrued Liabilities	$1,112	$ 712	$1,362
Deferred Revenue & Other Current Liabilities:			
Customer Advanced Billings & Deposits	$1,023	$ 0	$ 512
Other Current Liabilities	$ 325	$ 325	$ 325
Total Deferred Revenue & Other Current Liabilities	$1,348	$ 325	$ 837
Total for Both Accrued Liabilities & Deferred Revenue	$2,460	$1,037	$2,199
Difference with Base Case Company, SEB	n/a	$1,423	$ 262

The key takeaways from Exhibit 9.2 are as follows:

- The accrued liability balance for FB as of the FYE 12/31/23 is much lower than the similar balance for SEB and PEB. This makes sense given FB's accounting policy established of not accruing for potential PTO and vacation owed to employees. Also, please note the bump in PEB's accrued liability balance of $250,000, which, as previously disclosed, relates to estimated future costs associated with realizing an additional $1,000,000 in sales revenue during the FYE 12/31/23.
- FB has no liability set aside for customer advanced billings and deposits (for either FYE 12/31/22 or 12/31/23), as based on its policy, any amount billed to customers is recognized as sales revenue on the date of billing. PEB's balance is much lower than SEB's balance (for the FYE 12/31/22 and 12/31/23) because PEB uses a more aggressive revenue recognition and amortization policy. Again, these differences make sense based on the respective accounting policies established.
- FB's financial statements appear to contain errors and are not in compliance with GAAP. First, balances owed for PTO and vacation, as well as other direct employee benefits (e.g., sick time, potential 401(k) profit-sharing or matching, etc.), are required to be calculated, recorded, and disclosed. Second, advanced customer billings should be deferred and recognized as earned sales revenue over an appropriate period (generally over the period of services or software contracted by the customer). In both cases, FB has failed to implement proper accounting policies and as such, FB's errors have resulted in understatements of current liabilities by as much as $1,423,000 as of the FYE 12/31/23, a material misstatement.

In summary, the difference in the figures presented above between SEB and PEB is open for debate. The primary driver is the difference in accounting policies utilized by each company when recognizing advanced customer billings into earned revenue. For FB, there really is no debate that errors are present, but this does not imply fraud has been committed. (The company has established accounting policies that are being applied on a consistent basis.) Rather, errors have been made based on outdated accounting policies that need to be addressed and corrected by management moving forward.

Let's Crunch Some Numbers

Several financial analyses could be performed on accrued liabilities and deferred revenue, but to keep our number crunching focused, I'm going to target two key relationships for our case study companies. These are summarized in Exhibit 9.3.

First, I would like to focus on the relationship between accrued liabilities for payroll, wages, and burden, with the corresponding expense buckets in the income statement. What I'm interested in is just how much financial "float" (i.e., use of their cash) I can produce in the balance sheet by leaning on suppliers, vendors, and the company's employees (and associated wages and direct burden). Here's the basic formula that I'm applying to calculate the financial float related to accrued liabilities:

$$\frac{(\text{Total Accrued Liabilities, Payroll Related})}{\left(\frac{\text{Total Associated Expenses}}{12}\right)} \times \left(\frac{52}{12}\right) = \text{Financial Float}$$

The resulting figure represents the number of weeks on average I can expect each of our case study companies to maintain accrued liabilities for payroll and related direct burden. Using our case study company PEB's data, you can see that for the FYE 12/31/23, an average accrued liability financial float of 1.45 weeks is present (or basically 10 days). In relation to calculating this figure, the following two items should be kept in mind:

1. You will notice that I included the direct costs of sales revenue, minus product costs, in the analysis. This is because most of this expense amount of $14,624,000 relates to wages, bonuses, and direct payroll burden (e.g., payroll taxes) paid to staff for services that were billed to the customer for software and support services (e.g., training, installation, maintenance, etc.). As previously discussed, any cost or expense directly associated with sales revenue should be captured as costs of sales revenue (which PEB has done correctly).

2. You might wonder why only 1.45 weeks of float are available before the company has to remit payment for these accrued liabilities. The answer lies in the nature of payroll- and wage-related expenses, which are very often due within a short amount of time after each period end. Unlike a vendor that sells products to our case study companies and is willing to extend 30- to 60-day payment terms, employees are much less accommodating and need to be paid per set schedules, usually within a week of earning their wages. Needless to say, making sure your employees are paid on time is essential to any business and attempting to generate added float from the employees by deferring earned wages for two to three weeks is not a prudent strategy. (It may also draw the ire of governmental regulators.)

In Exhibit 9.1, the ending balance of accrued expenses payable (for our case study company PEB) includes $1,240,000 for

EXHIBIT 9.3—OTHER CURRENT LIABILITY FINANCIAL ANALYSES—THREE CASE STUDIES
Dollar Amounts in Thousands

Amounts—as of the FYE 12/31/22	SEB Base Case	FB Simple Case	PEB Aggressive Case
Total Accrued Liabilities—Payroll & Burden	$ 955	$ 605	$ 955
Expenses Associated with Payroll & Burden:			
Costs of Sales Revenue—Services	$12,882	$12,882	$12,882
Selling, General, & Administrative Expenses	$22,567	$22,525	$22,567
Research & Development Expenses	$ 5,692	$ 5,692	$ 4,192
Total Expenses Associated with Payroll & Burden	$41,141	$41,099	$39,641
Avg. Monthly Expenses Associated with P&B	$ 3,428	$ 3,425	$ 3,303
Avg. Weeks of "Float" in Accrued Liabilities—P&B	1.21	0.77	1.25
Other Current Liabilities—Deferred Revenue	$ 711	$ 0	$ 356
Total Sales Revenue	$54,210	$54,474	$54,342
Deferred Revenue % of Total Sales Revenue	1.31%	0.00%	0.65%

Amounts—as of the FYE 12/31/23	SEB Base Case	FB Simple Case	PEB Aggressive Case
Total Accrued Liabilities—Payroll & Burden	$ 990	$ 590	$ 1,240
Expenses Associated with Payroll & Burden:			
Costs of Sales Revenue—Services	$14,374	$14,374	$14,624
Selling, General, & Administrative Expenses	$25,289	$25,045	$25,089
Research & Development Expenses	$ 7,139	$ 7,139	$ 4,639
Total Expenses Associated with Payroll & Burden	$46,802	$46,558	$44,352
Avg. Monthly Expenses Associated with P&B	$ 3,900	$ 3,880	$ 3,696
Avg. Weeks of "Float" in Accrued Liabilities—P&B	1.10	0.66	1.45
Other Current Liabilities—Deferred Revenue:	$ 1,023	$ 0	$ 512
Total Sales Revenue	$59,494	$59,806	$60,650
Deferred Revenue % of Total Sales Revenue	1.72%	0.00%	0.84%

operating expenses and direct costs of sales revenue, minus product costs. Is approximately 10 days the right amount of accrued liability for this type of business? It's difficult to generalize from business to business, but the majority of these types of expenses are centered in payroll, wages, and direct burden, so the average payment cycle after the period end tends to be very short (i.e., one to two weeks).

It is not unusual that the ending balance of a company's accrued liabilities is larger than its accounts payable for unpaid operating expenses. For PEB, the ending balance of its accounts payable for operating expenses as of the FYE 12/31/23 is $748,000 (from Exhibit 7.1), which is roughly 60 percent of the $1,240,000 accrued liability balance for payroll and related expenses at the end of the year.

Speaking of accounts payable, some businesses elect to merge accrued expenses payable with accounts payable and report only one liability in their external balance sheets. Both types of liabilities are non-interest bearing. Both emerge out of the operations of the business, from manufacturing or purchasing products, or from performing services that are sold to a customer. For this reason, they are sometimes called spontaneous liabilities, which means they arise on the spot—not from borrowing money, but from operating the business. Grouping both types of liabilities in one account is acceptable under financial reporting standards, although many companies report them separately.

Next, I would like to highlight the relationship between the other current liability account, deferred revenue, and the income statement account total sales revenue, net. Referring again to Exhibit 9.3, you will notice that for our case study company SEB, deferred revenue amounted to 1.3 percent of total sales revenue, net for the FYE 12/31/22. This ratio increased to 1.72 percent for the FYE 12/31/23 and indicates that SEB is generating more advanced customer billings, which is most likely associated with increasing sales of software and services. The same relationship holds for PEB where you can see deferred revenue amounted to 0.65 percent of total sales revenue, net for the FYE 12/31/22. This ratio increased to 0.84 percent for the FYE 12/31/23. While these figures aren't huge, they do indicate that billing customers in advance for future software and services sales is becoming more prevalent. This trend warrants monitoring for two reasons. First, billing customers in advance and collecting the account receivables represents a prudent strategy to increase cash balances. Second, accounting risks may increase as our case study companies aim to properly recognize earned revenue from advanced billings in the correct period. Translation: When you come across companies that generate a significant amount of sales revenue from advanced customer billings, you should pay very close attention to the accounting policy for how they actually realize the deferred customer revenue into periodic earned sales revenue. (This represents an accounting area that is subject to management discretion and abuse.)

Accounting Issues

A primary accounting issue that is almost always present concerns the accrual of operating costs—and there are many such costs. I have to tell you that the accrual of the liability for unpaid expenses depends on the good faith of the business in doing the calculations of these amounts—many of which involve arbitrary estimates and forecasts. This step in the accounting process can be easily used for ***massaging the numbers***. This pejorative phrase refers to the deliberate manipulation of amounts recorded for sales revenue and expenses in order to record a higher (or lower) amount of profit for the period. (This unsavory topic is covered in Chapters 20 and 21 of *How to Read a Financial Report*, 10th Edition.)

Another example related to properly accruing expenses might be found in settling a legal dispute. If a company is involved in a legal proceeding that will likely result in a substantial loss, the company should accrue for an estimated settlement amount and record the expense. However, if the legal matter is still open and being actively disputed, a company may only elect to accrue an expense for the expected settlement. The amount of the expected settlement is open to debate, so you can imagine how this type of event and associated expense can be massaged by management. This underscores the importance of understanding that accounting is often based on estimates.

I caution you that some businesses lay a heavy hand on the amounts recorded in their sales revenue and expense accounts, in order to smooth profit year to year or to give the profit for the year an artificial boost. Of course, these companies do not disclose in their financial statements that they have manipulated their accounting numbers to nudge profit up (or down).

10

BRINGING IT ALL TOGETHER WITH CASH

If you haven't figured it out yet, let me give you a hint as to the management mentality and style of each of our case study companies, which you were first introduced to in Chapter 5.

Our simple Family Business (FB) is an honest and hardworking company that prides itself on loyalty (especially from family and friends that work in the business). FB's accounting and financial team and external resources have extensive hands-on accounting, finance, and taxation experience, but have not kept up with the latest rules, regulations, and standards that set base accounting guidelines to abide by. This includes their accounting firm, Dick & Jane Smith ABT Services, LLC, which provides support on an as-requested basis. This team does not include a qualified CFO and is a bit behind the times. They are also somewhat naïve but are very attentive and committed to their jobs. There's nothing inherently wrong with FB's accounting and financial reporting systems, but they are not technically in compliance with GAAP. For example, recall in Chapter 9 that FB does not properly defer and subsequently amortize advanced billings to customers for services that will be rendered over a future period. Finally, FB does not have audited financial statements prepared; only compiled financial statements are produced on an annual basis. Loyalty and commitment are the foundation of FB's culture.

Next up is our Steady Eddy Business (SEB), which is run by a disciplined, knowledgeable, experienced, and high-quality management team that includes a formal CFO with years of direct experience in complying with GAAP and managing debt and equity-based capital sources. The accounting, finance, and taxation team is talented and deep with a focus maintained on current topics, regulations, standards, and guidelines established by authoritative bodies. Further, SEB is actively supported by the CPA firm of Kleen, Kneet, and Tidey, LLC, which is engaged to complete the company's annual audited financial statements, annual income tax returns, periodic tax planning efforts, and a top-end review of SEB's internally prepared quarterly financial statements (to track any potential issues, variances, and/or negative trends). SEB's board of directors is actively involved in company affairs and they, along with the company's management team, tend to maintain a conservative approach to operating the business. Conservative and patience represent the culture of SEB.

Finally, our private equity business (PEB) has retained an executive management team that has extensive operating experience associated with managing rapidly growing businesses. The team includes a formal CFO and a accounting, finance, and taxation team that has a deep history of selling businesses. The team is aggressive, passionate, and experienced, but also has a habit and history of pushing the envelope when building a business. Top-line sales revenue growth and bottom-line net income targets are constantly emphasized, sometimes to the point of crossing a gray line with accounting policies and procedures. PEB is supported by a big name, high-profile board of directors that has a library full of successful exits under their belts and understands the importance of driving sales and net income growth to increase the company's enterprise value. PEB has retained the CPA firm of Dewey, Fixum, & Howe CPA, LLC to complete their annual audited financial statements and income tax returns. This CPA firm is known for their expertise in working with entrepreneurial businesses that are backed by private equity (PE) or venture capital (VC) and understand the pressurized and politicized environment to drive growth and value. From top to bottom, aggressive describes the culture of PEB.

You may wonder why I have made the effort to summarize our case study companies again. The point is to drive home critical concepts to help you truly understand financial reports and financial statements and the accounting systems on which they are based. First, a company's culture, management style, operating horizon, and exit objectives often play a significant role in the production of financial reports and financial statements, which are derived from the accounting system. Second, it should always be kept in mind that accounting, and the production of financial reports and financial statements, is as much of an art form as it is a science. What one party may view as a masterpiece another party may view as garbage. I cannot emphasize just how critical these two concepts are when it comes to not just reading, but, more importantly, truly understanding financial reports and financial statements.

Let's analyze our three case study companies side by side and determine each company's management mentality and style.

Accounting Adjustment Cheat Sheet

Before we complete our comparison of the financial statements for each of our case study companies, refer to Exhibit 10.1, which presents a summary of the accounting adjustments and differences between SEB, FB, and PEB. I use our base case company, SEB, as the baseline to calculate the differences in revenue and expenses between each company that then flow through to the respective financial statements.

I've provided a notes column that clarifies whether an accounting difference or adjustment increases sales, decreases expenses, or increases expenses. Each item on the following list corresponds to an adjustment in Exhibit 10.1 (see the "Ref" column). They summarize accounting differences outlined previously and identify the chapter where you can learn more.

1. The first adjustment relates to PEB recognizing $1,000,000 of additional revenue during the FYE 12/31/23 for what was deemed earned but not billed sales. This adjustment also triggered the need to accrue an additional $250,000 of payroll and burden costs, which I've captured in adjustment seven. (See Chapter 6, "Accounts Receivable.")
2. The second adjustment is associated with different accounting policies and estimates used to record customer bad debt expense during the FYE 12/31/23. (See Chapter 6, "Accounts Receivable.")
3. The third adjustment reflects the differences in accounting policies related to establishing reserves for slow-moving and obsolete inventory. As a reminder, FB writes off damaged/worthless inventory as identified whereas SEB and PEB establish estimated reserves for impaired inventory. (See Chapter 7, "Inventory.")
4. Adjustment number four is a doozy. SEB elected to set up an additional $2,000,000 reserve for worthless and obsolete inventory during the FYE 12/31/23 whereas FB and PEB did not deem it necessary to establish this reserve. (See Chapter 7, "Inventory.")
5. Adjustment number five accounts for the differences between the amortization periods used by each of our case study companies. (See Chapter 8, "Long-Term Capital Assets, Intangible Assets.")
6. In this adjustment, FB and SEB have elected to not capitalize any research and development costs as software development (as they didn't believe an asset of value was present) whereas PEB determined $2,500,000 of research and development costs should be capitalized as software development and amortized over an appropriate period. (See Chapter 8, "Long-Term Capital Assets, Intangible Assets.")

EXHIBIT 10.1—MASTER LIST OF ACCOUNTING ADJUSTMENTS—THREE CASE STUDIES

Dollar Amounts in Thousands

Amounts—as of the FYE 12/31/23	Ref.	SEB Base Case	FB Simple Case	PEB Aggressive Case	Notes --->
Accounts Receivable Related:					
Period Additional Sales Revenue Recognized	(1)	$ 0	$ 0	$ 1,000	n/a.
Difference from Base Case, SEB (FYE 12/31/23 only)		n/a	$ 0	$ 1,000	Inc. in Sales, period.
Period Bad Debt Expense Recognized	(2)	$ 219	$ 25	$ 19	n/a.
Difference from Base Case, SEB (FYE 12/31/23 only)		n/a	$ (194)	$ (200)	(Dec.)/Inc. in expenses, period.
Balance Sheet Cumulative Impact on Accounts Receivable		n/a	$ 220	$ 1,200	Inc. in A/R, end of period.
Inventory Related:					
Period Inventory Valuation Reserves & Write-offs		$ 197	$ 50	$ 197	n/a.
Difference from Base Case, SEB (FYE 12/31/23 only)	(3)	n/a	$ (147)	$ 0	(Dec.)/Inc. in expenses, period.
Period Additional Inventory Valuation Impairment		$2,000	$ 0	$ 0	n/a.
Difference from Base Case, SEB (FYE 12/31/23 only)	(4)	n/a	$(2,000)	$(2,000)	(Dec.)/Inc. in expenses, period.
Balance Sheet Cumulative Impact on Inventory		n/a	$ 2,238	$ 2,000	Inc. in Inventory, end of period.
Long-Term Capital Assets, Intangible Related:					
Period Amortization Expense		$1,643	$ 976	$ 1,776	n/a.
Difference from Base Case, SEB (FYE 12/31/23 only)	(5)	n/a	$ (667)	$ 133	(Dec.)/Inc. in expenses, period.
Period Capitalization of R&D Expense as Intangible Asset		$ 0	$ 0	$(2,500)	n/a.
Difference from Base Case, SEB (FYE 12/31/23 only)	(6)	n/a	$ 0	$(2,500)	(Dec.)/Inc. in expenses, period.
Balance Sheet Cumulative Impact on Intangible Assets		n/a	$ 2,667	$ 5,567	Inc. in Intang. Assets, end of period.
Other Current Liabilities Related:					
Accrued Liabilities Related:					
Period Payroll, Wages, & Burden, Net Annual Impact		$ 35	$ (15)	$ 285	n/a.
Difference from Base Case, SEB (FYE 12/31/23 only)	(7)	n/a	$ (50)	$ 250	(Dec.)/Inc. in expenses, period.
Balance Sheet Cumulative Impact on Accrued Liabilities		n/a	$ (400)	$ 250	(Dec.)/Inc. in accrued liabilities, end of period.
Deferred Revenue Related:					
Period Advanced Customer Billings, Net Annual Impact		$ (312)	$ 0	$ (156)	n/a.
Difference from Base Case, SEB (FYE 12/31/23 only)	(8)	n/a	$ 312	$ 156	Increase in sales, period.
Balance Sheet Cumulative Impact on Deferred Revenue		n/a	$(1,023)	$ (512)	(Dec.) in deferred revenue, end of period.

7. Adjustment seven accounts for differences in accounting policies between our case study companies in calculating and recording accrued payroll, wages, and related burden. (See Chapter 9, "Other Current Liabilities, Accrued Payroll and Deferred Revenue.")
8. Last but not least, adjustment eight calculates the differences realized by each of our case study companies by implementing different accounting policies related to recognizing sales revenue from advanced billings made to its customers. (See Chapter 9, "Other Current Liabilities, Accrued Payroll and Deferred Revenue.")

I would encourage you to revisit Chapters 6 through 9 as needed to review the respective accounting adjustments in more depth. It never hurts to improve your comfort level as we push forward through the remainder of this chapter.

Comparing the Income Statements

Exhibit 10.2 has been prepared to compare the respective income statements between each of our case study companies. I've placed SEB in the middle because it represents our baseline company. FB is presented in the left two columns with the adjustments summarized in the second column to equate to the third column (SEB). The right two columns present the adjustments between SEB and PEB and the income statement for PEB.

Before I move forward, I would like to address a calculation in Exhibit 10.1 that may seem confusing. It has to do with the calculation labeled "Balance Sheet Cumulative Impact." The differences in sales revenue and expenses for the FYE 12/31/23 calculated in Exhibit 10.1 relate only to the net impact on the specific accounts that occurred during the twelve months of operations for the FYE 12/31/23. The balance sheet cumulative impact is the result of multiple years of accounting policy and procedure differences that have accumulated since each case study companies' inception. In some situations, the impact of the accounting difference is felt 100% during the FYE 12/31/23 (e.g., the $2,000,000 write-off of inventory PEB recorded). In other situations, the impact of the accounting difference is felt over multiple years (e.g., recognizing deferred revenue from advanced billings to customers that have occurred for multiple years). For those of you who would like more detail and support for the calculations completed in Exhibit 10.1, please feel free to contact me directly at tagetracy@cox.net and I will forward an additional analysis. If not, please trust the numbers provided above, as they're accurate.

Visualizing the income statements in a side-by-side manner really helps capture the significance of the accounting differences and impact on the calculated net income after income taxes. You can trace each amount in the accounting differences columns back to Exhibit 10.1, but when taking a step back and evaluating the income statements between our case study companies, the following "big ticket" adjustments really move the needle:

- For FB, two accounting differences are responsible for the majority of the difference of $3,370,000 (between FB and SEB). First, amortization expense is $667,000 lower as a result of using a 15-year amortization period. Second, no write-off of worthless and obsolete inventory was realized, creating a positive impact of $2,000,000.
- On the PEB front, three accounting differences are doing the heavy lifting with the difference of $5,473,000 (between SEB and PEB). First, PEB elected to capitalize $2,500,000 of research and development costs (an expense) as software development costs (an asset). Second, no write-off of worthless and obsolete inventory was realized, creating a positive impact of

EXHIBIT 10.2—COMPARIABLE INCOME STATEMENTS—THREE CASE STUDIES

Dollar Amounts in Thousands

Income Statement For the Fiscal Years Ending	Ref.	FB 12/31/023	Accounting Difference	SEB 12/31/2023	Accounting Difference	PEB 12/31/2023
Sales Revenue, Net	(1), (8)	$ 59,806	$ 312	$ 59,494	$ 1,156	$ 60,650
Costs of Sales Revenue, Service	(7)	$(14,374)	$ 0	$(14,374)	$ 250	$(14,624)
Costs of Sales Revenue, Products	(3)	$ (7,245)	$ (147)	$ (7,392)	$ 0	$ (7,392)
Gross Profit (aka Gross Margin)		$ 38,188	$ 459	$ 37,728	$ 906	$ 38,634
Operating Expenses:						
Selling, General, & Administrative	(2), (7)	$ 25,045	$ (244)	$ 25,289	$ (200)	$ 25,089
Research & Development	(6)	$ 7,139	$ 0	$ 7,139	$(2,500)	$ 4,639
Depreciation & Amortization	(5)	$ 976	$ (667)	$ 1,643	$ 133	$ 1,776
Total Operating Expenses		$ 33,160	$ (910)	$ 34,071	$(2,567)	$ 31,504
Operating Income (Loss)		$ 5,027	$ 1,370	$ 3,658	$ 3,473	$ 7,130
Other Expenses (Income):						
Other Expenses or (Income)	(4)	$ 0	$ (2,000)	$ 2,000	$(2,000)	$ 0
Interest Expense		$ 407	$ 0	$ 407	$ 0	$ 407
Total Other Expenses (Income)		$ 407	$ (2,000)	$ 2,407	$(2,000)	$ 407
Net Income (Loss) before Income Taxes		$ 4,620	$ 3,370	$ 1,251	$ 5,473	$ 6,723
Income Tax Expense (benefit)		$ 438	$ 0	$ 438	$ 0	$ 438
Net Income (Loss) after Income Taxes		$ 4,182	$ 3,370	$ 813	$ 5,473	$ 6,285
Check/Balance Calculation				$ 0		$ 0

$2,000,000. And third, PEB realized an additional $1,000,000 of sales revenue during the year for a customer project that was deemed earned, but not officially billed.

There you have it. The three companies are basically the same but with significantly different income statements, especially when compared at the net income after income tax line item. Remember that income tax expense should be much higher for FB and PEB based on their net income before taxes, but as previously noted in the book, I've left the income tax expense consistent between our three case study companies to drive home a critical point related to cash (which will be highlighted in the next section).

Is any income statement better or more reliable than the other? It might be easy to conclude that our SEB case study has offered the most reliable income statement. An easy conclusion to make but one that may not necessarily be correct as there could be a very sound basis that PEB's accounting for capitalized software development costs and not reserving $2,000,000 for worthless inventory are correct (and that SEB is simply being overly conservative).

Comparing the Balance Sheets and Statements of Cash Flow

Now, let's turn our attention to Exhibits 10.3 and 10.4, which present comparable balance sheets and statements of cash flows (respectively) for our three case study companies.

For the balance sheet, I would direct your attention to three key items:

1. Look at how much larger the total assets are for FB and PEB compared to SEB ($5,125,000 and $8,767,000) respectively. Wow, where did these assets come from, and by now it should be clear, both FB and PEB have much higher asset balances in inventory and intangible assets as a result of their respective accounting policies and procedures.
2. Look at the significant increase in the retained earnings balance for FB and PEB compared to SEB. These significant balance increases resulted from the accumulation of years (i.e., from the FYE 12/31/20 through the FYE 12/31/23) of accounting policy differences and their related impact on increasing net after tax income, which flows through the balance sheet in the form of retained earnings.
3. Look at the ending cash balances for each case study company. They are all exactly the same. How is this possible? Refer to the statement of cash flows in Exhibit 10.4 for the answer.

Finally, for the statement of cash flows, I would direct your attention to the fact that for each of our case study companies, the net increase or decrease in cash for the FYE 12/31/23 is exactly the same, at $1,389,000. Even though differences are present in the income statements and balance sheets, what our three case study companies teach us is that net income or earnings from each case study company were consumed (in the form of cash) in different capacities.

For example, PEB generated net income after tax of $6,285,000 for the FYE 12/31/23 compared to SEB's net income after tax of $813,000 (for the same FYE), representing a difference of $5,473,000. How did this cash get used? PEB's accounts receivable and inventory balances consumed approximately $3,200,000 of cash compared to SEB as the ending balances in these accounts were significantly higher than SEB's ending balances (thus tying up cash in certain current assets). In addition, PEB invested an additional $2,500,000 in intangible assets (for a total of $7,500,000) compared to SEB's investment of $5,000,000. And just like that, PEB's cash flow statement for the FYE 12/31/23 tells us that roughly $5,700,000 of cash flow is consumed in higher inventory and accounts receivable balances, and added investments in intangible assets.

I'm going to close this section of the chapter with a statement I previously made in the book. Here is where it is extremely

EXHIBIT 10.3—COMPARIABLE BALANCE SHEETS—THREE CASE STUDIES

Dollar Amounts in Thousands

Balance Sheet as of the Fiscal Year Ending	Ref.	FB 12/31/2023	Accounting Difference	SEB 12/31/2023	Accounting Difference	PEB 12/31/2023
Assets						
Current Assets:						
Cash & Equivalents		$ 2,164	$ 0	$ 2,164	$ 0	$ 2,164
Accounts Receivable	(1), (2)	$ 8,229	$ 220	$ 8,009	$1,200	$ 9,209
Inventory	(3), (4)	$ 3,944	$ 2,238	$ 1,706	$2,000	$ 3,706
Prepaid Expenses		$ 625	$ 0	$ 625	$ 0	$ 625
Total Current Assets		$14,963	$ 2,459	$12,504	$3,200	$15,704
Long-Term Operating & Other Assets:						
Property, Machinery, & Equipment		$ 4,500	$ 0	$ 4,500	$ 0	$ 4,500
Less: Accumulated Depreciation		$ (2,214)	$ 0	$ (2,214)	$ 0	$ (2,214)
Net Property, Machinery, & Equipment		$ 2,286	$ 0	$ 2,286	$ 0	$ 2,286
Other Assets:						
Intangible Assets, Net	(5), (6)	$ 8,667	$ 2,667	$ 6,000	$5,567	$11,567
Other Assets		$ 100	$ 0	$ 100	$ 0	$ 100
Total Long-Term Operating & Other Assets		$11,052	$ 2,667	$ 8,386	$5,567	$13,952
Total Assets		$26,015	$ 5,125	$20,889	$8,767	$29,656
Liabilities						
Current Liabilities:						
Accounts Payable		$ 1,459	$ 0	$ 1,459	$ 0	$ 1,459
Accrued Liabilities Payable	(7)	$ 858	$ (400)	$ 1,258	$ 250	$ 1,508
Short-Term Loans Payable		$ 2,400	$ 0	$ 2,400	$ 0	$ 2,400
Other Current Liabilities & Deferred Revenue	(8)	$ 325	$(1,023)	$ 1,348	$ (512)	$ 837
Total Current Liabilities		$ 5,042	$(1,423)	$ 6,465	$ (262)	$ 6,204
Long-Term Liabilities:						
Loans Payable & Other Long-Term Debt, Less ST Loans		$ 2,500	$ 0	$ 2,500	$ 0	$ 2,500
Total Liabilities		$ 7,542	$(1,423)	$ 8,965	$ (262)	$ 8,704
Stockholders' Equity						
Capital Stock		$10,000	$ 0	$10,000	$ 0	$10,000
Retained Earnings		$ 8,473	$ 6,549	$ 1,924	$9,028	$10,953
Total Stockholders' Equity		$18,473	$ 6,549	$11,924	$9,028	$20,953
Total Liabilities & Stockholders' Equity		$26,015	$ 5,126	$20,889	$8,766	$29,656
Check/Balance Calculation				$ (0)		$ 0

EXHIBIT 10.4—COMPARIABLE STATEMENTS OF CASH FLOW—THREE CASE STUDIES

Dollar Amounts in Thousands

Statement of Cash Flows For the Fiscal Years Ending	Ref.	FB 12/31/2023	Accounting Difference	SEB 12/31/2023	Accounting Difference	PEB 12/31/2023
Net Income (Loss) after Income Taxes		$ 4,182	$ 3,370	$ 813	$ 5,473	$ 6,285
Operating Activities, Cash provided (used):						
Depreciation & Amortization		$ 976	$ (667)	$ 1,643	$ 133	$ 1,776
Decrease (increase) in accounts receivables		$(1,427)	$ (194)	$(1,233)	$(1,200)	$(2,433)
Decrease (increase) in inventory		$ (31)	$(2,147)	$ 2,116	$(2,000)	$ 116
Decrease (increase) in other current assets		$ (25)	$ 0	$ (25)	$ 0	$ (25)
Increase (decrease) in accounts payables		$ 54	$ 0	$ 54	$ 0	$ 54
Increase (decrease) in accrued liabilities		$ (8)	$ (50)	$ 42	$ 250	$ 292
Increase (decrease) in other liabilities		$ 157	$ (312)	$ 469	$ (156)	$ 313
Net Cash Flow from Operating Activities		$ 3,879	$ (0)	$ 3,879	$ 2,500	$ 6,379
Investing Activities, Cash provided (used):						
Capital Expenditures		$ (500)	$ 0	$ (500)	$ 0	$ (500)
Investments in Intangible & Other Assets		$(5,000)	$ 0	$(5,000)	$(2,500)	$(7,500)
Net Cash Flow from Investing Activities		$(5,500)	$ 0	$(5,500)	$(2,500)	$(8,000)
Financing Activities, Cash provided (used):						
Dividends or Distributions Paid		$ (250)	$ 0	$ (250)	$ 0	$ (250)
Sale (repurchase) of Equity		$ 2,500	$ 0	$ 2,500	$ 0	$ 2,500
Proceeds from Issuance of Loans (i.e., debt)		$ 3,000	$ 0	$ 3,000	$ 0	$ 3,000
Repayments of Long-Term Loans		$(1,250)	$ 0	$(1,250)	$ 0	$(1,250)
Net Borrowings (Repayments) of Short-Term Loans		$ (990)	$ 0	$ (990)	$ 0	$ (990)
Other Financing Activities		$ 0	$ 0	$ 0	$ 0	$ 0
Net Cash Flow from Financing Activities		$ 3,010	$ 0	$ 3,010	$ 0	$ 3,010
Other Cash Flow Adjustments—Asset Impairment		$ 0	$ 0	$ 0	$ 0	$ 0
Net Increase (decrease) in Cash & Equivalents		$ 1,389	$ (0)	$ 1,389	$ (0)	$ 1,389
Beginning Cash & Equivalents Balance		$ 775	$ (0)	$ 775	$ (0)	$ 775
Ending Cash & Equivalents Balance		$ 2,164	$ (0)	$ 2,164	$ (0)	$ 2,164
Check/Balance Calculation				$ 0		$ (0)

important to: (a) understand the income statement, (b) trust the balance sheet, and (c) most critically, rely on the statement of cash flows. As you can tell, the statement of cash flows can help root out potential accounting issues and valuation risks within the balance sheet. What is interesting in our case study companies is that here we have SEB, generating just $813,000 of net income after tax for the FYE 12/31/23 but still able to produce positive cash flow of $1,389,000. With some small changes and variations in asset and liability accounts, this relationship seems reasonable. But when we turn our attention to PEB, we see it generated net income after tax of $6,285,000 for the FYE 12/31/23 compared to producing just $1,389,000 of positive cash flow. This relationship appears suspect because net income after tax is far greater than the internal positive cash flow. This is how the statement of cash flows can be used as a sounding board to evaluate if a company may be massaging its financial results in the income statement and balance sheet. To quote Tony Montana (played by Al Pacino) from the movie *Scarface*, "I always tell the truth, even when I lie." Translation, the statement of cash flows can help tell the truth, even if the balance sheet and income statement are lying.

History, Cash, and Artistry

Three similar companies have very different financial statements and operating reuslts. Are FB's financial statements more reliable than SEB's, or are SEB's financial statements better than PEB? Only time will tell. Each company's operating results for 2024 and beyond should prove or disprove the financial statements presented in Exhibits 10.2 through 10.4. We must interpret the financial statements and financial reports based on what is known today, which includes using estimates often based on the present information and data available. However, these could be significantly impacted by future events that nobody could possibly predict.

To this point, I refer to the Great Recession, which basically ran from 2007 through 2010 and took down major financial institutions such as Lehman Brothers and Bear Stearns. If you asked basically anyone in 2005 or 2006 about the likelihood of these two companies going bankrupt, you probably would have heard crickets. This drives home a critical point about financial reports and financial statements. That is, financial reports and financial statements are a reflection of the past (i.e., *history*) but are not a precursor to the future.

Now to consider the role of cash. Remember how important it is to understand the purpose of each financial statement, how the financial statements are connected, and how critical it is to truly appreciate how a business generates and consumes *cash* as reported in the statement of cash flows. When you master comprehending this financial statement, you will finally learn to appreciate its real beauty.

Finally, I'm sure you now understand that the three case study companies I've presented have been done so by applying a certain amount of *artistry* to the accounting policies and resulting financial reports and financial statements. Some of the greatest financial masterpieces, which some may also refer to as the greatest financial cons ever undertaken, have been done so by those parties that applied the concept of accounting artistry a little too aggressively.

I would like to affirm that the financial statements presented for our three case study companies do not imply fraud has been committed. Rather, the financial statements for the three case studies were presented from the context of potential errors being present (in the case of FB) or accounting policies being used overly aggressively (in the case of PEB). If you would like to dive into the concepts of financial fraud or financial engineering, I would direct you back to Chapters 21 and 20 in *How to Read a Financial Report*, 10th Edition, where these subjects are covered in more depth.

Part Three

FINANCIAL ANALYSIS AND BONUS MATERIAL

11

FINANCIAL STATEMENT RATIOS AND ANALYSIS: STRENGTH

Financial Reporting Ground Rules

The main purpose of external financial reporting is to provide up-to-date, complete, accurate, reliable, and timely financial information from a business to shareholders, investors, lenders, analysts, and the like. Investors and lenders are critical external parties who need accurate information. They represent potential sources of capital (debt and equity) and have a right to financial data that is complete and correct. Other parties are also interested in the financial affairs of a business—for example, its employees, other creditors, analysts (who provide independent assessments of its financial performance), regulatory groups, and so on. When they read financial reports, they should keep in mind that these communications are primarily directed to the owner-investors of the business and its lenders. External financial reporting standards have been developed with this primary audience in mind.

A company's financial report may not be the first source of information about its profit performance. In the United States, most public corporations issue press releases about their most recent earnings results, but it is important to remember that these may not have been audited by an independent CPA firm. These press releases precede the mailing of hard copies of the company's financial report to its stockholders, lenders, and other parties. Most public companies put their financial reports on their websites at the time of or soon after the press releases. Private businesses do not usually send letters to their owners and lenders in advance of their financial reports, although they could. As a rule, private companies do not put their financial reports on publicly accessible websites.

This chapter as well as Chapter 12 examines what stockholders, lenders, and analysts do with financial reports once they have access to them. The chapter centers on the *annual* financial report. (Quarterly financial reports are abbreviated versions of the annual reports.) In particular, this chapter focuses on financial *statement ratios* that are widely used by investors, lenders, and analysts to evaluate the company's performance and help formulate an opinion on its overall operations.

Financial Statement Preliminaries

Exhibit 11.1 presents the annual financial statements for our base case company, Steady Eddy Business (SEB). This is the same company example used throughout earlier chapters and represents our baseline company example.

SEB is privately owned and its common stock ownership shares are not traded in a public market. The business has about 50 shareholders; some are managers of the business, including the CEO, the president, and several vice presidents. A business this size could go into the public marketplace for equity capital through an initial public offering (IPO) of capital stock shares and become publicly owned. However, the company has decided to remain private.

This chapter does not pretend to cover the field of *securities analysis* (i.e., the analysis of stocks and debt instruments issued by corporations), which is broad and includes the analysis of competitive advantages and disadvantages, domestic and international economic developments, business combination possibilities, general economic conditions, and much more. The key ratios explained in this chapter are basic building blocks in securities analysis.

Also, this chapter does not discuss trend analysis, which involves comparing a company's latest financial statements with its previous years' statements to identify important year-to-year changes. For example, investors and lenders are very interested in the sales growth or decline of a business, and the resulting impact on profit performance, cash flow, and financial condition.

This chapter has a more modest objective: to explain basic ratios used in financial statement analysis and what the ratios indicate about a business. Only a handful of ratios are discussed in the chapter, but they are fundamentally important and represent those most widely used by industry professionals.

Upon opening a company's financial report, probably one of the first things most investors do is a fairly quick scan of them. What do most financial report readers first look for? In our experience, they look first at the bottom line of the income statement to see if the business made a profit or suffered a loss for the year.

As one sports celebrity explained how he keeps tabs on his various business investments, he looks first to see if the bottom line has "parentheses around it." Thankfully SEB does not because it made a profit during the FYE 12/31/23. Its income statement reports that the business earned $813,000 net income (i.e., bottom-line profit) for the year. Is this profit performance good, mediocre, or poor? Ratios help answer this question.

After reading the income statement, most financial statement readers probably take a quick look at the company's assets and compare them with the liabilities of the business. Are the assets adequate to the demands of the company's liabilities? Ratios help answer this question.

EXHIBIT 11.1—SUMMARIZED EXTERNAL FINANCIAL STATEMENTS OF BUSINESS (WITHOUT FOOTNOTES)—BASE CASE (SEB)

Dollar Amounts in Thousands Except Earnings Per Share

INCOME STATEMENT FOR THE FYE 12/31/23

Sales Revenue, Net	$ 59,494
Costs of Sales Revenue, Products	$(21,766)
Gross Profit (aka Gross Margin)	$ 37,728
Selling, General, & Administrative	$ 25,289
Research & Development	$ 7,139
Depreciation & Amortization	$ 1,643
Total Operating Expenses	$ 34,071
Operating Income (Loss)	$ 3,658
Other Expenses or (Income)	$ 2,000
Interest Expense	$ 407
Net Income (Loss) before Income Taxes	$ 1,251
Income Tax Expense (Benefit)	$ 438
Net Income (Loss) after Income Taxes	$ 813
Basic Earnings Per Share	$ 1.25

STATEMENT OF CHANGES IN STOCKHOLDERS' EQUITY FOR YEAR

	Capital Stock	Retained Earnings
Beginning Balances	550,000	$1,362
Net Income (Loss) after Income Taxes		$ 813
Shares Issued during Year	100,000	
Dividends Paid during Year		$ (250)
Ending Balances	650,000	$1,924

BALANCE SHEET FOR THE FYE 12/31/23

Assets		
Cash & Equivalents		$ 2,164
Accounts Receivable		$ 8,009
Inventory		$ 1,706
Prepaid Expenses		$ 625
Total Current Assets		$12,504
Property, Machinery, & Equipment	$ 4,500	
Less: Accumulated Depreciation	$ (2,214)	$ 2,286
Intangible Assets, Net		$ 6,000
Other Assets		$ 100
Total Assets		$20,889
Liabilities & Stockholders' Equity		
Accounts Payable		$ 1,459
Accrued Liabilities Payable		$ 1,258
Short-Term Loans Payable		$ 2,400
Other Current Liabilities & Deferred Revenue		$ 1,348
Total Current Liabilities		$ 6,465
Loans Payable & Other Long-Term Debt, Less ST Loans		$ 2,500
Total Liabilities		$ 8,965
Capital Stock	$10,000	
Retained Earnings	$ 1,924	
Total Stockholders' Equity		$11,924
Total Liabilities & Stockholders' Equity		$20,889

STATEMENT OF CASH FLOWS FOR THE FYE 12/31/23

Net Income (Loss) after Income Taxes	$ 813
Depreciation & Amortization	$ 1,643
Decrease (increase) in accounts receivables	$ (1,233)
Decrease (increase) in inventory	$ 2,116
Decrease (increase) in other current assets	$ (25)
Increase (decrease) in accounts payables	$ 54
Increase (decrease) in accrued liabilities	$ 42
Increase (decrease) in other liabilities	$ 469
Net Cash Flow from Operating Activities	$ 3,879
Investing Activities, Cash provided (used):	
Capital Expenditures	$ (500)
Investments in Intangible & Other Assets	$ (5,000)
Net Cash Flow from Investing Activities	$ (5,500)
Financing Activities, Cash provided (used):	
Dividends or Distributions Paid	$ (250)
Sale (repurchase) of Equity	$ 2,500
Proceeds from Issuance of Loans (i.e., debt)	$ 3,000
Repayments of Long-Term Loans	$ (1,250)
Net Borrowings (Repayments) of Short-Term Loans	$ (990)
Cash Flow From Financing Activities	$ 3,010
Net Increase (decrease) in Cash & Equivalents	$ 1,389
Beginning Cash & Equivalents Balance	$ 775
Ending Cash & Equivalents Balance	$ 2,164

A New Financial Statement

Exhibit 11.1 introduces a new financial statement—the *statement of changes in stockholders' equity for year*—that I have not presented before in the book. In some respects, this is not really a financial statement; it's more of a supporting schedule that summarizes changes in the stockholders' equity accounts. The business issued 100,000 additional shares of capital stock during the year. The $2,500,000 cash from issuing the shares are reported in the statement of changes in stockholders' equity as well as the statement of cash flows (see Exhibit 11.1). Net income for the year is reported as an increase in retained earnings, and cash dividends paid to stockholders are a decrease.

The statement of changes in stockholders' equity is needed when a business has a capitalization (ownership) structure that includes two or more classes of stock and when a business owns some of its own capital stock shares (called *treasury stock*). I cover the topic of how a business is capitalized in Chapter 15, which includes additional bonus material on this somewhat complex but very important topic.

This financial statement is also needed when a business has recorded certain types of losses and gains that bypass the income statement. The amounts of any such special gains and losses are recorded in a special stockholders' equity account called "Accumulated Other Comprehensive Income." The term *comprehensive income* denotes that, in addition to net income that flows through the income statement into the retained earnings account, additional gains and losses have been recorded that have not been reported in the income statement. The accumulated other comprehensive income account serves as a second retained-earnings–type account, which holds the cumulative result of recording certain types of gains and losses. Exploring these special gains and losses would take us into technical territory beyond the scope of this book.

The statement of changes in stockholders' equity can be complex and highly technical. In the following discussion, I focus on the most widely used ratios calculated from data in the three primary financial statements (i.e., balance sheet, income statement, and statement of cash flows).

Benchmark Financial Ratios: Strength

Stock analysts, investment managers, individual investors, investment bankers, economists, and many others are interested in the fundamental financial aspects of a business. Ratios are a big help in analyzing a business's financial situation and performance. So far in the book, two financial statement ratios have been covered at length: the *accounts receivable days sales outstanding ratio* in Chapter 6 and the *inventory days outstanding ratio* in Chapter 7. You might be anticipating that I will begin with profit analysis. No, I start with *solvency*, also known as financial strength.

Solvency refers to the ability of a business to pay its liabilities when they come due. If a business is insolvent and cannot pay its liabilities on time, its continuance is at stake. In many respects, solvency comes first and profit second (as the first rule in business is never to run out of cash to operate). The ability to earn profit rests on the ability of the business to continue on course and avoid being shut down or interfered with by its lenders. In short, earning profit demands that a business remains solvent. Maintaining solvency (its debt-paying ability) is essential for every business. If a business defaults on its debt obligations, it becomes vulnerable to legal proceedings that could stop the company in its tracks or interfere with its normal operations.

Bankers and other lenders, when deciding whether to make and renew loans to a business, direct their attention to certain key financial statement ratios to help them evaluate the business's solvency situation and prospects. These ratios provide a useful financial profile of the business in assessing its creditworthiness and judging its ability to pay interest and repay the principal of its loans on time and in full.

For the rest of this chapter, all amounts from the financial statements are in thousands of dollars, except earnings per share (EPS). Instead of reminding you every time, I assume that you remember that the data is taken from Exhibit 11.1. In addition, while Exhibit 11.1 provides financial information for only the most recent FYE 12/31/23, for comparison purposes I've included the ratio calculations for the prior FYE 12/31/22 and all our case study companies. The figures for the FYE 12/31/22 can be found in Exhibits 5.1 through 5.9 for all three of our case study companies. In addition, the figures for our two other case study companies, FB and PEB, can be found in Exhibits 5.1 and 5.2 (for FB) and 5.7 and 5.8 (for PEB).

Net Working Capital

To start, I will present a simple yet critical analysis that calculates a company's net working capital, defined as total current assets less total current liabilities. Expanding on this analysis, I then examine the net working capital level in relation to average monthly sales (a measurement of a company's ability to ensure ample net working capital is available to support sales revenue growth).

For our case-study companies, the acid-test or quick ratio has been calculated and presented on page 162.

This analysis indicates our case study companies maintain ample levels of net working capital as, on average, current assets are range from roughly 1.75 to 3.00 times the amount of current liabilities (supporting its ability to pay current liabilities on time). However, this analysis doesn't tell us if our case study companies' net working capital is adequate to support continued business growth, so I've expanded our analysis as follows:

Net Working Capital, FYE:	*SEB 31-Dec-2022*	*SEB 31-Dec-2023*	*FB 31-Dec-2022*	*FB 31-Dec-2023*	*PEB 31-Dec-2022*	*PEB 31-Dec-2023*
Total Current Assets	$11,973	$12,504	$12,091	$14,963	$11,973	$15,704
Total Current Liabilities	$ 6,890	$ 6,465	$ 5,829	$ 5,042	$ 6,535	$ 6,204
Net Working Capital	$ 5,083	$ 6,039	$ 6,262	$ 9,921	$ 5,439	$ 9,500
Average Monthly Sales revenue, Net	$ 4,518	$ 4,958	$ 4,539	$ 4,984	$ 4,528	$ 5,054
Net Working Capital to Sales Revenue Ratio	1.13	1.22	1.38	1.99	1.20	1.88

Current Ratio, FYE:	*SEB 31-Dec-2022*	*SEB 31-Dec-2023*	*FB 31-Dec-2022*	*FB 31-Dec-2023*	*PEB 31-Dec-2022*	*PEB 31-Dec-2023*
Total Current Assets	$11,973	$12,504	$12,091	$14,963	$11,973	$15,704
Total Current Liabilities	$ 6,890	$ 6,465	$ 5,829	$ 5,042	$6,535	$ 6,204
Current Ratio	1.74	1.93	2.07	2.97	1.83	2.53

I will tell you that the expanded net working capital analysis provided is not as commonly utilized as other benchmark financial ratios covered in this chapter, but it does provide an important piece of financial information. That is, a company must be able to maintain a proper balance between ensuring it remains solvent and can pay its liabilities while, at the same time, proactively managing its net working capital to support continued business growth. Looking at it slightly differently, it becomes exceedingly difficult for companies to support elevated business growth rates (as measured by increases in annual sales revenue) if this ratio decreases, indicating short-term financial pressure and solvency issues may be present.

For SEB, you can see that the ratio of net working capital to sales revenue increased from 1.13 for the FYE 12/31/22 to 1.22 for the FYE 12/31/23, a positive sign that indicates the company can continue to grow at a moderate rate with the net working capital available. For our family business (FB) and private equity business (PEB), the ratios and year-over-year (YOY) trending is even stronger. This ratio can vary across industries and companies. While there are no set rules as to what it should be, keeping it above 1.00 is prudent for most businesses.

Current Ratio

The current ratio (which is highly correlated to the net working capital analysis previously discussed) tests a business's ability to pay its short-term liabilities. It is calculated by dividing total current assets by total current liabilities, using the figures from a company's most recent balance sheet. The current ratio for our example company is computed as follows:

Quick or Acid Test Ratio, FYE:	*SEB* *31-Dec-2022*	*SEB* *31-Dec-2023*	*FB* *31-Dec-2022*	*FB* *31-Dec-2023*	*PEB* *31-Dec-2022*	*PEB* *31-Dec-2023*
Total Current Assets	$11,973	$12,504	$12,091	$14,963	$11,973	$15,704
Less: Inventory & Other Current Assets	$(4,422)	$ (2,331)	$ (4,513)	$ (4,569)	$ (4,422)	$(4,331)
Net Current Assets	$ 7,551	$10,173	$ 7,578	$10,393	$ 7,551	$11,373
Current Liabilities	$ 6,890	$ 6,465	$ 5,829	$ 5,042	$ 6,535	$ 6,204
Quick or Acid Test Ratio	1.10	1.57	1.30	2.06	1.16	1.83

The current ratio is hardly ever expressed as a percent (which would be 193 percent for SEB as of the FYE 12/31/23). The current ratio for SEB would be 1.93:1.00, or more simply just 1.93.

The common opinion is that the current ratio for a business should be 2-to-1 or higher; however, this depends on the company's industry. In some instances, current ratios closer to 1.25 to 1.00 are acceptable. Most businesses find that their creditors expect this minimum current ratio. In other words, short-term creditors generally like to see a business limit its current liabilities to one-half or less of its current assets.

Why do short-term creditors put this limit on a business? The main reason is to provide a safety cushion of protection for the payment of the company's short-term liabilities. A current ratio of 2-to-1 means $2 of cash and assets should be converted into cash in the near future that will be available to pay each $1 of current liabilities that come due in roughly the same time period. Each dollar of short-term liabilities is backed up with $2 of cash on hand or in near-term cash inflows. The extra dollar of current assets provides a margin of safety for the creditors.

A company may be able to pay its liabilities on time with a current ratio that is less than 2-to-1, or perhaps even if its current ratio were as low as 1-to-1. In our SEB case study for the FYE 12/31/23, the company has borrowed $2,400,000 on the basis of short-term loans payable, which equals 19 percent of its total current assets. Its short-term lenders may not be willing to lend the business much more—although perhaps the business could persuade its lenders to go up to, say, $4 million or $5 million on short-term loans payable.

In summary, short-term sources of credit are generally comfortable with a company's current assets being double its current liabilities (again, depending on the industry). After all, creditors are not owners—they don't share in the profit the business earns. The income on their loans is limited to the interest they charge (and collect). As creditors, they quite properly minimize their loan risks; as limited-income (fixed-income) investors, they are not compensated to take on much risk.

Acid Test Ratio (Quick Ratio)

Inventory is many weeks or months away from conversion into cash. Products are typically held two, three, or four months before being sold. If sales are made on credit, which is normal when one business sells to another business (also called a B-to-B business model), there is a second waiting period before the receivables are collected. In short, inventory is not nearly as liquid as accounts receivable; it takes much longer to convert inventory first into sales and then into cash. Furthermore, there's no guarantee that all the products in inventory will be sold because items can become obsolete, spoiled, lost, stolen, and so on.

A more severe measure of a business's short-term liability-paying ability is the *acid test ratio*, which excludes inventory and prepaid expenses. Only cash, short-term marketable securities investments (if any), and accounts receivable are counted as sources to pay the current liabilities of the business.

This ratio is also called the *quick ratio* because only cash and assets that can be quickly converted into cash are included in the amount available for paying current liabilities. It's more like a liquidity ratio that focuses on how much cash and near-cash assets a business possesses to pay all of its short-term liabilities.

For our case study companies, the acid test or quick ratio has been calculated and presented on page 162.

The general rule is that a company's acid test ratio should be 1-to-1 or better, although you find many exceptions. As you can see with FB and PEB, their respective acid test ratios appear stronger than SEB's.

Debt-to-Equity Ratio

Some debt is generally good, but too much debt is dangerous. The debt-to-equity ratio is an indicator of whether a company is using debt prudently, or perhaps has gone too far and is overburdened with debt that may cause problems. 'Our case study companies' debt-to-equity and tangible debt-to-equity ratio calculations are presented below:

This ratio tells us that SEB is using $0.75 of liabilities in addition to each $1 of stockholders' equity in the business as of the FYE 12/31/23. Notice that all liabilities (noninterest bearing as well as interest bearing, and both short term and long term) are

Debt-to-Equity Ratio, FYE:	***SEB 31-Dec-2022***	***SEB 31-Dec-2023***	***FB 31-Dec-2022***	***FB 31-Dec-2023***	***PEB 31-Dec-2022***	***PEB 31-Dec-2023***
Total Liabilities	$7,640	$ 8,965	$ 6,579	$ 7,542	$ 7,285	$ 8,704
Total Stockholders' Equity	$8,862	$11,924	$12,040	$18,473	$12,417	$20,953
Debt-to-Equity Ratio	0.86	0.75	0.55	0.41	0.59	0.42

Debt-to-Tangible-Net-Equity Ratio, FYE:	***SEB 31-Dec-2022***	***SEB 31-Dec-2023***	***FB 31-Dec-2022***	***FB 31-Dec-2023***	***PEB 31-Dec-2022***	***PEB 31-Dec-2023***
Total Liabilities	$ 7,640	$ 8,965	$ 6,579	$ 7,542	$ 7,285	$ 8,704
Total Stockholders' Equity	$ 8,862	$11,924	$12,040	$18,473	$12,417	$ 20,953
Less: Intangible Assets, Net	$(2,000)	$(6,000)	$ (4,000)	$ (8,667)	$ (5,200)	$(11,567)
Tangible Net Stockholders' Equity	$ 6,862	$ 5,924	$ 8,040	$ 9,806	$ 7,217	$ 9,386
Debt-to-Tangible-Net-Equity Ratio	1.11	1.51	0.82	0.77	1.01	0.93

included in this ratio, and that all owners' equity (i.e., invested capital stock and retained earnings) is included.

SEB—with its 0.75 debt-to-equity ratio—would be viewed as moderately leveraged. *Leverage* refers to using the equity capital base to raise additional capital from nonowner sources. In other words, the business is using $1.75 of total capital for every $1 of equity capital. The business has $1.75 of assets working for it for every dollar of equity capital in the business.

Historically, most businesses have tended to stay below a 1-to-1 debt-to-equity ratio. They don't want to take on too much debt or they cannot convince lenders to put up more than one-half of their assets. However, some capital-intensive (asset-heavy) businesses such as public utilities and financial institutions operate with debt-to-equity ratios much higher than 1-to-1. In other words, they are highly leveraged.

I offer a word of caution: In the years following the Great Recession of 2007 through 2009 and the Covid-19 pandemic, the world has been flooded with massive cash infusions from global central banks, which undertook highly accommodative monetary policies to drive interest rates down. By some estimates, over $15 trillion of cash/currency has been injected into the global economy by the world's leading central banks. This resulted in a drastic decline in interest rates that, unbelievable as it may sound, resulted in over $15 trillion of global debt. In 2020, this aggressive monetary policy generated negative interest rates (yes, you heard us right). Since then, central banks have implemented monetary tightening policies that have, for the most part, eliminated negative interest rates as more normalized interest rate levels are currently in place. But what a time it was as just about everyone got punch drunk on the crazy, low interest rates from 2020 through 2022!

These policy changes have encouraged businesses to secure new and very cheap debt to be used for business purposes ranging from investing in capital equipment to repurchasing its issued shares, helping drive up EPS (earnings per share, referenced in Exhibit 11.1). This so-called *easy* monetary environment has, unfortunately, also produced two unwanted side effects:

1. First, historical "norms" (for lack of a better term) of debt-to-equity ratios of less than about 1-to-1 (as previously noted) have been sacrificed for debt that is cheap (i.e., low interest rates), abundant (i.e., large amounts of fresh/new capital), and easy (i.e., limited financial performance covenant requirements) debt. Not only are companies becoming more and more leveraged, but the quality of the debt is being reduced or, in some cases, eliminated by efforts to establish covenants to ensure a company's performance is acceptable. It doesn't take a genius to quickly conclude that a more leveraged company with lower-quality debt is generally a recipe for disaster.
2. Second, when companies use debt to repurchase their own shares (a very common practice over the past three years), the number of shares outstanding when calculating its EPS decreases. For example, Company XYZ had 1 million shares outstanding and elected to repurchase 100,000, leaving 900,000 shares remaining as outstanding. With fewer outstanding shares and a relatively constant net profit, the company provides the appearance, or some may say illusion, that its EPS is increasing even though its net profit has not changed. This concept is a perfect example of what is commonly referred to as *financial engineering*, a topic that is covered in *How to Read a Financial Report*, 10th Edition, Chapter 20. It is something that is extremely important to understand in today's global economy.

Debt-to-Tangible-Net-Worth Ratio

Another common ratio is the debt-to-tangible-net-worth ratio, which is very similar to the debt-to-equity ratio but takes it one step further. In this calculation, total stockholders' equity is reduced by the net value of any intangible assets to calculate total tangible stockholders' figure. Then, the same total liabilities figure is divided by total tangible stockholders' balance to produce a debt-to-tangible-net-worth ratio.

When comparing this revised ratio of 1.51 for SEB to the basic debt-to-equity ratio of 0.75 for the FYE 12/31/23, you can see a considerable difference is present. One reason external parties, and especially lenders, calculate this figure is to evaluate the so-called hard or tangible assets owned by a company in relation to its debt load and stockholders' equity. Some capital sources and lenders get a little more nervous when they see large amounts of intangible assets on the balance sheet that can sometimes lose their value extremely quickly due to rapidly changing technology or consumer tastes and preferences. Thus, this ratio is used to assess the potential risks associated with a company with significant investments in intangible assets.

Final Comments

Many other ratios can be calculated from the data in financial statements. For example, the *asset turnover ratio* (annual sales revenue divided by total assets) and the *dividend yield* (annual cash dividends per share divided by market value per share) are two ratios often used in securities analysis. There is no end to the ratios that can be calculated.

The trick is to focus on those ratios that have the most interpretive value. It's not easy to figure out which ratios are the most important. In my opinion, professional investors seem to use too many ratios rather than too few. However, you never know which ratio might provide a valuable clue to a stock's future market value direction.

In general, the ratio calculations for our case study companies FB and PEB are stronger than for SEB. This is the result of many factors, including: (a) higher net income levels achieved over the previous four years of operations, (b) the accounting treatment of worthless and obsolete inventory (which SEB elected to take as a large $2,000,000 expense in the FYE 12/31/23), and (c) the accounting for intangible assets. Thus, a word of caution is warranted because, while financial strength ratio analysis is a useful assessment tool, it must be applied with a thorough understanding of the financial reports and financial statements and where the source accounting information originates.

12

FINANCIAL STATEMENT RATIOS AND ANALYSIS: PERFORMANCE

Financial Performance versus Financial Strength

In Chapter 11, I introduced you to the standard ratios used by external parties to analyze a company's financial strength, solvency, and liquidity. By and large, the financial strength ratios are centered on the company's balance sheet. In this chapter, I'll turn our attention to financial performance ratios, which are primarily centered on the income statement as well as the balance sheet. Then, I'll finish with a couple of cash flow–based ratios that can be very useful in understanding a company's ability to generate cash and cover debt obligations.

To start, direct your attention to Exhibit 11.1, which I've included again for ease of reference.

Gross Margin and Breakeven

I start our discussion of financial performance ratios and analysis by revisiting each case study company's gross profit and sales revenue figures to calculate its gross margin and then estimate its breakeven operating level. As a side note, the terms *gross profit* and *gross margin* are often used interchangeably in the financial world. I would like to clarify that for the purposes of our ratio analysis, the term *profit* refers to an actual dollar figure, whereas the term *margin* refers to a percentage figure.

Calculating a company's gross margin is very easy. It is nothing more than taking its gross profit (which is net sales revenue less direct costs of sales revenue) and dividing this by net sales revenue as follows:

	SEB	*SEB*	*FB*	*FB*	*PEB*	*PEB*
Gross Margin, FYE:	*31-Dec-2022*	*31-Dec-2023*	*31-Dec-2022*	*31-Dec-2023*	*31-Dec-2022*	*31-Dec-2023*
Gross Profit	$30,288	$37,728	$30,544	$38,188	$30,420	$38,634
Sales Revenue, Net	$54,210	$59,494	$54,474	$59,806	$54,342	$60,650
Gross Margin	55.87%	63.41%	56.07%	63.85%	55.98%	63.70%

EXHIBIT 12.1—SUMMARIZED EXTERNAL FINANCIAL STATEMENTS OF BUSINESS (WITHOUT FOOTNOTES)—BASE CASE (SEB)

Dollar Amounts in Thousands Except Earnings Per Share

INCOME STATEMENT FOR THE FYE 12/31/23

Sales Revenue, Net	$ 59,494
Costs of Sales Revenue, Products	$(21,766)
Gross Profit (aka Gross Margin)	$ 37,728
Selling, General, & Administrative	$ 25,289
Research & Development	$ 7,139
Depreciation & Amortization	$ 1,643
Total Operating Expenses	$ 34,071
Operating Income (Loss)	$ 3,658
Other Expenses or (Income)	$ 2,000
Interest Expense	$ 407
Net Income (Loss) before Income Taxes	$ 1,251
Income Tax Expense (Benefit)	$ 438
Net Income (Loss) after Income Taxes	$ 813
Basic Earnings Per Share	$ 1.25

STATEMENT OF CHANGES IN STOCKHOLDERS' EQUITY FOR YEAR

	Capital Stock	Retained Earnings
Beginning Balances	550,000	$1,362
Net Income (Loss) after Income Taxes		$ 813
Shares Issued during Year	100,000	
Dividends Paid during Year		$ (250)
Ending Balances	650,000	$1,924

BALANCE SHEET FOR THE FYE 12/31/23

Assets		
Cash & Equivalents		$ 2,164
Accounts Receivable		$ 8,009
Inventory		$ 1,706
Prepaid Expenses		$ 625
Total Current Assets		$12,504
Property, Machinery, & Equipment	$ 4,500	
Less: Accumulated Depreciation	$ (2,214)	$ 2,286
Intangible Assets, Net		$ 6,000
Other Assets		$ 100
Total Assets		$20,889
Liabilities & Stockholders' Equity		
Accounts Payable		$ 1,459
Accrued Liabilities Payable		$ 1,258
Short-Term Loans Payable		$ 2,400
Other Current Liabilities & Deferred Revenue		$ 1,348
Total Current Liabilities		$ 6,465
Loans Payable & Other Long-Term Debt, Less ST Loans		$ 2,500
Total Liabilities		$ 8,965
Capital Stock	$10,000	
Retained Earnings	$ 1,924	
Total Stockholders' Equity		$11,924
Total Liabilities & Stockholders' Equity		$20,889

STATEMENT OF CASH FLOWS FOR THE FYE 12/31/23

Net Income (Loss) after Income Taxes	$ 813
Depreciation & Amortization	$ 1,643
Decrease (increase) in accounts receivables	$ (1,233)
Decrease (increase) in inventory	$ 2,116
Decrease (increase) in other current assets	$ (25)
Increase (decrease) in accounts payables	$ 54
Increase (decrease) in accrued liabilities	$ 42
Increase (decrease) in other liabilities	$ 469
Net Cash Flow from Operating Activities	$ 3,879
Investing Activities, Cash provided (used):	
Capital Expenditures	$ (500)
Investments in Intangible & Other Assets	$ (5,000)
Net Cash Flow from Investing Activities	$ (5,500)
Financing Activities, Cash provided (used):	
Dividends or Distributions Paid	$ (250)
Sale (repurchase) of Equity	$ 2,500
Proceeds from Issuance of Loans (i.e., debt)	$ 3,000
Repayments of Long-Term Loans	$ (1,250)
Net Borrowings (Repayments) of Short-Term Loans	$ (990)
Cash Flow From Financing Activities	$ 3,010
Net Increase (decrease) in Cash & Equivalents	$ 1,389
Beginning Cash & Equivalents Balance	$ 775
Ending Cash & Equivalents Balance	$ 2,164

In the calculations provided, notice the improvement in each case study company's gross margin, which ranges from 55.87 percent for the FYE 12/31/22 to 63.41 percent for the FYE 12/31/23 (for SEB and similar improvements for FB and PEB). This increase is due to the change in sales mix toward more software and services, which have higher profitability fundamentals, and away from low-profit product sales.

This sounds good and makes sense, but how do I use this information to analyze the company's operating results further? Here, I introduce the company's operating breakeven point. The breakeven point is the sales revenue required to ensure the company can produce an operating income of $0. The breakeven calculation takes a company's total annual operating expenses and divides it by the gross margin as follows:

There are some points to keep in mind when calculating the breakeven level. First, this analysis is completed at the base operating level and does not consider interest expense, income tax expense, and other or one-time expenses. It's designed to evaluate just the core operations. Second, you will notice from the calculation that for SEB, its breakeven net sales revenue level is roughly the same between the two years presented, yet its total annual fixed operating expenses increased by slightly over $4,000,000. How is it possible that the net sales revenue breakeven level remains unchanged with such a large increase in fixed operating expenses? The answer lies in the improved gross margin, which generates higher gross profits from more profitable software and service sales, improving the company's financial performance.

Breakeven Level, FYE:	*SEB* *31-Dec-2022*	*SEB* *31-Dec-2023*	*FB* *31-Dec-2022*	*FB* *31-Dec-2023*	*PEB* *31-Dec-2022*	*PEB* *31-Dec-2023*
Total Fixed Expenses (Op Ex. & SG&A, Exc. D&A exp.)	$28,259	$32,428	$28,217	$32,184	$26,759	$29,728
Gross Margin	55.87%	63.41%	56.07%	63.85%	55.98%	63.70%
Breakeven Level, Net Sales Revenue	$50,579	$51,136	$50,325	$50,404	$47,802	$46,668

Operating Margin and EBITDA

Another margin analysis often utilized to analyze a company's financial performance compares its operating income against total sales revenue. Operating income excludes expenses such as interest, income taxes, and other one-time costs. The idea is to evaluate the company's core operations against sales revenue by removing the noise.

For our case study companies, I've prepared the following operating margin analysis for your review:

As you can see, each of our case study companies' operating margin improved significantly between the two years presented, from SEB's razor-thin level of less than 1 percent for the FYE 12/31/22 to approximately 6 percent for the FYE 12/31/23. For PEB, the improvement appears even more significant as its operating margin has increased from approximately 4.5 percent for the FYE 12/31/22 to almost 12 percent for the FYE 12/31/23. Internal and external parties should view the improvement in the company's operating margin as good news. It is largely centered on the company's ability to increase sales revenue and improve its gross margin (discussed earlier).

Operating Margin, FYE:	*SEB* *31-Dec-2022*	*SEB* *31-Dec-2023*	*FB* *31-Dec-2022*	*FB* *31-Dec-2023*	*PEB* *31-Dec-2022*	*PEB* *31-Dec-2023*
Operating Income (loss)	$ 457	$ 3,658	$ 1,421	$ 5,027	$ 2,456	$ 7,130
Sales Revenue, Net	$54,210	$59,494	$54,474	$59,806	$54,342	$60,650
Operating Margin	0.84%	6.15%	2.61%	8.41%	4.52%	11.76%

Taking this analysis one step further, I also present an adjusted operating margin analysis based on calculating EBITDA (earnings before interest, taxes, depreciation, amortization, and other one-time expenses). Here is the adjusted operating or EBITDA margin analysis for your review:

Using this data, you can see again the year-over-year improvement in the EBITDA margin for all three of our case study companies and that for the FYE 12/31/23, SEB is approaching a 9 percent EBITDA margin compared to PEB's EBITDA margin of almost 15 percent. Again, the company's operating results are trending in a positive direction, but the interpretation as to whether reaching a 9 percent EBITDA margin is acceptable is open for debate. For example, an external analyst may compliment the company's management on improving the EBITDA margin but may also note that its competitors are producing 15 percent EBITDA margins, so the company would appear to have more wood to chop to improve operating results. Likewise, internal management may have only forecast a 6 percent EBITDA

Adjusted Operating (EBITDA) Margin, FYE:	***SEB 31-Dec-2022***	***SEB 31-Dec-2023***	***FB 31-Dec-2022***	***FB 31-Dec-2023***	***PEB 31-Dec-2022***	***PEB 31-Dec-2023***
Operating Income (loss)	$ 457	$ 3,658	$ 1,421	$ 5,027	$ 2,456	$ 7,130
Depreciation & Amortization Expense	$ 1,571	$ 1,643	$ 905	$ 976	$ 1,205	$ 1,776
Adjusted Operating Income or EBITDA	$ 2,029	$ 5,301	$ 2,326	$ 6,004	$ 3,661	$ 8,907
Sales Revenue, Net	$54,210	$59,494	$54,474	$59,806	$54,342	$60,650
Adjusted Operating (EBITDA) Margin	3.74%	8.91%	4.27%	10.04%	6.74%	14.69%

The primary difference between the operating margin calculation and the EBITDA margin calculation is that I add back depreciation and amortization expense to generate EBITDA, which is often viewed as the company's ability to generate internal positive cash flow (refer to Chapter 8 about depreciation and amortization). Further, any noise associated with one-time or non-recurring expenses is not included, as this distorts the calculation.

margin during the FYE 12/31/23, so in their eyes, the company is ahead of plan. It's important to emphasize that when analyzing financial information, trends, and ratios, it's critical to understand how the change in performance should be benchmarked against industry data, internal forecasts, and similar financial data points to provide a complete understanding of the company's financial performance.

Return-on-Sales Ratio

Making sales while controlling expenses is how a business generates profit. The profit residual slice from a company's total sales revenue pie is expressed by the ***return-on-sales ratio***, which is profit divided by sales revenue for the period. Our case study companies' return on sales ratio for its latest year are:

Return-on-Sales Revenue, FYE:	***SEB*** ***31-Dec-2022***	***SEB*** ***31-Dec-2023***	***FB*** ***31-Dec-2022***	***FB*** ***31-Dec-2023***	***PEB*** ***31-Dec-2022***	***PEB*** ***31-Dec-2023***
Net Income (Loss) after Income Taxes	$ 77	$ 813	$ 1,041	$4,182	$ 2,076	$ 6,285
Sales Revenue, Net	$54,210	$59,494	$54,474	$59,806	$54,342	$60,650
Return-on-Sales Revenue	0.14%	1.37%	1.91%	6.99%	3.82%	10.36%

There is another way of explaining the return-on-sales ratio. For each $100 of sales revenue for the FYE 12/31/23, SEB earned $1.37 net income—and had expenses of $98.63. Return on sales varies quite markedly from one industry to another. Some businesses do well with only a 2 percent return on sales; others need more than 10 percent to justify the large amount of capital invested in their assets.

Return on Equity (ROE)

Owners take the risk of whether their business can earn a profit and sustain its profit performance over the years. How much would you pay for a business that consistently suffers a loss? The value of the owners' investment depends first and foremost on the business's past and potential future profit performance—specifically on profit relative to the capital invested to earn that profit.

For instance, suppose a business earns $100,000 annual net income for its stockholders. If its stockholders' equity is $250,000, then its profit performance relative to the stockholders' capital used to make that profit is 40 percent, which is very good indeed. If, however, stockholders' equity is $2,500,000, then the company's profit performance equals only 4 percent of owners' equity, which is weak relative to the owners' capital used to earn that profit.

In short, profit should be compared with the capital invested to earn it. Profit for a period divided by the amount of capital invested to earn that profit is generally called return on investment (ROI). ROI is a broad concept that applies to almost any sort of capital investment.

The owners' historical investment in a business is the total of the owners' equity accounts in the company's balance sheet. Their profit is the bottom-line net income for the period—well, maybe not all of it. A business corporation may issue *preferred stock* on which a fixed dividend amount must be paid each year. The preferred stock shares have the first claim on dividends from net income. Therefore, preferred stock dividends are subtracted from net income to determine the *net income available for the common stockholders*. Our case study company SEB has issued only one class of stock shares. The company has no preferred stock, so all net income belongs to its common stockholders.

Dividing annual net income by stockholders' equity gives the *return-on-equity* (ROE) ratio. The calculation for our case study companies' ROE are as follows:

Return on Stockholders' Equity, FYE:	***SEB 31-Dec-2022***	***SEB 31-Dec-2023***	***FB 31-Dec-2022***	***FB 31-Dec-2023***	***PEB 31-Dec-2022***	***PEB 31-Dec-2023***
End of Year Total Stockholders' Equity	$8,862	$11,924	$12,040	$18,473	$12,417	$20,953
Net Income (Loss) after Income Taxes	$ 77	$ 813	$ 1,041	$ 4,182	$ 2,076	$ 6,285
Return on Average Stockholders' Equity	0.87%	6.82%	8.65%	22.64%	16.72%	30.00%

Note: I use the ending balance of stockholders' equity to simplify the calculation. Alternatively, the weighted average during the year could be used—and should be if significant changes exist.

By most standards, SEB's 6.82 percent annual ROE for the FYE 12/31/23 would be acceptable (accounting for the other expenses of $2,000,000) but not impressive. However, everything is relative. ROE should be compared with industry-wide averages and with investment alternatives. Also, the risk factor is important. Just how risky is the stockholders' capital investment in the business?

We must know much more about the history and prospects of the business to reach a final conclusion regarding whether its 6.82 percent ROE is good, mediocre, or poor. We should also consider the *opportunity cost of capital*—that is, the ROI the stockholders could have earned on the next-best use of their capital. Furthermore, I have not considered the personal income tax on dividends paid to its individual stockholders. In summary, judging ROE is not a simple matter!

Return on Assets (ROA)

Here's another useful profit performance ratio:

Return on Assets, FYE:	***SEB 31-Dec-2022***	***SEB 31-Dec-2023***	***FB 31-Dec-2022***	***FB 31-Dec-2023***	***PEB 31-Dec-2022***	***PEB 31-Dec-2023***
End of Year Total Assets	$16,502	$20,889	$18,619	$26,015	$19,702	$29,656
Net Income (Loss) Before Interest, Income Taxes, & Other Expenses	$ 457	$ 3,658	$ 1,421	$ 5,027	$ 2,456	$ 7,130
Return on Average Assets	2.77%	17.51%	7.63%	19.33%	12.47%	24.04%

The *return-on-assets* (ROA) ratio reveals that SEB earned $17.51 before interest, other, and income tax expenses on each $100 of assets for the FYE 12/31/23. The ROA is compared with the annual interest rate on the company's borrowed money. In this case study, the SEB's annual interest rate on its short-term and long-term debt is 9.0 percent. SEB earned 17.51 percent on the money borrowed, as measured by the ROA. The difference or spread between the two rates is a favorable spread equal to 8.51 percentage points, which increases the earnings after interest for stockholders. This source of profit enhancement is called *financial leverage gain*. In contrast, if a company's ROA is less than its interest rate, it suffers a financial leverage loss.

In our ROA calculation, I use an adjusted operating earnings figure of $3,658,000 compared to the net income figure of $813,000. This is to focus on the business's core operating earnings in relation to its total assets and remove any noise associated with other one-time expenses.

Earnings Per Share (EPS)

In contrast to the ratios discussed earlier in the chapter, public companies report the earnings-per-share (EPS) ratio at the bottom of their income statements. You don't have to calculate it. Given its importance, you should understand how it is calculated. Private companies are not required to report EPS, but many larger, more sophisticated private companies do. As a stockholder of a private company, you may find it helpful to calculate EPS.

The capital stock shares of roughly 3,750 domestic business corporations are traded in public markets—the New York Stock Exchange, Nasdaq, and electronic stock exchanges. The day-to-day, even minute-by-minute market price changes of these shares receive a great deal of attention. More than any other single factor, the market value of capital stock shares depends on a business's past and forecast net income (earnings).

Suppose I tell you that the market price of a stock is $20 and ask you whether this value is too high or too low, or just about right. You could compare the market price with the stockholders' equity per share reported in the balance sheet—called the *book value per share*, which is about $18.35 for SEB as of the FYE 12/31/23. (Recall that a company's total assets minus its total liabilities equal its stockholders' equity.) The book value method has a respectable history in securities analysis. Today, however, the book value approach plays second fiddle to the earnings-based approach. The starting point is to calculate *earnings (net income) per share*.

EPS is one of the most widely used ratios in investment analysis. The essential calculation of earnings per share for our case study companies is as follows:

Earnings Per Share, FYE:	*SEB 31-Dec-2022*	*SEB 31-Dec-2023*	*FB 31-Dec-2022*	*FB 31-Dec-2023*	*PEB 31-Dec-2022*	*PEB 31-Dec-2023*
Net Income (Loss) for Common Stockholders	$ 77	$ 813	$1,041	$4,182	$2,076	$6,285
Common Shares Outstanding	550,000	650,000	550,000	650,000	550,000	650,000
Basic Earnings Per Share	$ 0.14	$ 1.25	$ 1.89	$ 6.43	$ 3.77	$ 9.67
Book Value Per Share	$16.11	$18.35	$21.89	$28.42	$22.58	$32.23

To be technically accurate, the weighted average number of shares outstanding during the year should be used—based on the actual number of shares outstanding each month (or day).

Notice that the numerator (top number) in the EPS ratio is *net income available for common stockholders*, which equals bottom-line net income less any dividends paid to the business's preferred stockholders. As mentioned earlier, many corporations issue preferred stock that requires a fixed annual dividend payment. The mandatory annual dividends to the preferred stockholders are deducted from net income to determine the net income available for the common stockholders.

Second, please notice the word *basic* in front of *earnings per share*, which means that the actual number of common stock shares in the hands of stockholders is the denominator (bottom number) in the EPS calculation. Many business corporations have entered into contracts of one sort or another that require the company at some time in the future to issue additional stock shares at prices below the market value of the stock shares at that time. The shares under these contracts have yet to be actually issued but probably will be in the future.

For example, business corporations award managers *stock options* to buy common stock shares of the company at fixed prices (generally equal to the present market price or current value of the shares). If, in the future, the market value of the shares rises over the fixed option prices, the managers will exercise their rights and buy capital stock shares at a bargain price. With stock options, therefore, the number of stock shares is subject to inflation. When (and if) the additional shares are issued, EPS will suffer because net income will have to be spread over a larger number of stock shares. EPS will be diluted, or thinned down, because of the larger denominator in the EPS ratio.

Basic EPS does not recognize the additional shares that will be issued when stock options are exercised. It also does not take into account the potential dilution effects of any convertible bonds and convertible preferred stock issued by a business. These securities can be converted at the option of the security holders into common stock shares at predetermined prices.

To warn investors of the potential effects of stock options and convertible securities, a second EPS is reported by public corporations, called fully *diluted* EPS. This lower EPS takes into account the potential dilution effects caused by issuing additional common-stock shares under stock-option plans, convertible securities, and any other commitments a business has entered into that could require it to issue additional stock shares at predetermined prices in the future.

Basic EPS and fully diluted EPS (if applicable) must be reported in the income statements of publicly owned business corporations. This indicates the importance of EPS. In contrast, none of the other ratios discussed in this chapter must be reported, although many public companies report selected ratios.

Price/Earnings (P/E) Ratio

The market price of stock shares of a public business corporation is compared with its EPS and expressed in the *price/earnings (P/E) ratio* as follows:

$$\frac{\text{Current Market Price of Stock Shares}}{\text{Earnings Per Share}} = \text{Price / Earnings Ratio}$$

Suppose a public company's stock shares are trading at \$30 per share, and its basic EPS for the most recent year (called the *trailing 12 months*) is \$2. The company does not report a diluted EPS. Thus, its P/E ratio is 15. Like other ratios discussed in this chapter, the P/E ratio should be compared with industry-wide and market-wide averages to judge whether it is acceptable, too high, or too low. At one time, a P/E ratio of 8 was considered suitable. As I write this sentence, P/E ratios in the range of 15 to 20 (or higher) are considered acceptable and nothing to be alarmed about, especially for high-growth, technology-based companies.

Here's a problem in calculating the P/E ratio for a public company: Should you use its *basic* EPS or its fully *diluted* EPS? If the business reports only basic EPS, there is no problem. But when a public company reports both, which EPS should you use? Well, it is done both ways. Our advice is to check the legend in the stock market tables in the *Wall Street Journal* and *The New York Times* to find out which EPS the newspaper uses in reporting the P/E ratios for companies. Using diluted EPS is more conservative; that is, it gives a higher P/E ratio.

The market prices for stock shares of private businesses are not available to the public at large. Private company shares are usually not actively traded; when they are traded, the price per share is not made public. Nevertheless, stockholders in these businesses are interested in what their shares are worth. A multiple P/E can be used to estimate the value of stock shares. SEB's EPS is $1.25 for the FYE 12/31/23 (see Exhibit 11.1). Suppose you own some of the capital stock shares, and someone offers to buy your shares. You could establish an offer price at, say, 20 times basic EPS. This would be $25.00 per share. The potential buyer may not be willing to pay this price, or they might be willing to pay 15 or 18 times basic EPS.

Market Cap

Suppose the stock shares of a public company are currently trading at $65 per share, and the business has 10 million shares outstanding. The *market cap*, or total market value capitalization of the company, is $650 million ($65 market value per share × 10 million capital stock shares = $650 million). I'd bet you dollars to doughnuts that if you compared the market cap of most businesses with the shareholders' equity amounts reported in their latest balance sheets, the market caps would be considerably higher—perhaps *much* higher.

The book value (balance sheet value) of shareholders' equity is the historical record of the amounts invested in the business by the owners' past plus its retained earnings accumulated over the years. Over time, these amounts become more and more out of date. In contrast, the market cap is based on the current market value of the company's stock shares. If a business gets into financial straits, its market cap may drop below the book value of its owners' equity—at least for the time being. In rare cases, a company's cash balance may exceed its market cap.

Two Cash Flow Ratios to Chew On

The ratios associated and analyzed so far have focused on the income statement and balance sheet (ignoring the cash flow statement). This is traditionally where most parties focus their attention because the information gleaned from the calculations is very useful. But cash flow ratios and analyses are just as informative and, in today's world, have become mainstays when evaluating a company's operating performance and financial viability. Here, I present two cash-flow–based ratios and analysis tools that are widely used in the market.

Debt Service Coverage Ratio and EBITDA

To pay principal and interest (combined referred to as *debt service*) on its outstanding loans, a business needs to have sufficient earnings before interest expense, income tax expense, other one-time expenses (usually non-cash in nature), and depreciation and amortization expense, a metric referred to as *adjusted EBITDA*. The debt service coverage ratio is calculated to test the ability to pay interest and principal from earnings. Annual earnings before interest expense, income tax expense, other expenses, and depreciation and amortization expense is divided by interest expense, plus annual loan principal payments.

There is no standard or general rule for this particular ratio, although obviously, the ratio needs to be higher than 1.00:1.00 and really should be north of 2.00:1.00. For our case study company SEB, its adjusted EBITDA is 2.35:1.00 its annual interest expense and estimated loan principal payments for the FYE 12/31/23, which is comforting to its lenders. Lenders would be more alarmed with SEB's debt service coverage ratio of 1.05 for the FYE 12/31/22, as it indicates the business barely generates enough cash to cover its annual interest expense and loan principal payments. (The company's management and stockholders should be equally alarmed.) For our other case study companies, FB and PEB, the same trends are present, as their DSCRs for the FYE 12/31/22 are on the low side but have improved significantly for the FYE 12/31/23. But I must caution you that looks can be deceiving, especially with our case study company PEB (as you will find in our final ratio analysis, following).

Debt Service Coverage Ratio, FYE:	*SEB 31-Dec-2022*	*SEB 31-Dec-2023*	*FB 31-Dec-2022*	*FB 31-Dec-2023*	*PEB 31-Dec-2022*	*PEB 31-Dec-2023*
Net Income (Loss) Before Income Taxes	$ 118	$1,251	$1,082	$4,620	$2,117	$6,723
Depreciation & Amortization Expense	$1,571	$1,643	$ 905	$ 976	$1,205	$1,776
Interest Expense	$ 339	$ 407	$ 339	$ 407	$ 339	$ 407
Other (Income) Expenses	$ 0	$2,000	$ 0	$ 0	$ 0	$ 0
Adjusted Operating Income or EBITDA	$2,029	$5,301	$2,326	$6,004	$3,661	$8,907
Debt Service Requirements:						
- Interest Expense	$ 339	$ 407	$ 339	$ 407	$ 339	$ 407
- Principal Payment, Long-Term Debt	$ 750	$1,250	$ 750	$1,250	$ 750	$1,250
- Estimated Principal Payment, Current Debt (4 yr)	$ 848	$ 600	$ 848	$ 600	$ 848	$ 600
- Total Debt Service Payments	$1,937	$2,257	$1,937	$2,257	$1,937	$2,257
Debt Service Coverage Ratio	1.05	2.35	1.20	2.66	1.89	3.95

Adjusted EBITDA

To recap, EBITDA stands for earnings before interest, taxes, depreciation, and amortization expense and is a calculation that attempts to measure a company's ability to generate positive cash flow from normalized operations. Typically, EBITDA is not separately disclosed in a company's financial report or required to be reported in audited financial statements, so it must be calculated independently. Seeing that EBITDA is not governed by GAAP and is not verified during an audit, the best advice I can give you is to understand the concept of EBITDA but always take it with a grain of salt. This figure can easily be manipulated based on different interpretations of the facts present. You may ask why I have elected to offer a discussion on EBITDA, and the answer lies in two key facts. First, EBITDA provides a base estimate of how much cash a company can generate from normalized internal operations on a periodic basis. Second, it is widely used in today's financial world, so the more you understand its value and limitations, the better.

Taking EBITDA one step further, adjusted EBITDA is calculated by first increasing EBITDA for expenses or charges that are considered non-recurring or one-time in nature (which I've already completed by adding back the $2,000,000 of one-time expenses for SEB for the FYE 12/31/23). Then, EBITDA is decreased for normal and customary capital expenditures that must be incurred to ensure continued operating performance levels. For example, a manufacturing company must constantly invest in new equipment to support business operations (as the old equipment becomes obsolete or is worn-out through depreciation), or a technology company must continuously invest in intangible assets such as patents, new software code, and so on to maintain its status as a cutting-edge technology company.

In our case study companies, adjusted EBITDA has been calculated as follows (refer to subsequent page for calculation).

So far this doesn't look so bad. SEB's adjusted EBITDA for the FYE 12/31/23 is $2,801,000 (a significant improvement over the negative figure of $221,000 for the FYE 12/31/22). But upon closer look, when evaluating this figure against total debt service requirements of $2,257,000, dividends paid of $250,000 (Exhibit 12.1), and income tax expense of $438,000, I can determine that the company's total normalized cash needs amounted to $2,945,000 for the FYE 12/31/23, which is slightly higher than the adjusted EBITDA figure of $2,801,000.

I might also draw your attention to our case study company PEB, as you will notice that normalized intangible asset purchases are set at $4,500,000 compared to the $2,000,000 figure used for SEB and FB. Why the difference and the answer lies in its software development capitalization policy (covered in Chapter 8). PEB is really saying that its normalized intangible asset investment requirement is greater than SEB and FB as neither of these companies capitalize software development costs (but instead absorb the expenses into the income statement each year). As such, PEB's adjusted operating income has been inflated during the year (via reducing research and development expenses), which must be properly reflected as additional annual intangible asset investment requirements. In summary, PEB cannot have its cake and eat it too!

So, the real question with this calculation is: Does this indicate a problem? The company didn't generate enough internal cash flow for the year to cover all expenses, support required capital expenditures, meet total debt service during the year, and pay a small dividend. This, of course, could be an anomaly for the current year, or it could highlight a deeper problem with cash and capital management, leading to the need to eliminate dividends,

Adjusted EBITDA & DSCR, FYE:	SEB 31-Dec-2022	SEB 31-Dec-2023	FB 31-Dec-2022	FB 31-Dec-2023	PEB 31-Dec-2022	PEB 31-Dec-2023
Adjusted Operating Income or EBITDA (from above)	$ 2,029	$ 5,301	$ 2,326	$6,004	$ 3,661	$ 8,907
Normalized Capital Expenditures:						
- Tangible Fixed Asset Purchases, Normalized	$ (250)	$ (500)	$ (250)	$ (500)	$ (250)	$ (500)
- Intangible Asset Purchases, Normalized	$(2,000)	$ (2,000)	$(2,000)	$(2,000)	$(4,500)	$(4,500)
Adjusted EBITDA	$ (221)	$ 2,801	$ 76	$ 3,504	$(1,089)	$3,907
Total Debt Service Payments (from above)	$1,937	$2,257	$1,937	$2,257	$1,937	$2,257
Adjusted Debt Service Coverage Ratio	(0.11)	1.24	0.04	1.55	(0.56)	1.73

restructure long-term debt (to be paid over a longer period), and so on. In any case, this result warrants a deeper dive into the company's financial reports and plans to gain additional clarity on any potential issues or problems that might be coming down the road.

I would also like to point out two critical assumptions with this calculation that represent internal management estimates and why I previously highlighted the importance of understanding EBITDA with a grain of salt.

1. You will notice that the term *normalized* relates to tangible and intangible asset investments. Referring to Exhibit 12.1 (in the cash flow statement), you will see that SEB invested $5,000,000 in intangible asset purchases during the FYE 12/31/23, yet only $2,000,000 is reflected in our adjusted EBITDA analysis. Why the difference? Per management, this is simple: The $5,000,000 current-year intangible asset investment was elevated as normal, and recurring annual

investments in intangible assets should be approximately $2,000,000 (to maintain the business and support future growth). Thus, to properly calculate adjusted EBITDA, an arbitrary figure of $2,000,000 was used (as provided by management). Is this too high or too low? It's hard to say since it is not an audited figure and represents an internal management estimate. Often EBITDA is debated between professionals.

2. Referring to the debt-service coverage ratio, an estimate was made related to repaying short-term loans over four years. Based on the estimate provided, SEB's management team assumed that the short-term loans would have a normalized repayment term of four years for the adjusted EBITDA calculation. Once again, does four years represent a correct period? While it seems reasonable, could there be instances where it is too short (e.g., the company gets into financial trouble, resulting in the lenders requiring immediate repayment) or too long (e.g., the working capital short-term loan could be converted to a long-term loan payable over eight years)?

It should go without saying that even making small adjustments to the financial estimates used in calculating EBITDA and adjusted EBITDA can significantly impact the calculations, altering the financial analyses completed and conclusions drawn as to the company's financial and operating performance and, ultimately, its value. Hence, I cannot emphasize enough the importance of utilizing EBITDA (to analyze a company's financial performance) with an abundance of caution!

13

HOW TO MANUFACTURE CASH FROM THE BALANCE SHEET

I want to pause and summarize what has been covered and from what perspective (i.e., the outside looking in). Chapters 1 through 4 provide a crash course on financial reports, financial statements, and how the big three financial statements are connected. Chapters 5 through 10 take a deeper dive into the numbers presented in financial reports and financial statements for our three fictional but also very realistic case study companies. Chapters 11 and 12 focus on completing additional financial analyses on our three case study companies using various financial statement ratios. All of these chapters take an external perspective; that is, how an individual might review and analyze a company's financial reports and statements from the outside looking in.

I will shift gears for the remainder of this book, and I'm including bonus material not covered in the 10th edition of *How to Read a Financial Report*. These topics are extremely important, highly relevant in today's economy, and slightly more complex than those covered to this point. The material covered in Chapters 13 through 15 take a more internal perspective, like how a business manager might utilize critical (usually confidential) business financial information and data to assist with making business decisions. As such, you will notice that I make subtle changes to the presentation of the material, including:

- Numbers and figures are presented in a more detailed and expanded format, which is often how internal business managers work with financial information and data. For example, the external presentation of our case study companies was presented in figures rounded to the thousands of dollars. Moving forward, I present the entire number without rounding.
- I've expanded the use of fictional businesses beyond our three case study companies to drive home key concepts in the exhibits and financial analyses presented. I've included a reference to an e-commerce company as well as a local professional service business (e.g., an architectural firm), as these types of businesses are widely prevalent in the economy and are ideally suited to highlight key business decision-making scenarios.
- The subject matter presented in these three chapters tends to be at the center of every business manager and owner's mind every day. They ask: "How do I increase sales and profits?" (Chapter 14), "How can I improve liquidity and generate more cash in a business?" (Chapter 13), and "How can I protect ownership and management control of the business?" (Chapter 15).

Let's dive right into these discussions and focus on how a company can manufacture or generate cash from its financial statements, specifically the balance sheet.

When Capital Markets Turn Hostile

For our analysis and the exhibits presented in this chapter, I will use our base case company (i.e., SEB) and provide some additional perspective on what the executive management team anticipates for the coming years (in a macroeconomic environment). Long story short, SEB's board of directors, owners, and executive management team are expecting some significant turbulence in the national economy as a deep recession looks to be on the horizon. SEB is preparing for hostile debt markets (making it more difficult to secure loans), "frozen" equity markets (i.e., sources of capital from equity investors will either be unavailable or brutally expensive), and company insiders or "friendlies" not being able to step up with extra cash. With this in mind, the board of directors has tasked the executive management team with two extremely important jobs. First, build a low or worst-case financial forecast model for the FYE 12/31/24 that assumes a 20 percent reduction in sales revenue and corresponding expense reductions, focusing on wage and employee reductions. Second, improve the company's liquidity position and cash balance by $3,000,000 in the FYE 12/31/23 to support future operating needs. These mandates were developed and placed on SEB's executive management team as of the third quarter ending 9/30/23 (giving them just 90 days to execute). Wow, that's quite a request, but let's face it: In today's rapid-fire economy, businesses must remain extremely nimble and flexible to adapt, survive, and prosper.

For our discussion and analysis in this chapter, a financial forecast for the FYE 12/31/24 will not be provided (as it is beyond the scope of the primary purpose of this chapter). I should note that over a period of time (e.g., one year), cash can be generated by reducing expenses and cutting costs, but these generally take a while to materialize and actually can have negative short-term impacts on cash if one-time buyout-type transactions are required (e.g., employee severance packages, buyout of facility leases, etc.). Rather, the need for immediate cash generation means we're going to focus on the balance sheet and squeeze it to drive fast cash over 90 days by using the following tactics/strategies:

1. Liability, Loan Line of Credit: SEB has ample ability to borrow on its line of credit, given the strength of the loan collateral. The company will increase the amount borrowed from the line of credit by $1,000,000 to improve its cash position. You may ask why SEB would do this, knowing that it will incur additional interest expense. The answer is centered on strategically increasing the line of credit usage to avoid possibly having its lender reduce or restrict borrowing capacity in the future (for any number of reasons).
2. Liability, Accounts Payable: PEB completed an analysis of its suppliers and vendors and will be pushing them a bit more

on payment terms. Critical suppliers and vendors will not see any changes in their payment terms, but non-essential and discretionary vendors will see payments, in general, stretched out another 2 to 4 weeks. This strategy is anticipated to generate an additional $175,000 of cash. Still, it will be implemented carefully to avoid agitating any vendors and suppliers and in a manner that does not raise any significant flags (which could be problematic for the company if the suppliers and vendors raise concerns). Some small fees are anticipated to be incurred as certain suppliers and vendors tack on late fees.

3. Liability, Deferred Revenue: The company implemented an aggressive early-bird software and services renewal sale that provided a 10 percent discount to customers that renewed sales contracts for 2024 (which only applies to customers that pay before the end of the year). The sales promotion was effective as it enticed advanced sales of $750,000 prior to the FYE 12/31/23. No additional expense is anticipated to be realized in the FYE 12/31/23 as the discount provided will be absorbed in 2024, the year the sales revenue will be recognized as earned.

4. Asset, Accounts Receivable: A 2 percent early-pay discount was offered to customers that paid their outstanding invoices within 15 days of the invoice date. A number of customers took advantage of this offer as $500,000 of additional customer payments were received prior to the FYE 12/31/23, generating $490,000 of cash and resulting in $10,000 of discount expense.

5. Asset, Inventory: PEB evaluated an offer by a third party to purchase $3,000,000 of finished goods inventory for 25% on the dollar (for a cash sale, no credit terms provided). The company accepted this offer as it already had set aside a reserve for $2,000,000. PEG will receive $750,000 of cash but will absorb another $250,000 loss on the inventory. PEB's executive management team had already decided to phase out the reselling of various technology products. It felt it was worth exiting the business more aggressively based on the company's 2024 business plan. This decision is risky as the company will absorb an additional one-time expense of $250,000. Not only does the strategy generate immediate cash, but carrying/management costs associated with inventory should also be reduced. Sometimes, you have to take the money and run.

6. Asset, Prepaid Expenses: In the past, SEB paid for certain prepaid expenses in advance, such as its general liability and property insurance, various software licenses, and similar items. The company has elected to set up installment payments for these expenses in 2024, which will increase expenses slightly during FYE 12/31/24 as the insurance and software license companies will include an additional fee to accommodate PEB's request. This strategy change freed up $250,000 of cash as of FYE 12/31/23.

There you have it; the cash-generating strategy has been set and executed during the fourth quarter of operations ending 12/31/23. Please refer to the next section to evaluate the results and impact on the SEB's financial statements. One note: The company elected not to sell or liquidate any long-term tangible and intangible assets for a couple of reasons. First, selling these types of assets often takes added time as generating quick cash is usually difficult (but not impossible). Second, if certain long-term capital assets are sold, it may damage the company's strategic business plan down the road (which PEB's management team is keenly aware of).

Crunching the Numbers: Let's Visualize SEB's Efforts

Please refer to Exhibit 13.1, which presents the evolution of SEB's balance sheet (in numbers) from our base case operating scenario (as previously presented in Exhibit 5.5) to our low or worst-case scenario for the business. I've included references to the previously discussed cash-raising strategies to help you track the impact on the balance sheet and income statement.

SEB's management team accomplished its mission by increasing the company's cash balance by roughly $3,200,000 as of FYE 12/31/23. This did come at a cost (refer to Exhibit 13.2), but the additional expenses incurred of $177,000 were digestible by the company and manageable with its external capital sources.

Now, let's also examine the impact on SEB's revised income statement for FYE 12/31/23, assuming the company's executive management team implemented the tactics/strategies summarized in the previous section.

SEB's net income decreased from roughly $813,000 in our original base case scenario to approximately $636,000 in our alternative ending scenario, representing a decrease of roughly $177,000, or 22 percent. While no company likes to intentionally realize additional expenses, in this situation, sacrificing $177,000 of net income to raise over $3,000,000 of cash was deemed an appropriate strategy by SEB's executive management team. Will implementing these strategies pay off in 2024? Only time will tell, but having an extra cash war chest to navigate what could be a turbulent year provides extra comfort for the company.

The financial information presented in Exhibits 13.1 and 13.2 represents an alternative ending for SEB. The financial reports and statements offered previously for SEB were prepared to help you understand different strategies related to increasing cash balances from internal financial business sources. Other strategies could have been presented in addition to the six I provided, but the idea remains the same. At some point, just about every business will have to implement strategies to generate increases in cash balances when times are tough.

EXHIBIT 13.1—ALTERNATIVE ENDING BALANCE SHEET—BASE CASE (SEB)

Unaudited—Prepared by Company Management (for internal review & discussion only)

Balance Sheet as of the Fiscal Year Ending	Ref.	Original 12/31/2023	Change	Alternative 12/31/2023	
Assets					
Current Assets:					
Cash & Equivalents		$ 2,163,748	$ 3,247,875	$ 5,411,623	Target cash increase of $3 million achieved.
Accounts Receivable	(4)	$ 8,009,000	$ (500,000)	$ 7,509,000	Customer early pay amount, discount in P&L.
Inventory	(5)	$ 1,706,000	$(1,000,000)	$ 706,000	Bulk inventory sale, added loss in P&L.
Prepaid Expenses	(6)	$ 625,000	$ (250,000)	$ 375,000	Installment agreements, no 2023 P&L impact.
Total Current Assets		$12,503,748	$ 1,497,875	$14,001,623	
Long-Term Operating & Other Assets:					
Property, Machinery, & Equipment		$ 4,500,000	$ 0	$ 4,500,000	
Less: Accumulated Depreciation		$ (2,214,285)	$ 0	$ (2,214,285)	
Net Property, Machinery, & Equipment		$ 2,285,715	$ 0	$ 2,285,715	
Other Assets:					
Intangible Assets, Net		$ 6,000,000	$ 0	$ 6,000,000	
Other Assets		$ 100,000	$ 0	$ 100,000	
Total Long-Term Operating & Other Assets		$ 8,385,715	$ 0	$ 8,385,715	
Total Assets		$20,889,463	$ 1,497,875	$22,387,338	
Liabilities					
Current Liabilities:					
Accounts Payable	(2)	$ 1,459,000	$ 175,000	$ 1,634,000	Pushing on vendor terms, small P&L impact.
Accrued Liabilities Payable		$ 1,258,000	$ 0	$ 1,258,000	
Short-Term Loans Payable	(1)	$ 2,400,000	$ 1,000,000	$ 3,400,000	Added borrowings, increased interest expense in P&L.
Other Current Liabilities & Deferred Revenue	(3)	$ 1,348,148	$ 500,000	$ 1,848,148	Early-bird sales success, no 2923 P&L impact.
Total Current Liabilities		$ 6,465,148	$ 1,675,000	$ 8,140,148	
Long-Term Liabilities:					
Loans Payable & Other Long-Term Debt, Less ST Loans		$ 2,500,000	$ 0	$ 2,500,000	
Total Liabilities		$ 8,965,148	$ 1,675,000	$10,640,148	
Stockholders' Equity					
Capital Stock		$10,000,000	$ 0	$10,000,000	
Retained Earnings		$ 1,924,315	$ (177,125)	$ 1,747,190	
Total Stockholders' Equity		$11,924,315	$ (177,125)	$11,747,190	
Total Liabilities & Stockholders' Equity		$20,889,463	$ 1,497,875	$22,387,338	

Confidential—Property of QW Example Tech, Inc.

EXHIBIT 13.2—ALTERNATIVE ENDING INCOME STATEMENT—BASE CASE (SEB)

Unaudited—Prepared by Company Management (for internal review & discussion only)

Income Statement For the Fiscal Years Ending	Ref.	Original 12/31/2023	Change	Alternative 12/31/2023	
Sales Revenue, Net	(4)	$ 59,494,321	$ (10,000)	$ 59,484,321	Added sales discount on early pays.
Costs of Sales Revenue, Service		$(14,374,000)		$(14,374,000)	
Costs of Sales Revenue, Products		$ (7,392,000)		$ (7,392,000)	
Gross Profit (aka Gross Margin)		$ 37,728,321	$ (10,000)	$ 37,718,321	
Operating Expenses:					
Selling, General, & Administrative	(2)	$ 25,288,772	$ 5,000	$ 25,293,772	Added fees from vendors for longer payment terms.
Research & Development		$ 7,139,000		$ 7,139,000	
Depreciation & Amortization		$ 1,642,856		$ 1,642,856	
Total Operating Expenses		$ 34,070,628	$ 5,000	$ 34,075,628	
Operating Income (Loss)		$ 3,657,694	$ (15,000)	$ 3,642,694	
Other Expenses (Income):					
Other Expenses or (Income)	(5)	$ 2,000,000	$250,000	$ 2,250,000	Additional write-off of value related to bulk sale.
Interest Expense	(1)	$ 407,000	$ 7,500	$ 414,500	Additional interest expense on loan advance.
Total Other Expenses (Income)		$ 2,407,000	$257,500	$ 2,664,500	
Net Income (Loss) before Income Taxes		$ 1,250,694	$(272,500)	$ 978,194	
Income Tax Expense (Benefit)		$ 438,000	$ (95,375)	$ 342,625	Lower tax expense as a result of added losses.
Net Income (Loss) after Income Taxes		$ 812,694	$(177,125)	$ 635,569	

Confidential—Property of QW Example Tech, Inc.

PEB's Unintended Consequences

I would be remiss if I didn't include an analysis of the irony associated with our aggressive case study, PEB. If you recall, I kept income tax constant to drive home the key point related to cash balances in Chapter 10. Now, let's change this and assume that PEB has income tax expense of 35 percent of net pre-tax income during the FYE 12/31/23. Please refer to Exhibits 13.3 and 13.4, which represent PEB's income statement and balance sheet for the FYE 12/31/22 and 12/31/23, paying close attention to three items: income tax expense, retained earnings, and the company's cash balance. Note: I have not represented the statement of cash flows to maintain the focus on income tax expense and cash balances. This same analysis could be completed for our case study company, FB, with results similar expected. I elected not to include additional exhibits for FB as the same logic would apply.

In this adjusted and revised scenario, you will notice that PEB's income tax expense has increased significantly, both in the FYEs 12/31/22 and 12/31/23 (by approximately $700,000 and $1,915,000, respectively), with a corresponding decrease in net income. I've kept the connection to the balance sheet very simple and have assumed the entire increase in income tax expense was paid during the year, so the resulting impact is to reduce the cash balance at the end of each year and the retained earnings balances by the same amount. The end result is that PEB has little to no cash on its balance sheet as of the FYE 12/31/22 and 12/31/23, which may create concerns with external parties.

EXHIBIT 13.3—ADJUSTED & REVISED AUDITED FINANCIAL STATEMENTS—INCOME STATEMENT, AGGRESSIVE CASE (PEB)

Dollar Amounts in Thousands

Income Statement		
For the Fiscal Years Ending	**12/31/2022**	**12/31/2023**
Sales Revenue, Net	$ 54,342	$ 60,650
Costs of Sales Revenue, Service	$(12,882)	$(14,624)
Costs of Sales Revenue, Products	$(11,040)	$ (7,392)
Gross Profit (aka Gross Margin)	$ 30,420	$ 38,634
Operating Expenses:		
Selling, General, & Administrative	$ 22,567	$ 25,089
Research & Development	$ 4,192	$ 4,639
Depreciation & Amortization	$ 1,205	$ 1,776
Total Operating Expenses	$ 27,964	$ 31,504
Operating Income (Loss)	$ 2,456	$ 7,130
Other Expenses (Income):		
Other Expenses or (Income)	$ 0	$ 0
Interest Expense	$ 339	$ 407
Total Other Expenses (Income)	$ 339	$ 407
Net Income (Loss) before Income Taxes	$ 2,117	$ 6,723
Income Tax Expense (Benefit)	*$ 741*	*$ 2,353*
Net Income (Loss) after Income Taxes	$ 1,376	$ 4,370
Increase in Income Tax Expense	*$ 700*	*$ 1,915*

See Notes to Financial Statements

EXHIBIT 13.4—ADJUSTED & REVISED AUDITED FINANCIAL STATEMENTS—BALANCE SHEET, AGGRESSIVE CASE (PEB)

Dollar Amounts in Thousands

Balance Sheet as of the Fiscal Year Ending	12/31/2022	12/31/2023
Assets		
Current Assets:		
Cash & Equivalents	$ 75	$ 249
Accounts Receivable	$ 6,776	$ 9,209
Inventory	$ 3,822	$ 3,706
Prepaid Expenses	$ 600	$ 625
Total Current Assets	$11,273	$13,789
Long-Term Operating & Other Assets:		
Property, Machinery, & Equipment	$ 4,000	$ 4,500
Less: Accumulated Depreciation	$ (1,571)	$ (2,214)
Net Property, Machinery, & Equipment	$ 2,429	$ 2,286
Other Assets:		
Intangible Assets, Net	$ 5,200	$11,567
Other Assets	$ 100	$ 100
Total Long-Term Operating & Other Assets	$ 7,729	$13,952
Total Assets	$19,002	$27,741

Balance Sheet as of the Fiscal Year Ending	12/31/2022	12/31/2023
Liabilities		
Current Liabilities:		
Accounts Payable	$ 1,405	$ 1,459
Accrued Liabilities Payable	$ 1,084	$ 1,508
Short-Term Loans Payable	$ 3,390	$ 2,400
Other Current Liabilities & Deferred Revenue	$ 656	$ 837
Total Current Liabilities	$ 6,535	$ 6,204
Long-Term Liabilities:		
Loans Payable & Other Long-Term Debt, Less ST Loans	$ 750	$ 2,500
Total Liabilities	$ 7,285	$ 8,704
Stockholders' Equity		
Capital Stock	$ 7,500	$10,000
Retained Earnings	$ 4,217	$ 9,037
Total Stockholders' Equity	$11,717	$19,037
Total Liabilities & Stockholders' Equity	$19,002	$27,741

See Notes to Financial Statements

The irony should be self-evident as here we have PEB, our most profitable business (of the three case studies), with almost no cash remaining at the end of the year. This is the unintended consequence of the aggressive case business: Without thinking through the full impact of its decisions, PEB's strategy could actually drain cash and liquidity from the business. Yes, PEB has probably developed strategies to manage this situation, but from a capital management perspective, there's nothing worse than coughing up cash for the government when it could be used for internal operating purposes. This highlights another lesson about how important it is for a business to manage its liquidity and cash proactively.

Raising Cash Quickly, Not for the Faint of Heart

Operating businesses in difficult economic times is not the most pleasant experience, and squeezing balance sheets is not for the faint of heart. It takes significant experience, thick skin, confidence, solid financial information, a delicate management balance, and a bit of luck to navigate these situations. But, as previously communicated earlier in this book, manufacturing cash from the balance sheet highlights exactly why I made the statement about the balance sheet being where losses go to hide, cash goes to die, and the bullshit goes to lie.

When a strategy is implemented to squeeze the balance sheet to generate cash, a well-thought-out plan must be implemented and executed well in advance. If you wait too long and let your lenders, suppliers, and customers drive the process and dictate terms (or suspect that the business may be entering a difficult operating period), then the business will most likely find itself with limited options and flexibility (to manufacture cash). As the old saying goes, banks and lenders want to lend money when you need it the least and never seem to provide new loans when you need it the most.

When running a business, it is essential to maintain proper levels of liquidity and cash to manage through the good times and the bad. Trust me when I say that there is nothing worse than running out of cash, except being surprised that you have run out of cash. When this happens, be prepared to have to accept extremely expensive terms to bring in cash quickly, as the vultures will no doubt be waiting to feast!

14

NET PROFITS AND CASH FLOW: REAL OR IMAGINARY

Introductory courses in business or economics generally start by introducing principles or concepts that are universal in nature, simple to understand, and extremely important. In Economics 101, the central concept is supply and demand; that is, higher supply combined with lower demand results in falling prices, and vice versa when supply is constrained and demand is high. For Business 101, the central concept is that all companies must generate a profit to remain in business. Translation: Annual sales revenue must exceed annual expenses, equating to an annual profit.

It seems simple enough, but in today's economic environment, the public equity markets continue to provide opportunities for companies like Uber to remain in business even though they consume hefty amounts of cash and generate large losses. After 15 years in business, Uber generated its first profit ever in 2022. Can this go on forever? Probably not (unless, of course, you are the United States government, which racks up huge deficits and debt that will most likely never be repaid), but when public equity markets are operating in an optimistic mindset, companies like Uber can continue to raise capital (i.e., cash) in hopes of eventually being profitable. Unfortunately, most companies cannot operate like Uber and absorb years of losses covered by round after round of financing. Yes, they exist, but no, that is not the real world.

Seldom does a newly launched business or operating unit generate a net profit right out of the gate. It usually takes a lot of time to create a business plan, launch the business, develop markets, and deliver reliable products (or services) in ample volume to cover all expenses and generate a profit. This is generally the rule rather than the exception, and kudos to those businesses that can generate real profits out of the gate, but rarely, and I mean rarely, is this the case. Companies must grow, adapt, and adjust their business models over a period of time to eventually reach profitability that can be delivered in a reliable, year-over-year fashion. The balance of this chapter focuses on profit-generating strategies, both real and illusory, that companies utilize to improve profitability.

Fixed, Variable, and Semi-Variable Expenses

The next section of this chapter delves into a deeper analysis of how companies make various business decisions to improve profitability. But before I discuss various profit-making strategies, a quick refresher course is warranted on the three primary types of expense a business incurs: fixed, variable, and semi-variable.

1. ***Fixed:*** Fixed expenses represent costs that are fixed, set, or firm over an extended period (e.g., a year or more) and are often referred to as period expenses. A perfect example of a fixed expense would be a building lease requiring a company to pay $10,000 a month for the next 60 months (representing a five-year lease), regardless of how much sales the company generates or profits it earns. Depreciation expense is another example of a period or fixed expense. For example, if a company has a $1,000,000 asset and depreciates it over 60 months, each month the company will record depreciation expense of $16,667. Further examples of fixed costs include subscription or technology support contracts that may run a year or longer and wages paid to company executives that may have a long-term guaranteed employment agreement.
2. ***Variable:*** Variable expenses represent costs that vary directly with sales revenue levels based either on the number of units sold or the price realized. For example, an e-commerce retailer that sells clothing should know that for each pair of a specific type of shoe sold, the cost of each pair is $12. If the retailer sells 100 pairs of shoes, it incurs $1,200 in expenses; if zero pairs of shoes are sold, it incurs $0 in expenses. It is important to note that the variable nature of expenses is not related to unit volume alone, as some expenses are associated with price and not volume. An example of this would be merchant fees paid to credit card processing companies that charge 2.5 percent for every dollar a company receives from credit card sales.
3. ***Semi-variable:*** Semi-variable expenses are fixed over the short term (e.g., 90 days or less), but over the medium or longer term, can increase or decrease with some degree of proactive control by company management as business conditions dictate. Regular employee wages and burden (e.g., payroll taxes, health insurance, etc.) provide an example of this, as a company may establish a staff level of 10 full-time employees operating in a customer support and service function based

on an anticipated sales range of $3 million to $5 million over a 90-day period. The company may commit to this staffing level for the first 90 days and then adjust its headcount based on actual sales revenue achieved and revised outlooks.

Smart businesses realize that it is just as important to understand business expenses by function (e.g., costs of goods sold or costs of sales, direct operating expenses, corporate overhead, general, and administrative, and other expenses) as it is to recognize the implications of fixed, variable, or semi-variable expenses. This allows companies to adjust operations and pivot or adapt quickly to changing business conditions, cutting expenses when needed and adding expenses if warranted.

Generating Real Profits

It is important to understand the business economics of attempting to improve profits by driving top-line sales, which is not as easy as simply increasing sales to increase profits. As will be clear in Exhibit 14.1, there are situations in which driving higher sales can lead to increased losses. I should note that I've elected to deviate from our case study companies and present another fictional business, one that operates in the direct-to-consumer (DTC) or e-commerce retail industry. The reason for this is twofold. First, even though the company presented in Exhibit 14.1 is fictional, the financial analysis and decisions it faces are very, very real. Second, the DTC/e-commerce industry is extremely large and continues to experience rapid growth, so our fictional example is very relevant to today's economy.

Exhibit 14.1 provides a simple example of an e-commerce company attempting to drive top-line sales to increase operating profits by increasing sales price (scenario #3) or sales volume (scenario #2). This exhibit also presents a summarized income statement that incorporates the concepts of fixed, variable, and semi-variable expenses.

What do the results of our analysis tell us? Should our e-commerce company drive sales or profits? Consider the following:

- Scenario 1 displays a company that can generate a reasonable operating profit of roughly $202,000 on approximately $7.5 million of sales revenue. It's not a horrible performance, but it is something management would like to improve, as a 4.28 percent operating margin will not cut it with the investors (as well as the industry standard being closer to 10 percent). Please note that the company's corporate overhead or fixed annual costs are expected to remain at $1.5 million under all the scenarios. This is because the company's corporate infrastructure has been designed to support annual sales levels ranging from $5 to $10 million.
- In Scenario 2, unit sales volumes are increased by 10 percent, but this comes at a significant cost. Not only is the average selling price reduced from $215 to $204 (as more aggressive discounting is required to sell more units), but the company incurs higher direct selling expenses (i.e., advertising and commissions) to push 10 percent more units out the door. The result speaks for itself. Even though the company increased top-line sales, it swung from an operating profit to an operating loss via the increased direct selling expenses combined with the lower net sales price per unit. This scenario highlights the impact of stable variable unit costs at $75 per unit, but with a lower average sales price, the company's gross margin decreases from 62.6 percent to 60.8 percent.
- Scenario 3 is our surprise. Even with lower top-line sales revenue, the company was able to generate a higher gross margin,

EXHIBIT 14.1—E-COMMERCE PROFITABILITY ANALYSIS

Unaudited—Prepared by Company Management (for internal review & discussion only)

Description	Scenario #1 Amount	% of Sales	Scenario #2 Amount	% of Sales	Scenario #3 Amount	% of Sales
Selling KPIs, Annual:						
Number of Units Sold	35,000		38,500		31,500	
Average Selling Price	$ 215		$ 204		$ 226	
Average Cost of Unit, Fully Loaded	$ 75		$ 75		$ 75	
Average Merchant Fee, % of Sales	2.50%		2.50%		2.50%	
Average Direct Selling Expense, Adv. & Comm.	40.00%		42.00%		38.00%	
Summary Income Statement, Annual:						
Sales Revenue	$ 7,525,000	100.00%	$ 7,863,625	100.00%	$ 7,111,125	100.00%
Costs of Goods Sold, Unit	$(2,625,000)	–34.88%	$(2,887,500)	–36.72%	$(2,362,500)	–33.22%
Costs of Sales, Merchant Fee	$ (188,125)	–2.50%	$ (196,591)	–2.50%	$ (177,778)	–2.50%
Gross Profit	$ 4,711,875	62.62%	$ 4,779,534	60.78%	$ 4,570,847	64.28%
Gross Margin	62.62%		60.78%		64.28%	
Direct Selling Expenses, Advertising & Commissions	$ 3,010,000	40.00%	$ 3,302,723	42.00%	$ 2,702,228	38.00%
Corporate Overhead (Fixed Costs)	$ 1,500,000	19.93%	$ 1,500,000	19.08%	$ 1,500,000	21.09%
Operating Profit (EBITDA)	$ 201,875	2.68%	$ (23,188)	–0.29%	$ 368,619	5.18%
Operating Margin (EBITDA Margin)	4.28%		–0.49%		8.06%	

Confidential—Property of XYZ DtoC Example, Inc.

which, when combined with lower direct selling expenses and a static fixed cost structure, achieved an operating profit of roughly $370,000. This amounts to an operating margin of 8.06 percent, which is more in line with industry standards. Of particular importance is that the company's direct selling expenses for advertising and commissions decreased to 38 percent from 42 percent (in Scenario 2). This was achieved by proactively reducing semi-variable advertising and commission expenses by eliminating ineffective advertising and unproductive sales representatives.

This example was provided to highlight a common trap or mistake companies make with their business models. Companies will often try to impress investors by highlighting rapid sales growth without paying attention to the bottom line. They do this in an attempt to attract investors and raise capital by basically saying, "Look how fast I'm growing. You'd better get on the bandwagon." They also hope to dispel worries about profits by implying they will come as the business matures. Translation: I will grow our way into profits. This makes no sense because the company loses money on each incremental unit sale.

This growth-at-all-cost mentality can excite investors, but it quickly becomes apparent that chasing incremental sales by targeting weaker customers with more aggressive selling strategies will generally lead to increased losses, higher cash burn rates, and the need for ever more financial capital to stay afloat.

Exhibit 14.2 provides a second perspective on how operating profits can be increased, even though direct costs of sales have increased and the company's gross margin has decreased. Our example this time is presented for a fictional professional service company (again, very real business model in today's economy) that bills out its staff on various consulting projects.

Here are the key outputs indicating why this company would be willing to operate with an overall lower gross margin (decreasing from 37.5 percent to 35.06 percent) for the benefit of increasing top-line sales and operating profits:

- Note that the company's average bill rate decreased from $200 per hour to $175 per hour, but at the same time, the company was able to secure large new consulting projects, enabling it to increase annual billable hours by 13,312. Further, the average hourly fully burdened staff cost (which includes wages, payroll taxes, insurance, training, paid time off, etc.) decreased from $125 to $114. This decrease did not come from paying employees less; rather, the company realized that by taking on additional consulting projects, the staff's productivity level would increase by 7.5 percent (i.e., the company can keep their staff busier and bill more hours of work). Translation, the staff is being managed and billed to jobs more efficiently.
- Another key to the company's improved operating performance is that direct operating and corporate overhead expenses only increased slightly between the scenarios (by roughly $68,000). The reason is that the company realized it had adequate infrastructure to support the increase in sales, thus spreading more sales revenue over a relatively constant expense structure. Even though the incremental gross margin for the increase in business amounted to only 24.24 percent, by leveraging fixed expenses more efficiently, the company could improve annual operating profits by $295,000 and increase its operating margin from 13.24 percent to 21.87 percent.

A key concept illustrated in Exhibit 14.2 is the theory of economies of scale. When a company has made a fixed investment in infrastructure or capital assets, it should be able to gain efficiencies by utilizing or leveraging the fixed investment more efficiently with marginal increases in sales. Economies of scale take hold in manufacturing companies, considering how significant certain periods or fixed expenses can be, such as building leases or equipment depreciation. If a manufacturing company can increase production (and sales) by 25 percent, but its fixed expenses remain largely the same, it can spread higher sales volumes at the same expense level. This should drive higher profits (assuming the ultimate sales price is adequate to cover variable product costs).

I close this section by highlighting three critical concepts. First, completeness is essential. Focusing on only one line item of operating results (e.g., top-line sales revenue) can be dangerous.

EXHIBIT 14.2—LOCAL PROFESSIONAL SERVICE COMPANY PROFITABILITY ANALYSIS

Unaudited—Prepared by Company Management (for internal review & discussion only)

Description	Scenario #1 Amount	% of Sales	Scenario #2 Amount	% of Sales	Variance Amount
Selling KPIs, Annual:					
Hours of Staff Time Billed	33,280		46,592		13,312
Average Hourly Bill Rate	$ 200		$ 175		$ (25)
Average Hourly Staff Cost, Fully Burdened	$ 125		$ 114		$ 11
Direct Operating & Account Mgmt. Expenses	10.00%		9.00%		1.00%
Summary Income Statement, Annual:					
Sales Revenue	$ 6,656,000	100.00%	$ 8,153,600	100.00%	$ 1,497,600
Costs of Sales, Staff Wages & Burden	$(4,160,000)	-62.50%	$(5,294,545)	-64.94%	$(1,134,545)
Gross Profit	$ 2,496,000	37.50%	$ 2,859,055	35.06%	$ 363,055
Gross Margin	37.50%		35.06%		24.24%
Direct Operating & Account Mgmt. Expenses	$ 665,600	10.00%	$ 733,824	9.00%	$ (68,224)
Corporate Overhead (Fixed Costs)	$ 1,500,000	22.54%	$ 1,500,000	18.40%	$ 0
Operating Profit (EBITDA)	$ 330,400	4.96%	$ 625,231	7.67%	$ 294,831
Operating Margin (EBITDA Margin)	13.24%		21.87%		8.63%

Confidential—Property of Local Sample Service Co, Inc.

When completing profitability analyses, understanding the impact on sales is just the start of the food chain, as flowing the analysis through gross profits and operating profits is critical.

Second, it's essential to have a clear understanding of the three primary expense types of variable, fixed, and semi-variable, and how these expenses relate to both volume and price changes. Third, improving real profits should drive real cash flow and thus improve the real value of a business. No accounting or financial gimmick here, as the goal is to ensure that sound economic business decisions can be made to increase real profits and cash.

Manufacturing Imaginary Profits

Chapter 20 of *How to Read a Financial Report*, 10th Edition, presents the concept of financial statement engineering. I take this opportunity to expand on how profits can be "manufactured" by using accounting strategies. (This idea contrasts with the previous section, where I discussed generating real profits and cash flow.) I would also like to be clear that the content provided in this section should not be confused with accounting or financial fraud. Rather, the concepts highlighted below originate from companies adjusting or changing specific accounting policies, procedures, use of estimates, and so on over several years as business conditions or operating circumstances change. These are legitimate (per GAAP) but warrant a closer look by internal and external parties when companies move down this path. I have provided four examples for you to chew (or maybe the more appropriate word would be gag) on:

1. ***Change in estimate:*** Chapter 8 provided insight into a company's investment cycle related to intangible assets, including selecting appropriate depreciation and amortization estimates (to appropriately expense the consumption of an asset over a period of time). Companies may elect to revise these estimates based on changes to their operating environment. For example, suppose an asset was anticipated to be fully consumed and depreciated over a five-year period. However, revised management estimates indicate that the asset has a longer life, so the life was extended to seven years. As a result, the period depreciation expense would decrease because the asset would be depreciated over a longer period. The same logic could apply when amortizing intellectual property. The point is that a simple change in an estimate from five to seven years could impact operating performance significantly. Other examples include a company changing an estimate for potential sales returns or future warranty-related costs as they scrub operating results to be more accurate. I will let you decide if a company scrubbing operating results is being done legitimately or to achieve a specific performance target, but as I noted in Chapter 9 (when I discussed the use of estimates when calculating accrued liabilities), accounting estimates are always an area that should demand attention.

2. ***Change in policy:*** A change in accounting estimate should not be confused with a change in accounting policy. For example, a company may change its policy of capitalizing assets on the balance sheet versus expensing costs in the income statement. Research and development costs that were expensed historically may now be capitalized as an intangible asset and amortized over an appropriate period (as management has determined that the R&D costs are a valuable long-term asset). In either case, cash still flows out

the door, but companies may want to "park" the capitalized asset on the balance sheet and then depreciate or amortize the asset over a period of time, helping improve the income statement.

3. ***Interest rates:*** Interest rates were at historic lows (some would say artificially low, manipulated by the Fed), really dating all the way back to 2008 and running through 2021 (until the Fed started to raise rates in 2022). Interest rates significantly impact business valuations, with low interest rates having the effect of increasing business valuations (above reasonable levels). The same logic applies to specific assets, such as intellectual property or proprietary content that will generate future cash flows. In effect, low interest rates prop up asset values by discounting the future cash flow at a low rate (which increases the asset's future value). Companies may attempt to justify using lower interest rates to support a higher asset value and avoid writing off the asset or having to expense the asset over a shorter period.
4. ***Cleaning house:*** The three previous examples focused on how a company may inflate operating profits and earnings. The concept of cleaning house does the exact opposite. A common strategy companies use when they need to deliver bad news (to the market or investors) is to deliver all the bad news at once. Simply put, let us clean house with all potential write-offs, adjustments, losses, and so on in one time period to sacrifice the current year and build a clean basis to drive profits in future years. Mind you, no cash changes hands with these types of events; rather, the balance sheet is simply adjusted to eliminate the crap (e.g., worthless inventory, unsupportable assets, quickly fading IP/content, etc.). If you refer back to our example company SEB and its story, a similar cleaning house strategy was used but slightly differently. You will notice a large decrease in the inventory value as of the FYE 12/31/23 compared to the FYE 12/31/22, dropping from $3,822,000 to $1,706,000 (refer to Exhibit 5.5). You might also note an "other expense" of $2,000,000 in the FYE 12/31/23 (which, as a reminder, represents writing off worthless inventory of $2,000,000). For the company to stay profitable each year, (for whatever reason) management elected to write-off the inventory and record the adjustment during the FYE 12/31/23 when higher profits were present (to absorb the hit). Further, management concluded that this represents a one-time expense from a discontinued product line that will be nonrecurring (thus, it is captured below the operating income or EBITDA line).

I would like to emphasize two important points related to manufacturing profits. First, in the four examples provided above, no cash changes hands. None, zero, zip! This is to say that the losses are not real, as somewhere in the past, cash was impacted by either investing in a long-term asset or buying inventory (to provide two examples). Yes, the losses are very much real and the company's management team needs to be held accountable for any performance issues. But the adjustments noted above represent a sleight of accounting hand to move expenses or costs between the balance sheet and income statement in a manner that is, for lack of a better term, *desirable* (to achieve certain goals or confirm a story).

Second, there is nothing inherently wrong with these strategies, especially when a company's external CPA auditor has agreed to the changes and confirms that the changes comply with GAAP. But you should always watch for these items in relation to the size of adjustments, the frequency, and the reasoning/validity. These clues may indicate a management effort to massage the financial results or, worse yet, weaknesses in the company's internal accounting system and financial information reporting.

Cash Flow as Our Validation

This should sound familiar by now: Understand the income statement, trust the balance sheet, and, most importantly, rely on the statement of cash flows. Given the amount of leeway companies have with preparing the balance sheet and income statement, the statement of cash flows can help root out inconsistencies or peculiarities in a company's financial results by following the flow of cash. In a sense, the statement of cash flows acts as a de facto audit mechanism to help validate the economic viability of the business.

You may hear statements from time to time such as "in the black but where's the green," which refers to a company generating a profit but experiencing cash flow difficulties. This may be fully explainable and perfectly normal for a high-growth business that is consuming large amounts of capital and internal earnings to finance growth. But the company's operating story, financial statements, reports, and financial information should all be aligned in a manner that makes sense. When financial imbalances arise, they can usually be traced directly to a company's ability to generate positive cash flows.

15

DECIPHERING THE CAP TABLE AND CAP STACK

I have elected to hold our final discussion and addition of bonus material to the last section of the balance sheet, owners' or stockholders' equity. I've elected to include this bonus material because, although it represents more complex financial information that appears in financial reports and financial statements, for any of you aspiring entrepreneurs, it offers absolutely critical information and concepts related to helping you understand and maintain ownership control of a business. This is pretty darn important financial information because it not only reveals who is in control of a business from an ownership perspective, but it also illuminates the motivations of ownership in terms of establishing accounting policies and procedures and how these impact preparing financial reports and financial statements. If nothing else in this book, you should have gained an additional appreciation of how financial reports and financial statements are impacted based on different ownership structures for FB (our family-owned and operated business), SEB (our Steady Eddy controlled and operated business that takes a more conservative approach), and PEB (our private equity controlled and operated business that focuses on growing the business aggressively).

As a reminder, the stockholders' equity section of the balance sheet appears on the bottom of the right-hand side of the balance sheet (from a horizontal perspective) or at the bottom of the second page (from a vertical perspective). It is no coincidence that I have saved this topic for the end of the book. After learning the whats, whens, wheres, and hows of financial information, I focus on who owns and controls a business (and why this is so critical, beyond the obvious reasons).

Before I dive into explaining owners' equity in more depth, I would like to preface our discussion by highlighting two points:

1. For those readers who are operating a business unit or division of an existing business, our discussion on owners' equity and business capitalization may not appear to be all that relevant. (*Why bother? The corporate mothership raises capital and manages the owners and creditors.*) The topics covered in this chapter could be useful for you to understand beyond just how your organization is capitalized. It is important to clearly understand that whether it be working with customers, suppliers, strategic partners, or the like, any third party's ownership can have a huge influence on future decision-making (and your relationship with these parties).
2. Most small businesses tend to be closely held and formed as either partnerships, subchapter S corporations, or single-owner limited liability companies (LLCs). For these entities, owners' equity is often an afterthought, as the net equity of these types of businesses is usually just comprised of two components: retained earnings and common equity. For these companies, retained earnings are nothing more than a business's cumulative net profits and losses, less any distributions of earnings paid (made over the year). Common equity captures the amount of capital contributed by the company's owners, who generally (and legally) should have the same rights to profits, distributions, voting, and so forth on a prorated basis to their actual ownership. That is, if one owner invested $20,000 in exchange for 2,000 common stock shares and another owner invested $10,000 in exchange for 1,000 common stock shares, the first owner should maintain rights to distributions of earnings, profits, and voting of 66.67 percent (2,000 shares owned out of 3,000 shares issued in total). Again, and by reading on, you as a small business owner will gain additional knowledge that may be useful when dealing with third parties or, better yet, if considering raising more complex forms of capital (and their pros and cons).

Our discussion on owners' equity will move well beyond smaller businesses and be directed toward more complex business capital structures that involve multiple types of equity and even quasi-forms of equity disguised as debt. All businesses will have retained earnings or, in the case of multiple years of losses, accumulated deficits, where cumulative losses are greater than cumulative profits. However, when companies utilize more complex legal entities such as C corporations or LLCs they also tend to use a wider range of equity to capitalize their business. This is commonly referred to as the capitalization table or (*cap table*).

The cap table is nothing more than a table or spreadsheet that spells out exactly who owns what in terms of the equity issued by a company as presented or listed by what type of equity has been issued. On the surface, reading a cap table should be relatively straightforward, as it should list various parties and their respective ownership percentage in the company's owner equity. However, the devil is absolutely in the details when understanding cap tables and the potential impact of what owners truly control the company and have the most advantageous ownership stakes.

I have laid out the topics covered in this chapter from the perspective of the equity owner's rights to claims against the company instead of the total amount of equity owned. This may seem somewhat convoluted, but you will quickly understand why it is important to understate rights and preferences in lockstep with total ownership interest. For simplicity, our discussion focuses on three main components of a typical cap table:

1. Risk-based debt (e.g., convertible notes)
2. Preferred equity
3. Common equity, options, and warrants

Before I dive into these topics in more depth, a quick word is warranted on the primary available sources of equity capital (from the market). Raising equity can be achieved by pursuing different sources of capital ranging from tapping what I like to refer to as FF&CBAs (family, friends, and close business associates) who are often unsophisticated when making investment decisions through to taking a company public through an IPO (a complex process targeting sophisticated investors).

In between these two extremes is equity capital, which is usually raised from groups that have a keen expertise in providing the right financial capital at the right time and include VCs (venture capitalists), PEs or PEGs (private equity or private equity groups), HNWIs (high-net-worth individuals, sometimes referred to as angel investors), HFs (hedge funds), and other similar types of capital sources. These groups tend to specialize by industry or company stage. They usually have significant capital to deploy and employ highly qualified management teams to assess investment opportunities.

Equity Disguised as Debt

Companies that cannot raise capital from traditional debt sources, such as banks or alternative-based lenders, and which do not want to raise equity capital (over fears of diluting the ownership and control of the company) will often use what is commonly referred to as convertible debt (a hybrid form of debt and equity that has characteristics of both).

Convertible debt is a form of actual debt (i.e., a loan to the company) that is reported on a company's balance sheet as a liability, similar to a note or loan payable. Most convertible debt is structured to be long term, with typical repayment terms of two to five years. At the option of the party providing the loan or if a specific event occurs (e.g., a qualified financing event occurs such as the company raises over $10,000,000 of new equity), convertible debt can be converted into the company's common or preferred equity. The conversion of the debt may occur for any number of reasons, including the company achieving a milestone such as a predetermined sales revenue level being met or if the company raises a large amount of equity (the triggering event), the company is sold, or if the due date of the convertible debt is reached and the debt cannot be repaid.

A logical question at this point is why would a company want to raise money using convertible debt and, conversely, why would an external party want to invest in convertible debt? I answer both questions as follows:

1. ***Issuing convertible debt to raise capital:*** Raising capital through issuing convertible debt is often used by companies that need to bridge the business (by providing a capital infusion) to get from point D to point F to help substantiate a higher valuation. If a company is worth $X at point D but can see itself worth three times more at point F (based on achieving key milestones), it will be able to raise equity capital at a much higher valuation and reduce the risk of ownership dilution. Further, when companies do not qualify for traditional bank or alternative-based loans, it can tap a more junior or subordinated type of debt by raising capital through convertible debt (and, if structured correctly by the company, it can avoid providing an actual secured interest in company assets).

   Like traditional bank loans, convertible debt requires interest payments and has set repayment terms, but, generally speaking, these are structured very favorably for the company. That is, a below-market interest rate is provided, which is accrued monthly and not paid until the due date of the convertible debt. Further, it is not uncommon for convertible debt to not require periodic payments but come 100 percent due at the end of the term. Under this structure, the company has the maximum flexibility to use the capital raised for the longest period of time (as the debt interest and principal will not be due until the very end).

2. ***Investing in convertible debt to provide capital:*** Why would a convertible debt investment be of interest to third parties? First, debt has a higher seniority or claim against company assets than equity. Although convertible debt is often structured in a junior position to bank or alternative lender loans (i.e., these lenders have a higher claim to company assets in case of a company liquidation or bankruptcy, so they get paid first, assuming cash is available), they sit higher in the cap stack as it relates to distributing company assets in the event of an unfortunate or depressed company sale. Second, convertible debt investors can earn a set return on their investments from the interest rate established (such as 8 percent per annum), even though this may not be paid until the due date. Third, and maybe most importantly, the convertible debt investors have additional return upside via being able to convert into the company's equity down the road. It is quite common for convertible debt to include a feature that allows the investors to convert into the company's equity at a discount to a future capital raise. For example, the convertible debt investors may be provided a 20 percent discount against the price of the company's equity value established in a large subsequent equity capital raise. If the company raised a large amount of capital at $20 per share, the convertible debt investors would be allowed to convert the debt principal and any accrued interest at $16 per share (thus realizing an additional 20 percent return on their invested capital).

Similar to convertible debt, a company may raise capital by issuing a junior tranche of debt that has set repayment terms and interest rates established. But unlike convertible debt, warrants to purchase equity in the company may be attached instead of allowing the debt to convert. For example, if our sample company needed to sweeten the deal to entice the third-party lender to provide the loan of $8 million, it could offer a warrant to purchase 50,000 common shares at $1 per share at the lender's choice. Similar to the 20 percent discount provided to the investors in the convertible debt, the common stock warrant provides for an equity kicker to enhance the overall investment return well above the stated interest rate.

The nuances, details, and specifics surrounding convertible or junior debt are extensive and complex, and well beyond the scope of this book. The goal of this overview was not to make you an expert, but rather to socialize the concept of debt/equity hybrid forms of capital and why they are attractive to both the company raising capital and the investors providing capital. In effect, these forms of capital represent a middle-of-the-road strategy to help balance the use of debt and equity in one type of financial capital. As with all forms of financial capital, there are pros and cons associated with each form, so the trick is knowing when to use each form and, in all cases, making sure you have proper professional counsel to navigate the capital-raising process.

Preferred Equity and the Real Control

I now move further down the cap table and explore the wonderful world of preferred equity. Before beginning, I will look at where I stand in the investor priority list to make sure I understand the basic order of potential claims that creditors, investors, and owners would have against the company in the event of a liquidation, dissolution, or bankruptcy. Exhibit 15.1 provides a simple summary of the cap stack for our sample company PEB.

I present our sample company PEB's cap table in Exhibit 15.2, which emphasizes equity ownership (i.e., who owns what). The cap stack presented in Exhibit 15.1 emphasizes the pecking order of creditors, investors, and owners who have claims against company assets. It provides some comments and thoughts on who would get what in the event of liquidation event. It should be obvious that the cap stack can be a very sobering analysis for equity investors as, in this case, if the company had to liquidate and received $14,000,000 for all its assets because of a forced liquidation proceeding, it would have enough to cover the total liabilities of approximately $8,700,000 with just enough left over to repay the preferred stock owners, including their exit preference of 1.50x (see below) of $3,750,000 (leaving roughly $1,546,000 for the common stock owners).

The cap stack highlights the priority status of the preferred stock owners, who are below debt but above common stock owners. This is the first and most critical concept to understand about preferred equity or stock: It almost always has a *preference* to common equity or stock when it comes to not just rights to dividends or earnings (before the common equity) but more importantly, claims against company assets. In our sample company, the preferred equity holders have the right to receive an 10 percent annual dividend before any company earnings are returned to common stock owners in the form of dividends. The preferred equity investors also negotiated terms in this capital offering that include a 1.5x preference upon a liquidating event. What this means is that after all debt is satisfied, the preferred equity investors receive 150 percent of their capital investment (in this case $3,750,000 million) along with any declared but unpaid preferred stock dividends before the common stock owners receive anything (which is also referred to having a *first out* exit provision as their money is first out of the deal). To sweeten the deal, the preferred equity investors included a provision that allows them to convert their preferred stock to common stock upon a qualified event (e.g., a company sale that achieves a specific exit value or a successful IPO).

The second critical concept about preferred equity is that, usually, the investors demand a certain amount of management control, either directly or indirectly, with the company's affairs. For large, preferred capital raises, it is quite common for investors to demand a seat (or possibly two) on the board of directors. For a company that has five board members prior to the preferred capital raise, the terms of the raise may require that

EXHIBIT 15.1—CAP STACK SUMMARY—AGGRESSIVE CASE (PEB) (cap is short for capital)

Unaudited—Prepared by Company Management (for internal review & discussion only)

Summary of Liabilities & Equity	Priority Status	Amount	Notes/Comments
Payroll, Taxes, & Burden Payable	High	$ 1,240,000	Employee obligations are generally at the top of the list.
Income Taxes Payable	High	$ 146,000	Governments make sure they get their money.
Loans & Notes Payable, Secured	High	$ 4,900,000	Senior debt/secured against company assets.
Trade Payables & Accrued Liabilities	High/Med.	$ 1,581,000	Depending on terms with vendors, could be high or med.
Deferred Revenue & Other Current Lia.	Medium	$ 836,574	Customer advance payments & deposits not secured.
Other Long-Term Debt	Medium	$ 0	Other contingent debt, limited rights to assets.
Subtotal Liabilities		$ 8,703,574	
Preferred Stock	Med/Low	$ 2,500,000	Higher preference than common but lower than debt.
Common Stock	Low	$ 7,500,000	Basically last in priority with rights to company assets.
Common Stock Options & Warrants	Bottom	$ 0	Value dependent on successful company only.
Subtotal Shareholders' Equity		$10,000,000	
Total Liabilities & Equity		$18,703,574	
Hypothetical Liquidation:			
Net Proceeds from Liquidating the Business		$14,000,000	Estimate—for presentation purposes only.
Repayment of All Debt		$ (8,703,574)	Total liabilities per above.
Repayment of Preferred Equity with 1.5x Pref.		$ (3,750,000)	Preferred stock investment times 1.5 preference.
Balance Remaining to Cover Common Investors		$ 1,546,426	Not much is left over.
Recovery Ratio		20.62%	Basically recovering just 20% of their investments, ouch!

Confidential—Property of QW Example Tech, Inc.

EXHIBIT 15.2—CAP TABLE SUMMARY—AGGRESSIVE CASE (PEB)

Unaudited—Prepared by Company Management (for internal review & discussion only)

Description	Number of Shares	Invested Amount	Voting Issued & O/S % Owned	Fully Diluted % Owned
Preferred Equity:				
H&H Test VC Firm, Fund V	100,000	$ 2,500,000	15.38%	13.33%
Subtotal—Preferred Equity	100,000	$ 2,500,000	15.38%	13.33%
Common Equity:				
Founders, Original	350,000	$ 3,500,000	53.85%	46.67%
Investors, Various Parties	200,000	$ 4,000,000	30.77%	26.67%
Subtotal—Common Equity	550,000	$ 7,500,000	84.62%	73.33%
Common Equity Options & Warrants:				
Stock Options Issued & Outstanding	75,000	$ 0	0.00%	10.00%
Warrants Issued for Common Stock Purchases	25,000	$ 0	0.00%	3.33%
Subtotal—Common Equity Options & Warrants	100,000	$ 0	0.00%	13.33%
Total, All Forms of Equity	750,000	$10,000,000	100.00%	100.00%

Confidential—Property of QW Example Tech, Inc.

the board of directors increase to seven, of which two will be appointed by the preferred equity investors. There are clear reasons preferred equity investors demand board participation, including the ability for them to monitor their investment more closely, as well as to provide valuable executive management insight they may bring to the table. The point is that board participation represents direct strategic management involvement in the company.

Indirectly, the preferred investors can (and usually do) include several negative control provisions that help protect their investment. A few examples of negative control provisions include:

- Requiring 100 percent board approval to raise capital through another equity offering (so that better terms cannot be offered to the next investors at the expense of the current preferred investors)

- Limitations on how much and what type of loans or notes payable can be secured (without their approval)
- 100 percent board authorization and approval in the event the company sells the majority of its business interests.

When capital is raised in the form of preferred equity, the structure of these deals tends to strongly favor the preferred equity investors by providing significant financial preferences (to enhance their return) and management involvement (to protect and control their investments).

There is so much information and knowledge surrounding the subject of preferred equity that an entire book could be written on the terms, conditions, provisions, pros, cons, dos, don'ts, and I should have known betters. In closing, I would like to leave you with this perspective on preferred equity investments, specifically, how the financial community can put a spin on a company and inflate its value.

The financial community (especially VCs and PEGs) often makes references to unicorns, which are nothing more than start-ups or young companies that have achieved an extremely lofty valuation (usually $1 billion or more). The high valuation is derived from the fact that if a $100 million investment is made in a company that is valued at $1 billion, then the party(ies) making the investment own 10 percent of the company.

What they do not tell you is that the $100 million investment was made in preferred equity that includes the protections discussed in this chapter. If the company is successful and sells for $2 billion, the preferred investors can convert their preferred shares into common shares, still own 10 percent of the company, and sell out for $200 million. Not bad for the investment, as this is the story everyone wants to hear and achieve. But if the company struggles and is ultimately sold off the scrap heap for $250 million (still a tidy sum), the preferred investors do not get 10 percent ($25 million) but rather are protected with a 1x preference and will get their $100 million back.

Remember this, as when you hear about unicorn valuations, this is the value the investors *hope* the company will be worth down the road (not what it is worth now). If the company doesn't make it, the investors can cover their downside by investing in preferred equity with favorable terms. In other words, this is just more financial lingo and terminology to familiarize yourself with to make sure you understand the never-ending flow of bullshit oozing from the financial community.

Common Equity, Options, and Warrants

I conclude our discussion of the cap table by briefly discussing common stock ownership and common stock options or warrants. There is really not a lot to discuss, as the reference to common says it all. That is, with common stock, everyone is basically in the same bucket with rights to earnings, voting on company matters, claims against company assets, and similar matters. Larger companies may issue multiple types of common stock with a common feature being that the class A common stock has voting rights and the class B common stock has no voting rights, but this type of equity complexity is generally only found in the largest and most powerful companies (e.g., Alphabet's Class A and C common stock).

Exhibit 15.2 presents PEB's cap table, which reflects ownership by what type of equity owns what percentage of the company.

The items of importance in the cap table are as follows:

- Two columns of ownership percentages have been provided, voting and fully diluted. Voting captures only the equity that is issued, outstanding, and has voting rights. Since common stock options and warrants are nothing more than rights to purchase common stock at a later date, they do not have voting rights (thus the 0 percent ownership in this column). The fully diluted column calculates the ownership percentages of the company if all forms of equity were issued and outstanding and held equal rights.
- An item of significant importance is the voting ownership percentage of 53.85 percent controlled by the common equity group referenced as founders. This indicates that the founders of the company have majority control (just over 50 percent) and, at least through the most recent preferred capital raise, still retain management control of the company (which is especially important for obvious reasons).
- Completing a little bit of math, you can calculate that the new preferred equity investors purchased their shares at $25 each compared to the original founders investing at $10 per common share and the other common stock owners at $20 per share. In other words, the preferred equity investors are breaking even, the original founders' shares have increased in value, and the other common equities investors are currently holding on to a small gain. Oh well, not every investment turns into a home run, and getting a single is better than grounding out. The other common equity investors are hopeful that management, by implementing its new business plan, can increase the value of the company so that all investors achieve a positive return on their investments.
- The final item in the cap table is the issuance of equity incentive grants in the form of common stock options or warrants. Common stock options and warrants are often

issued (with the right to exercise at a set price based on a future event) to key employees, board members, strategic third parties, and others to provide an extra monetary incentive to allow these parties to participate in the increase in a company's value (if all goes well). Almost all large companies utilize these types of incentives to attract top employee talent and keep parties engaged with the business to help build value and achieve a successful exit. If all goes well, everyone makes out, but if it does not, more than a few common stock options will be worthless. Options and warrants may have value to the recipient (eventually), but they only provide an option to purchase, so unless the option is exercised, these types of equity have no rights to earnings and cannot vote. Thus, I place them at the very bottom of the cap table, as this group of (potential) equity owners are truly last in line.

I have reached the bottom of the food chain as it relates to rights to both earnings and claims against assets. It may seem counterintuitive that the founders and the early other common equity investors along with key insiders (in control of common stock options and warrants), the ones that have poured their blood, sweat, and tears into building the business, stand last in line, but this is the reality of operating a business and building it into something of real value. When you raise capital and ask other parties to believe in your business, you must remember the golden rule: Whoever has the gold makes the rules!

My Final Raising Capital Tips, Tidbits, and Traps

In closing, I would like to leave you with these words of wisdom:

- *Cash is king.* Businesses must proactively, appropriately, and prudently manage cash resources or, to paraphrase the words of Warden Norton from the movie *Shawshank Redemption* (referring to the escape of Andy Dufresne), "Lord, it's a miracle, he just vanished like a fart in the wind." If not responsibly managed and protected, your cash will vanish like a fart in the wind!
- *Never run out of cash.* It is somewhat easy to discuss a miss or negative variance in the income statement, especially if you have best-in-class information to explain it. But if you run out of cash and must explain this to a capital source, get ready to have a rather unpleasant discussion that most likely involves some very restrictive and unfavorable terms (if they even consider providing more capital).
- *When capital sources offer extra cash, take it!* Yes, this may translate into more ownership dilution and/or added interest expense, but the ability to build a liquidity cushion for when a business hits the eventual speed bump (which it will), is invaluable. There is nothing worse than having to raise cash when times are tough.
- *Timing can be everything.* Companies will look to offer equity when the price is high (to limit ownership dilution). This is a quite common tactic with large, hot companies looking to raise extra cash for use down the road as evidenced by Tesla in 2020 (raising extra capital). You will need to pay close attention to economic and market cycles, which can change quickly.
- *When cash is tight, know how to squeeze your balance sheet.* You could incentivize customers to pay early or make deposits (e.g., a strategy used by Tesla) or push your vendors a bit (but not too much). You might also be able to work with key lenders or investors to have a bit of a slush fund to tap when needed. The key is to plan proactively, understand your cash flow statement, and communicate effectively. If you need a refresher on squeezing cash from the balance sheet, refer to Chapter 13, which is dedicated to this subject matter.
- *Most importantly, understand that who you take capital from is often more important than the amount, type, and structure of that capital.* Having the right financial partners who understand your business and timelines and have vast experience and resources can be invaluable. Securing capital from the right sources can really help turn a highly stressful process into a wonderful experience. Secure capital from the wrong source and get ready for hell.

For the last time, I emphasize the importance of understanding and relying on the statement of cash flows and retaining proper levels of liquidity to operate your business in good times or bad. There is nothing worse than having to tap capital markets in a hostile environment, as the terms will most likely be ugly (if you get them at all). Also, remember the adage about banks: They will lend when you do not need it, and when you do, they are nowhere to be found.

ABOUT THE AUTHOR

Tage C. Tracy (Anthem, Arizona) has operated a financial consulting firm focused on providing executive-level accounting, financial and risk management, and strategic business planning management support to private businesses, on a fractional basis. Tage specializes in businesses operating at distinct stages, including startups and launches, rapid growth, ramp-up and expansion management, and strategic exit. He also has expertise in acquisition preparedness and management, turnarounds, challenging environments, and survival techniques.

In addition to authoring *How to Write a Financial Report*, Tage was the lead author of *How to Read a Financial Report*, 10th Edition, *Business Financial Information Secrets*, and *Accounting Workbook for Dummies*, 2nd Edition. Further, Tage has co-authored a total of five books with his late father, John A. Tracy, including *Accounting for Dummies*, 7th Edition, *The Comprehensive Guide on How to Read a Financial Report*, *Cash Flow for Dummies*, *Small Business Financial Management Kit for Dummies*, and *How to Manage Profit and Cash Flow*.

Tage received his baccalaureate in accounting in 1985 with honors from the University of Colorado at Boulder. Tage began his career with Coopers & Lybrand (now part of PricewaterhouseCoopers) and obtained his CPA certificate in the state of Colorado in 1987 (now inactive). (His first name, pronounced *tog*, is of Scandinavian origin.)

You can find Tage online at: http://financemakescents.com/ or reach out directly to Tage at tagetracy@cox.net.

INDEX

Page numbers followed by *e* refer to exhibits.

B

C

E

Learn how to read, write and analyze financial reports with our full suite of titles

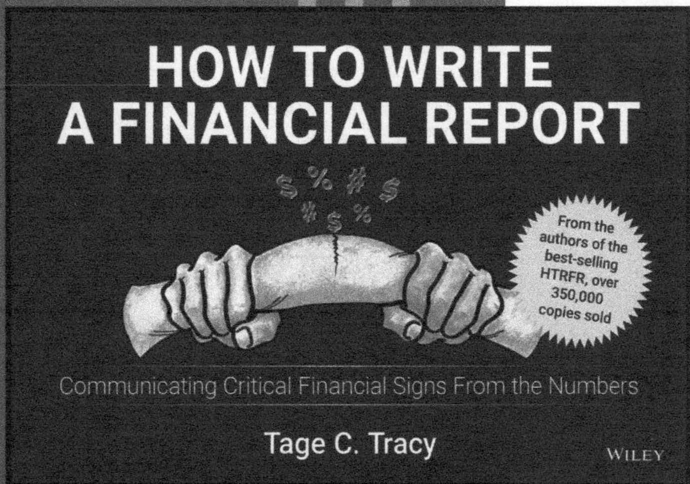

WILEY